MARGAI

Margaret Atwood

Second Edition

Coral Ann Howells

First edition published 1996
Second edition published 2005 by
PALGRAVE MACMILLAN
Houndmills, Basingstoke, Hampshire RG21 6XS and
175 Fifth Avenue, New York, N.Y. 10010
Companies and representatives throughout the world

PALGRAVE MACMILLAN is the global academic imprint of the Palgrave Macmillan division of St. Martin's Press, LLC and of Palgrave Macmillan Ltd. Macmillan® is a registered trademark in the United States, United Kingdom and other countries. Palgrave is a registered trademark in the European Union and other countries.

ISBN-13: 978 1–4039–2200–7 hardback
ISBN-10: 1–4039–2200–4 hardback
ISBN-13: 978 1–4039–2201–4 paperback
ISBN-10: 1–4039–2201–2 paperback

This book is printed on paper suitable for recycling and made from fully managed and sustained forest sources.

A catalogue record for this book is available from the British Library.

A catalog record for this book is available from the Library of Congress.

10   9   8   7   6   5   4   3   2   1
14   13   12   11   10   09   08   07   06   05

Printed in China

For Robin, Phoebe and Miranda

Contents

Contents

2000 AND AFTER

Acknowledgements

Since 1996 when the first edition of this book appeared, Margaret Atwood has published three new novels plus a collection of critical essays on writers and writing. *The Blind Assassin* won the Booker Prize in 2000, *The Handmaid's Tale* has been made into an opera by Danish composer Poul Ruders, at least eight new collections of critical essays by Canadian and international Atwoodians have been published, and a huge symposium on Atwood has taken place at the University of Ottawa in 2004. Taking all this into account, it is time for a second edition of *Margaret Atwood* which refocuses critical perspectives, always in the awareness that Atwood's shape-shifting profile makes any assessment provisional as she continues to explore the potential and possibilities of narrative with every new novel.

I am grateful to the many friends and colleagues who have encouraged and advised me in my continuing work on Atwood. My thanks are due to Ruth Blair at the University of Queensland, John Moss at the University of Ottawa, Pilar Somacarrera at the Universidad Autónoma de Madrid, Conny Steenman-Marcusse at the University of Leiden, and Héliane Ventura at the Université d'Orléans, all of whom have invited me to conferences to speak about Margaret Atwood; to Faye Hammill, formerly Reviews Editor of the *British Journal of Canadian Studies*; to my colleagues at the University of Reading, especially Maddi Davies and Patrick Parrinder, to my post-graduate student Michelle Reid for conversations about Canadian science fiction, and to the students in my Canadian women's fiction classes in Reading and in Madrid; also to my editors at Palgrave Macmillan, Anna Sandeman, Kate Wallis and Sonya Barker, for their enthusiasm and support. I am grateful to the School of English and American Literature (SEAL) at the University of Reading for teaching alleviation so that I could complete the revisions to this book, and to the SEAL Research Board and the Foundation for Canadian Studies in the United Kingdom for travel assistance on my research and conference visits. My special thanks yet again to Paula and Larry Bourne in Toronto and to Linda and Leslie Marshall in Guelph for their hospitality and for their continual supply of books and news-paper clippings related to my ongoing Atwood projects. Finally, my best thanks as always to my husband Robin and my daughters Phoebe and Miranda, and especially to Miranda for her expertise in preparing this typescript.

I am particularly grateful to Margaret Atwood's agent Vivienne Schuster for permission to quote from Atwood's published work, and to Margaret Atwood for permission to use Manuscript Materials.

In this second edition I have drawn on and developed some of my previously published Atwood materials. Thanks are due to the following for permission to reprint in part those materials here: Palgrave Macmillan, Basingstoke, for materials in my essay on *Cat's Eye* from *Margaret Atwood: Writing and Subjectivity*, ed. Colin Nicholson (1994); Palgrave Macmillan, New York, for material in my chapter on Margaret Atwood from Coral Ann Howells, *Contemporary Canadian Women's Fiction: Refiguring Identities* (2003); University of Wollongong Press, Wollongong, New South Wales, for material in my essay 'Sites of Desolation' from *Margaret Atwood: Entering the Labyrinth: The Blind Assassin*, ed. Gerry Turcotte (2003); York Press, London, for material in my York Notes Advanced on *The Handmaid's Tale* (2003).

Thanks are also due to Times Newspapers Ltd, for the extracts from a review by Philip Howard, *The Times*, 14 March 1980; copyright © Times Supplements Ltd, 1980.

'True Stories' is reprinted by permission of Margaret Atwood. It is available in the USA in the collection *Selected Poems II: Poems Selected and New, 1976–1986*, copyright 1981, 1987 by Margaret Atwood, from Houghton Mifflin Co., and in Canada in the collection *Selected Poems 1966–1984*, copyright 1981, 1990 by Margaret Atwood from McClelland & Stewart Ltd; reprinted by permission of Time Warner Book Group UK. It is available in the UK in *Eating Fire: Selected Poetry 1965–1995 by Margaret Atwood* (Virago, 1998).

1

Introduction: A Writer on Writing

Who are you writing for? Why do you do it? Where does it come from?

(Margaret Atwood, *Negotiating with the Dead*, p. xix)[1]

When Margaret Atwood as international literary celebrity lectured at the University of Cambridge in 2000, these were the three questions which she addressed. Those lectures, published under the Gothic title *Negotiating with the Dead*, combined personal anecdotes about her own life as a writer with less personal topics like authorship and creativity, fame, literary tradition and changing aesthetic fashions, and the writer's social responsibility. As she wryly remarked, she ought to know something about those topics as someone 'who's been laboring in the wordmines for, say, forty years' (*Negotiating with the Dead*, p. xvii). A versatile and prolific writer, Atwood has produced eleven novels and as many volumes of poetry, three collections of short stories, in addition to five important books of literary and cultural criticism as well as numerous essays, reviews and forewords to other people's books. She has also written three children's books, and compiled and illustrated *The CanLit Foodbook*, and is the editor of the *Oxford Book of Canadian Verse in English* and co-editor of the *Oxford Book of Canadian Short Stories in English*. Her work has been translated and published in more than thirty-five languages.

So what is the secret of Atwood's appeal? An important clue might be found in the comment made in 1980 in *The Times* by the reviewer of *Life Before Man*, the novel that brought her international recognition:

> In spite of the triple handicap of being a token 'feminist' author, a Canadian, and a poet, Margaret Atwood manages to be a true novelist. She opens our eyes to ways in which we think and behave,

1

irrespective of sex and nationality. Life among the dinosaurs may have been simpler. . . . But it cannot have been anything like as interesting.[2]

The Times's comment is significant for a number of reasons – not least because of its negative qualifications, which show the obstacles Atwood has had to overcome in her literary career. Ironically, that 'triple handicap' now spells out the distinctive marks of her fiction. Her writing is grounded in a strong sense of her own cultural identity as white, English-speaking, Canadian and female; but she also challenges the limits of such categories, questioning stereotypes of nationality and gender, exposing cultural fictions and the artificial limits they impose on our understanding of ourselves and others as human beings. As she wrote in 1982:

> If writing novels – and reading them – have any redeeming social value, it's probably that they force you to imagine what it's like to be somebody else.
> Which, increasingly, is something we all need to know.[3]

This leads us back to *The Times*'s comment on Atwood's being a 'true novelist' and, via the dinosaur reference, to the wider parameters of Atwood's search to find an adequate definition of what it means to be 'human', a question whose endless complexities she is still exploring in *Oryx and Crake*. In *Life Before Man* she engages with questions of human behaviour in relation to history and prehistory, as well as with the implied threat of human extinction, for 'You aren't and can't be apart from nature. We're all part of the biological universe: men as well as women.'[4] The dinosaurs signal an important fantasy dimension, for alongside her realistic representations of modern Toronto life there exist other, imagined worlds which belong to romance, fairy tale or to her characters' obsessional private agendas. These may be worlds of escape, but they may also be fantasies which exist alongside everyday life and which absorb the neuroses of contemporary Western society. As Atwood remarked, 'Ways of going crazy are culturally determined' (*Conversations*, p. 114). The social dimensions of Atwood's fiction are always underpinned and sometimes undermined by representations of individual behaviour, for if there is a single distinguishing Atwoodian marker, it is her insistently ironic vision, which challenges her readers' complacent acceptance of easy definitions about anything. As a novelist who was first and still is a poet with a poet's fascination with the endless possibilities of language, she also shows the same speculative interest in the possibilities of narrative, which she views as fictional space to be opened up beyond the constraints of traditional genre conventions. With their combination of empirical and speculative intelligence, her novels challenge her readers to see more by seeing differently. As the female artist in *Cat's Eye* realises when confronted by her brother's scientific perspective on the world, 'There are, apparently, a great many more dimensions than four.'[5]

Atwood, now in her mid-sixties, was born in 1939 in Ottawa, Canada. She spent her early childhood moving around in the forests and small settlements of Northern Ontario and Quebec with her parents and her elder brother (her younger sister was born in 1951), for her father was a field entomologist. It was not until after the end of the Second World War that her family settled in Toronto, where her father became a university professor. Atwood went to school there and then on to Victoria College, University of Toronto, where she took an Arts degree with honours in English. During that time she was busy writing and reviewing for her college magazine and designing programmes for the drama society. This visual dimension has remained an important feature of Atwood's work, where 'vision' is often elaborated to include insight and hallucination as well as merely seeing. In 1961, her graduation year, she had her first book of poems privately published, a collection called *Double Persephone*. But Atwood never felt at home in the city; she says she has always suffered from 'culture shock' after her bush childhood (*Conversations*, p. 121). Her first experience of the United States came when she went on a graduate fellowship to Radcliffe College, Harvard, where she studied Victorian and American literature and began her PhD thesis on 'The English Metaphysical Romance'. It was there that she had another culture shock when she realised that to the Americans Canada was invisible:

> It's not that the Americans I met had any odd or 'upsetting' attitudes toward Canada. They simply didn't have any attitudes at all. They had a vague idea that such a place existed – it was that blank area north of the map where the bad weather came from. (*Conversations*, p. 78)

Atwood's was the common colonial experience of moving to a metropolitan culture where people know nothing and care nothing about one's home place. Here might be located the roots of Atwood's Canadian nationalism, which developed in the late 1960s and frequently defined itself against the United States, a position which she scrutinises in her early 1970s work, _Surfacing_ and _Survival_. Atwood moved back to Canada without finishing her doctorate and spent the next ten years, her 'Rooming House' years as she describes them,[6] teaching in university English departments across Canada, from Vancouver to Montreal and Toronto, making her first trip to Europe, getting married for the first time, and writing her first novel.

During the 1970s Atwood was extremely productive, publishing three novels, a book of short stories, five books of poetry, a pioneering critical survey of Canadian literature, and a children's book. This was the period when her national and international reputation was made, and the stages of her rise to fame make an interesting chronicle, coinciding as they did with the rise of feminism and a resurgence of cultural nationalism centred on Canada's Centennial Year, 1967.[7] _The Edible Woman_ had been welcomed as the best first novel of 1969 – according to _The Times_'s critic in London, 'it stuck out above the rest like a sugar plum fairy on top of a Christmas cake'.[8] However, Atwood was still seen as a poet, as well as a colonial writer and a feminist. It was really with the double publication in 1972 of her second novel _Surfacing_ and her literary history _Survival: A Thematic Guide to Canadian Literature_ that she made her first serious claim for critical attention, though as she recalls, responses varied according to the different ideological perspectives of her reviewers. While, in the United States, _Surfacing_ was reviewed 'almost exclusively as a feminist or ecological treatise, in Canada it was reviewed almost exclusively as a nationalistic one' (_Conversations_, p. 117). In Britain those political implications were of less importance than its theme of psychological quest, and a reviewer in _The Sunday Times_ praised it for what has come to be recognised as Atwood's characteristic doubleness of vision, 'the balance between the narrator's interior vision and sharp observation of the real world outside her head'.[9] Her third novel, _Lady Oracle_ (1976), 'extravagant, macabre, and melodramatic', marked the shift to Atwood's decisive identification as a novelist, and was welcomed in _Newsweek_ as 'the kind of novel that makes reviewers send out fresh green sprouts'.[10] _Life Before Man_ (1979) received enthusiastic reviews in the United States and in Britain,[11] while in Canada Atwood was becoming a prominent figure in cultural politics. She was a founder member of the Writers' Union of Canada, on the editorial board of the newly established Anansi

Press in Toronto, and a member of Amnesty International. As she remarked, her involvement with 'political' issues was

> not separate from writing. When you begin to write, you deal with your immediate surroundings; as you grow, your immediate surroundings become larger. There's no contradiction.[12]

She has maintained an active engagement with political and human rights issues not only in Canada but on the international scene, as the title of her latest collection of essays indicates; it is called *Moving Targets: Writing with Intent 1982–2004.*

In the late 1970s Atwood began travelling extensively, reading and lecturing in Britain, Italy, Australia and Afghanistan in the late 1970s. During this period, Atwood, now divorced, met the Ontario novelist Graeme Gibson; their daughter was born in 1976. In 1980 Atwood moved with her family to Toronto, which has been their permanent home ever since. That combination of high literary productivity, Toronto home life and international travel has continued, with brief periods in the United States as Professor of Creative Writing at several university campuses, and two longish spells living away from Canada – first in England (1983–4) and then in France (1991–2). Her output as a novelist, poet, critic and essayist has been prodigious, a pattern that has continued up to the present day (see Bibliography, Primary Sources). When *The Handmaid's Tale* was published, it was shortlisted in Britain for the Booker Prize; in Canada it won Atwood her second Governor General's Award; in the United States it won the Arthur C. Clarke Science Fiction Prize and the *Los Angeles Times* Fiction Prize. All five of Atwood's most recent novels have been nominees for the Booker Prize, and *The Blind Assassin* won the Booker in 2000. She is the most written-about Canadian writer ever, and there is a thriving international Atwood industry, with at least eight critical anthologies published in English since 1996, and yearly updates on Atwood scholarship in the Newsletter of the Atwood Society (www.cariboo.bc.ca/atwood).

Atwood has become, in her own words, 'a sort of eminent fixture' not only in Canada but also internationally – 'A public face, a face worth defacing. This is an accomplishment,' as her woman artist wryly remarks in *Cat's Eye*.[13] Atwood is an extremely versatile writer, and in every novel she takes up the conventions of a different narrative form – Gothic romance, fairy tale, spy thriller, science fiction or historical novel – working within those conventions and reshaping them. Her writing insistently challenges the limits of traditional genres, yet this experimentalism is balanced against a strong continuity of interests, which are both aesthetic and social: 'I do see the novel as a vehicle for looking at society – an interface between language and what we choose to call reality, although even that is a very malleable substance' (*Conversations*, p. 246). Atwood has always believed in the social function of art and in the writer's responsibility to her readers:

> If you think of a book as an experience, as almost the equivalent of having the experience, you're going to feel some sense of responsibility.... You're not going to put them through a lot of blood and gore for nothing; at least I'm not. (*Conversations*, p. 151)

From *The Edible Woman* onwards, her novels have focused on contemporary social and political issues. 'And what do we mean by "political"?' she asks in an interview after *The Handmaid's Tale*: 'What we mean is how people relate to a power structure and vice versa' (*Conversations*, p. 185). This wide definition of politics accommodates Atwood's major thematic concerns: her scrutiny of relations between men and women, which she has always construed as a form of power politics; the representation of women's lives, their bodies, their fantasies and their search for identity; her engagement with questions of national identity and Canada's international relations, especially with the United States; her wider humanitarian concerns with basic human rights, and her environmental interests and increasingly urgent warnings about global warming, pollution and the risks of biotechnology. There are strong thematic continuities as Atwood refigures the same topics with different emphases and from multiple perspectives in different narrative genres. Her comment on memory in *Cat's Eye* is a perfect description of the way key themes recur in her novels: 'Sometimes this comes to the surface, sometimes that, sometimes nothing. Nothing goes away' (*Cat's Eye*, p. 3).

This introductory chapter provides a context for reading any one of Atwood's novels as it explores key issues related to themes, language and narratology, and by sketching some of the main terms in the critical debates around her work. These range from questions to do with feminism and generic experiment to more recent emphases on elements of postmodernism and postcolonialism in relation to her interests in historiography and speculative fiction. In this second edition I have adopted a chronological arrangement for my analyses of Atwood's novels, with one chapter per novel for all eleven of them, following their order of publication. In each chapter I offer a close reading which pays attention to thematics and narrative experiment, while also highlighting the specific interest of the novel under discussion. In some chapters I have referred in passing to other writings by Atwood or to manuscript materials, for the manuscripts provide valuable amplification on her working methods while the other texts offer a commentary on the different ways the same topic might be treated in a short story or a poem. At the end of every chapter I have included Suggestions for Further Reading as a quick guide to the main secondary sources for that particular novel. These individual chapters are set in a wider chronological pattern, marked out into the four decades of Atwood's writing career, from her first novel published in the late 1960s through to 2000 and since. This provides at a glance a comprehensive overview of her achievement, while it also suggests that each of Atwood's novels needs to be located in its specific historical and cultural context, a suggestion endorsed by Atwood herself when, speaking about her first historical novel, *Alias Grace*, she recalled the words of that other senior Toronto novelist Robertson Davies: 'We all belong to our own time, and there is nothing whatever that we can do to escape it. Whatever we write will be contemporary, even if we attempt a novel set in a past age.'[14]

In all my discussions, thematics are important but so too are questions of textuality, and with Atwood our attention is always directed back to the words on the page. Of course the reader's attention is seized by the plot, but Atwood is always conscious of the significant role that language plays in the appeal of a novel, for novels are made out of words alone.

Incidentally, Atwood has made one of the most sensible comments that one is likely to see on the best way to read novels. When asked how she envisaged her ideal reader, she replied:

> The Ideal Reader for me is somebody who reads the book on the first read-through to see what happens.... I read books to see what happens to the people in them. And after that I can sit back and admire how well it was done and what great skill was brought to bear. But the first time through I want to read the book. (*Conversations*, p. 168)

Her close attention to people and relationships in a particular historical and social location gives her novels the appeal of traditional

realistic fiction, even when she is presenting futuristic visions like
The Handmaid's Tale and *Oryx and Crake*. Any one of her novels shows
how Atwood challenges the conventions of realism while working
within them for she never pretends that words and stories offer an
unproblematic access to the real world. Instead, there are always
gaps to be negotiated, by the characters in the novels and also by the
reader. The Canadian critic Linda Hutcheon gives a precise description
of Atwood's fictional method in her analysis of the way postmodern
novelists 'use and abuse the conventions of the realist novel. They
ask us to rethink those conventions, this time *as conventions*, but
also as ideological strategies. Such novelists destabilize things we
used to think we could take for granted when we read novels.'[15]

Atwood's fiction draws attention not only to the ways in which
stories may be told but also to the function of language itself: the
slipperiness of words and double operation of language as symbolic
representation and as agent for changing our modes of perception.
As Atwood pointed out in an interview:

> The word *woman* already has changed because of the different
> constellations [of meaning] that have been made around it.
> Language changes within our lifetime. As a writer you're part of
> that process – using an old language, but making new patterns
> with it. Your choices are numerous.   (*Conversations*, p. 112)

That comment focuses the political dimensions of the question:
What does 'writing like a woman' mean, when language itself codes
in such ideological shifts? The greatest challenge for a woman writer
is how to position herself in response to changing cultural definitions
of 'woman' and its 'constellations' like 'feminine' and 'feminist'.
Atwood has constantly engaged with that challenge in a concerted
attempt to widen the dimensions of the debate.

If textuality is important so too is intertextuality, and many critics
have commented on Atwood's revision of traditional fictional genres
as she draws attention to the cultural myths they embody and to the
multiple inherited scripts through which our perceptions of ourselves and the world are structured. What does 'revision' mean in this
context? Perhaps the most quoted definition is the American poet
Adrienne Rich's in 'When We Dead Awaken: Writing as Re-Vision'.
Rich writes in a specifically feminist context, whereas for Atwood the
definition needs to be widened to include her Canadian postcolonial
context as well:

Re-Vision – the act of looking back, of seeing with fresh eyes, of entering an old text from a new critical direction – is for women more than a chapter in cultural history; it is an act of survival. . . . We need to know the writing of the past and to know it differently . . . not to pass on a tradition but to break its hold over us.[16]

In other words, revision involves a critical response to the traditional narratives of a culture and then a reinterpretation of them from a new perspective, which offers a critique of the value structures and power relations (the 'ideological implications') coded into texts. Revision does not break with tradition though it aims to 'break its hold over us'. As early as 1976, Atwood was describing the relation between her poetry and popular art in such revisionist terms as she explained how in *Power Politics* she explored relationships between men and women through allusions to stories like Bluebeard and *Dracula* and to horror comics.

Atwood's novels are criss-crossed with allusions to other texts, signalling her literary inheritance while at the same time marking significant differences from her predecessors. To illustrate the way this challenge to tradition operates, we might glance briefly at some of her different versions of Gothic romance, the genre to which Atwood has returned in every decade of her career. *Lady Oracle* (1976) is a very funny parody of the mass-market genre of popular Gothics known as 'bodice rippers', but at the same time as it exposes the artificiality of Gothic conventions with their female victim fantasies and their double dealing it also attempts to analyse the insidious appeal of Gothic for women readers. In *Bodily Harm* (1981), witty comedy changes to something far more threatening where classic female fears of male violence spill over from fiction into real life, first via pornographic fantasy and sexual abuse in Toronto, and then through the account of a military coup in a newly independent Caribbean republic, told by a woman who finds herself in jail there. Moving into the 1990s, *The Robber Bride* (1993) combines Gothic vampires and Frankenstein monsters with a feminised version of the 'Robber Bridegroom' fairy tale as it details the adventures of a demonic woman who returns from the dead to torment three female friends in Toronto. Through that story Atwood examines the role of the Other Woman, reflecting on fantasies of femininity but also on concepts of the uncanny Other and the return of the repressed. In *The Blind Assassin* (2000), Atwood is writing a Gothic version of Canadian history, uncovering carefully hidden secrets and scandals through the life story of an old woman who is haunted by ghosts. As private memoir and public memorial this is a novel concerned with questions of identity and inheritance which expands beyond the personal to include the history of the nation. Atwood has once again transformed her favourite genre, demonstrating that her fiction 'is both canonical and postcanonical, nationalistic and postnationalistic, realistic and postmodern'.[17]

Obviously, revisionist perspectives have narrative consequences not only for narrators but also for readers, turning our attention towards processes of deconstruction and reconstruction while emphasising the provisionality of any narrative structure. Atwood's novels are characterised by their refusals to invoke any final authority as their open endings resist conclusiveness, offering instead hesitation, absence or silence while hovering on the verge of new possibilities. Their indeterminacy is a challenge to readers, for one of the problems we have to confront is how to find a critical language to describe Atwood's distinctive brand of postmodernism with its ironic mixture of realism and fantasy, fictive artifice and moral engagement.

I wish to return to the other two elements of Atwood's 'triple handicap': her Canadianness and her feminism. A Canadian by birth and upbringing (her family traditions go back to the Empire Loyalists who left Massachusetts after the American Declaration of Independence), Atwood has done much through her writing and interviews to make Canadian culture visible outside her country. She began, however, by spelling out traditions to Canadians themselves in the early 1970s with her literary history *Survival* and her novel *Surfacing*. For an international readership her project has been that of 'translating' Canada, mapping its geography, its history of European exploration and settlement, its literary and artistic heritage, and its cultural myths. Her representation of Canada is a combination of documentary realism and imaginative interpretation from her own perspective as a white English-Canadian woman living in Ontario. She is not an immigrant or a Native Person, nor from western Canada or Quebec, any of which would make a difference to her representation of Canadianness. Several of her novels move outside Canada to the United States, the Caribbean, or to Europe, yet her fiction is based on a strong sense of local identity.

This sense of geographical location is the basis of Atwood's realism. She writes about Canadian cities and small towns, about the Canadian wilderness with its forests and lakes, and sometimes about the Arctic North. In her novels she continues to give updated versions of the city of Toronto from the mid-1940s to the late 1990s, and it is not difficult for a reader to chart that city's postwar history from *The Edible Woman* to *The Blind Assassin*. *Cat's Eye* features a woman painter brought up in Toronto in the 1950s and 1960s who returns 30 years later as a minor celebrity, only to find the place defamiliarised by time:

I've been walking for hours it seems, down the hill to the downtown, where the streetcars no longer run. It's evening, one of those grey watercolour washes, like liquid dust, the city comes up with in fall. The weather at any rate is still familiar.

Now I've reached the place where we used to get off the streetcar, stepping into the curbside mounds of January slush, into the grating wind that cut up from the lake between the flat-roofed dowdy buildings that were for us the closest thing to urbanity. But this part of the city is no longer flat, dowdy, shabby-genteel. Tubular neon in cursive script decorates the restored brick façades, and there's a lot of brass trim, a lot of real estate, a lot of money. Up ahead there are huge oblong towers, all of glass, lit up, like enormous gravestones of cold light. Frozen assets.

I don't look much at the towers though, or the people passing me in their fashionable get-ups, imports, handcrafted leather, suede, whatever. Instead I look down at the sidewalk, like a tracker. (*Cat's Eye*, pp. 8–9)

That imaginative reconstruction of place and the narrator's attempt to orientate herself in a wilderness of signs will be familiar to any Atwood reader. In Chapter 3 I shall discuss Atwood's treatment of wilderness landscape in *Surfacing* and *Survival*, which I believe to be the cornerstone in her representations of Canadianness up until the early 1990s. However, I wish to comment here on Atwood's position within the English-Canadian literary tradition and on her significance as a writer who is highly sensitive to the evolving Canadian narrative of national identity. Any nation's identity is an ideological construction by which it defines its difference from its neighbours and from the rest of the international community, an increasingly difficult thing to do in the late modern world of global communications and transnational economic relations. Canada's image as a bilingual multicultural nation contains within it the narratives of a colonial history as well as contemporary narratives of cultural difference within the country itself. Historically, Canada has been defined in relation to its two

European 'mother countries', Britain and France, and its southern neighbour the United States of America. This is an 'emergent nation' story which follows patterns characteristic of the shift from colonial status to postcolonial nationhood. In Canada's case the story is complicated by the pluralities within its own political discourse, where debates between anglophone and francophone communities are amplified by diverse voices representing different regions, different ethnic and immigrant groups, and the voices of Native peoples, all of which have implications for an evolving narrative of national identity.[18] In her fiction over almost 35 years Atwood has closely charted Canada's story with its political crises and shifts of ideological emphasis, as a novelist engaged in an ongoing project of cultural representation and critique. To encounter the nation as it is written by Atwood is to follow a history of shifting and often contradictory representations which range from 1970s English-centred cultural nationalism to more complex articulations of contemporary Canada as a postcolonial, multicultural nation. In Atwood's novels of the 1990s popular myths of heritage and identity are destabilised, and even the history of the nation is subjected to sceptical inquiry: 'We live in a period in which memory of all kinds, including the sort of large memory we call history, is being called into question' (*In Search of Alias Grace*, p. 7). The terms of debate have shifted, as Atwood points out in arguing for Canadians' need to refigure stories of nationhood and identity. With *Oryx and Crake*, national boundaries have blurred as Atwood responds to her widening international readership, arguing for a shared recognition of complicity in globalisation, which threatens human survival.

Although, as Atwood has said repeatedly, she had no reason in the late 1950s to believe that she would ever be able to make her living as a writer in Canada, she did in fact belong to a new generation who were 'busy discovering the fact of our existence as Canadians', and she was also one of the first generation of students who were taught that there was a Canadian literary tradition in poetry if not in fiction.[19] As an undergraduate in Toronto she was taught by the late Professor Northrop Frye and the poet Jay Macpherson, whose influence as role model Atwood gratefully acknowledges: 'to actually be able to look at someone and say, that person has published a book! You can't imagine how important that was to a Canadian living at that time' (*Conversations*, p. 112). It was in Macpherson's private library that Atwood read her way through Canadian poetry, while she was also influenced by Frye's myth-centred criticism and his efforts to translate European myths into a new Canadian cultural context. Given her background, it is not surprising that she would have begun by writing poetry, nor that her first critical work should have been an attempt to map a parallel Canadian tradition in fiction. Since the 1970s Atwood has maintained her active engagement with Canadian literary and cultural politics, though she is now so well known internationally that readers tend to forget where she comes from. Atwood herself never forgets this, and her fictions are pervaded by Canadian cultural codes. At the same time the meanings of her novels cannot be restricted to a Canadian frame of reference, for stories are fabrications made out of language and they use narrative conventions which transcend self-conscious political ideologies:

> I write for people who like to read books. They don't have to be Canadian readers. They don't have to be American readers....I don't get all the references in William Faulkner either. That doesn't mean I don't enjoy the books, or can't understand them. You can pick up a lot of things from context. (*Conversations*, p. 144)

It is a similarly non-exclusive attitude which has characterised Atwood's relation to feminism: 'Some people *choose* to define themselves as feminist writers. I would not deny the adjective, but I don't consider it inclusive' (*Conversations*, p. 139). Atwood is now perhaps the best known woman novelist writing in English, though this statement, made in 1979, still accurately describes her position. I believe there are two main reasons for this: first, because Atwood sees sexual politics as only one of the areas in which power relations are the crucial issue, and secondly, because as a novelist she insists on her aesthetic freedom to write from her 'sense of the enormous complexity, not only of the relationships between Man and Woman, but also of those between those other abstract intangibles, Art and Life, Form and Content, Writer and Critic, etcetera'.[20] Her novels might best be characterised as 'experiments' (to adopt her own scientific vocabulary and method of inquiry), always testing the limits of theory and exceeding ideological definitions. Her fiction canvasses such a comprehensive range of issues that it eludes the simplicity of any single 'feminist' position. That being said, it remains true that as she grew up in the late 1950s and early 1960s in Toronto and then went as a graduate student to Harvard, Atwood's formative years coincided with the emergence of 'second wave' North American feminism and her fiction reflects the changing climate when Women's

Liberation first became a political issue. Over the past 35 years, ever since *The Edible Woman*, which Atwood described as 'protofeminist', her novels have provided a chronicle and critique of the changing fashions within feminist politics.

The early 1960s signal the beginnings of a new, politically self-conscious phase of feminist awareness in North America at grassroots and institutional levels. A great deal has been written about the emergence of the Women's Liberation Movement in the United States, which was energised by the political radicalism of the American Civil Rights Movement. It is worth noting that the first phase of feminism was dominantly white and middle class, and it was not till the late 1970s and 1980s that Afro-Caribbean and Third World feminists began to spell out their very different agendas, where race was an important issue. There was a parallel feminist movement developing in Canada, though the distinctive outlines of the Canadian women's movement are only now being extensively documented by collectives of women scholars in Ottawa and Toronto;[21] 1960 was the year that the Voice of Women, the first Canadian national women's organisation, was founded as a group to lobby federal and provincial governments on women's issues and peace issues, and in 1967 the first Canadian Royal Commission on the Status of Women was set up. The distinctively 'political' feature of women's struggle was the shift away from private experience to the recognition of the relatedness between domestic and social structures as women were encouraged to reflect on their position in postwar North American society. As Betty Friedan phrased it in her polemical treatise *The Feminine Mystique* (1963), in a first chapter entitled 'The Problem that Has No Name':

> The problem lay buried unspoken for many years in the minds of American women. It was a strange stirring, a sense of dissatisfaction, a yearning that women suffered in the middle of the twentieth century.[22]

Friedan's book signalled the shift from individual women's discontents to a collective gender consciousness which came to characterise 'second wave' feminism.[23] Friedan, following in the footsteps of Simone de Beauvoir's *The Second Sex* (1949; translated into English in 1953), mounted the first popular critique of North American cultural myths of femininity, reminding women how much they had lost by allowing their lives to be restricted to the suburbs in the 1950s following the return to civilian life after the war. Atwood refers to Simone de Beauvoir and Betty Friedan as the two most significant influences on her thinking as a young woman in early 1960s.[24] In the States, Friedan founded her political pressure group NOW (National Organization for Women) in 1966; in Canada, the Royal Commission's report on women was published in 1970. Meantime, in London in 1966, Juliet Mitchell's New Left-inspired study *Women: The Longest Revolution* was published, and in 1969 Mitchell began teaching the first Women's Studies course in Britain. In 1970, Robin Morgan's *Sisterhood is Powerful: An Anthology of Writings from the Women's Liberation Movement* was published in New York, the same year as Germaine Greer's *The Female Eunuch* in London. Feminist newspapers and periodicals began to appear and the number of reformist women's groups grew remarkably during the 1970s. It is within this historical context of women's dissent that *The Edible Woman* assumes its proper significance for us, and as I shall argue in Chapter 2, *The Feminine Mystique* provides a powerful lens through which Atwood's first novel may be read. Both texts focus on the predicament of young white university-educated women trapped in social myths of femininity, though *The Edible Woman* is a novelist's imaginative response, cast as comic social satire in vividly metaphorical language. This is sociology translated into the private idiom of one fictive female character, where unconscious resistance to her social destiny takes the form of a hysterical eating disorder. Written in 1965 and published in 1969, Atwood's novel represents an imaginative response to a current social malaise. It is parallel to, not a product of, the new Women's Movement, although that movement created the conditions for its popular reception. Atwood has always been seen as a feminist icon, albeit a resistant and at times an inconvenient one.

During the 1970s there was a flood of feminist writing in North America, England and France as women sought to define their positions on social and political issues within every discipline (literary criticism and the media, history, psychoanalysis, anthropology, science, theology). The most startling innovation was in the explicit treatment of female sexuality and desire, for suddenly those hitherto unspoken territories were mapped and written about: Shulamith Firestone's *The Dialectic of Sex* (1970), the Boston Women's Book Collective's *Our Bodies Our Selves* (1971), and Hilda Bruch's study of anorexia nervosa, *The Golden Cage* (1975), focused on women's bodies; while feminist revisions of Freudian theories of femininity appeared in Phyllis Chesler's *Women and Madness* (1972) and Juliet Mitchell's *Psychoanalysis and Feminism* (1974). Adrienne Rich's *Of Woman Born* (1976) and Nancy Chodorow's *The Reproduction of Mothering* (1978) scrutinised women's experiences of motherhood (Atwood reviewed Rich's *Of Woman Born*, in the *Toronto Globe and Mail*, 11 November 1976); while the darker areas of male violence against women began to be explored by Susan Brownmiller in *Against Our Will: Men, Women and Rape* (1975). Laura Mulvey's study of the male gaze in *Visual Pleasure and Narrative Cinema* (1975) analysed the politics of male dominance within the media, which in turn is related to the analysis of male fantasies of aggression and violence in Andrea Dworkin's *Pornography: Men Possessing Women* (1981). In the field of literary criticism, the most significant innovations were the theorising of a feminist writing practice and the establishment of a female literary tradition such as we find in Ellen Moers's *Literary Women* (1976) and Elaine Showalter's *A Literature of Their Own* (1977), both of which were supplemented by Tillie Olsen's *Silences* (1978), one of the first feminist studies to combine an analysis of class and gender when speaking about the erasure of traditions of women's creativity.

These innovative texts provide an historical framework within which to read Atwood's fiction of the 1970s, and a similar pattern of dialogue may be traced through the 1980s to the present. 'Context is all,' as the Handmaid asserted. A complex web of interrelatedness is developed as the novelist responds to her changing cultural climate and to the writings produced by the most significant social movement of the past 40 years. All the representative feminist as well as many of the anti-feminist positions could be illustrated with examples from Atwood's novels, which have insistently challenged traditional male power structures while giving readers some of their funniest and most trenchant models for a feminist critique. Just as feminist theory has developed strong historical and cultural dimensions through its investigation of the institutions of marriage and mother-hood, so Atwood has explored similar territory in her represent-ations of 'female, feminine and feminist' positions. On the question of women's relation to language and literary conventions Atwood has been constantly engaged in the revision of traditional genres, opening up spaces for women as subjects speaking and writing about their own experience, though still forced to acknowledge what Linda Hutcheon described as 'the power of the (male/"universal") space in which it [women's writing] cannot avoid, to some extent, operating'.[25]

However, readers of Atwood need to be as discriminating as Atwood herself when describing her as a feminist writer, for her fiction is a combination of engagement, analysis and critique of the changing fashions within feminism. In there from the beginning, Atwood realised very clearly the implications of the early 1970s feminist slogan 'The Personal is Political', and she has been exploring this interdependence ever since. Feminism cannot be reduced to parodic slogans like 'the oppression of women by men' or 'women are always right'. Certainly, feminism has always insisted that women have rights in the sense of individual human rights (which immediately relates 'the woman question' to wider political issues), but feminism also means looking at the ways in which women use the powers traditionally granted to them and how they have attempted to enlarge the scope of their influence; it also means looking at the effects on women of not having legitimised power. That lack can turn them into victims or manipulators, or it can launch them into guerrilla warfare, all of which are positions explored in Atwood's fiction. At every stage, Atwood has speculated beyond the issues addressed by the feminist movement with her awkward and daring questions, not only about relations between women and men, but about relations between women and women. She has explored the relations between mothers and daughters and sisters or between little girls or adult female friends, and the challenge posed by a *femme fatale* to members of both sexes. With every novel Atwood ventures into new and dangerous territory, exposing the blind spots within feminist ideology:

> As for Woman, capital W, we got stuck with that for centuries. Eternal Woman. But really, 'Woman' is the sum total of women. It doesn't exist apart from that, except as an abstracted idea. (*Conversations*, p. 201)

In *The Handmaid's Tale* and *The Robber Bride* Atwood has taken an historical view of the North American feminist movement, charting some of the ways in which feminism has changed from Women's Liberation to the more theorised and subtly politicised feminism of the late 1980s and 1990s. Her analysis is a cultural one, which traces patterns of social interaction and consequences, for just as feminism has contributed to shifts in social ideology so has feminism itself been transformed into 'feminisms' in order to include the different agendas of other formerly marginalised groups of women: Black women in America, Third World women, female immigrants from racial minority groups, and lesbians whose interests are closer to Gay Rights than to traditional liberal feminist agendas. In Toronto, which is Atwood's 'home ground', the first generation inspired by Friedan and De Beauvoir are now middle-aged (white) women in positions of power, like Atwood herself, who writes about middle-aged successful women artists (such as Elaine Risley in *Cat's Eye*) or businesswomen and university professors (such as Roz and Tony in *The Robber Bride*), well aware that the idioms of feminism have changed; Atwood recognises this in the presence of Shanita in *The Robber Bride*, a Toronto-born woman of South Asian origin. Though she does not attempt to negotiate racial politics, Atwood's fiction gestures towards those othered identities in Canadian society. Her main emphasis, however, is not on gender but on race as she satirises the 'everyday racism' to which so many non-white Canadian writers have drawn attention.

It is symptomatic of her double vision that with one eye on the present Atwood is also aware of the long history of exceptional women's achievements in the past, and *The Robber Bride* ends by tracking back through history to celebrate the name of a medieval French female military commander, Dame Giraude, who defended her fortified castle to the death in 1211, then even further back to recall the figure of Jezebel whose story is told in the Old Testament – no doubt to remind readers not to fall into any blinkered attitude of presentism. In her recent historical novels, *Alias Grace* and *The Blind Assassin*, her protagonists are dissident if not actually criminal women: a mid-nineteenth-century Irish working-class immigrant and a Toronto high society relic of the 1920s and 1930s. Both their stories reflect on women's lives across social classes in Canada, while the enigmatic South Asian woman in *Oryx and Crake* eludes any attempts to define her (though we should remember that the point of view here is entirely that of a male narrator).

Atwood's resistance to generalisations about 'Woman' is a crucial feature in her feminist understanding of the importance of history and culture in shaping women's lives. In her interviews over the years she has insisted on specifying the context before defining feminism:

> *Feminist* is now one of the all-purpose words. It really can mean anything from people who think men should be pushed off cliffs to people who think it's O.K. for women to read and write. All

those could be called feminist positions. Thinking that it's O.K. for women to read and write would be a radically feminist position in Afghanistan. So what do you mean? (*Conversations*, p. 140)

When asked in Australia, in 2001, if she was a feminist, Atwood replied:

My bottom line is that women are human beings, a fact that is disputed elsewhere on the globe, and that if they're human beings they also have human rights and human frailties. And then we can go on talking about the rights and frailties but if we don't take 'human beings' as the axiom we won't get anywhere.[26]

In Atwood's fiction there are no essentialist definitions of 'woman' or 'feminism' or even 'Canadian', but instead representations of the endless complexity and quirkiness of human behaviour, which exceeds ideological labels and the explanatory power of theory. As a political writer she is interested in an analysis of the dialectics of power and shifting structures of ideology; as a creative writer she is interested in the dynamic powers of language and story; and what is more, as a 'true novelist' she is interested in her readership:

So that is who the writer writes for: for the reader. For the reader who is not Them, but You. For the Dear Reader. . . . And this ideal reader may prove to be anyone at all – any *one* at all – because the act of reading is just as singular – always – as the act of writing.[27]

2
The Edible Woman

As a woman writer Atwood has always been intensely aware of the significance of the female body, in terms both of a woman's sense of her own identity and of the cultural meanings that are coded into representations of female bodies:

> The body as a concept has always been a concern of mine. It's there in *Surfacing* as well. I think that people very much experience themselves through their bodies and through concepts of the body which get applied to their own bodies. Which they pick up from their culture and apply to their own bodies. It's also my concern in *Lady Oracle* and it's even there in *The Edible Woman*. (*Conversations*, p. 187)

Atwood directs our attention to her first novel, published in 1969, which marks the beginning of her explorations of sexual power politics through her comic exposure of the contradictions within social myths of femininity, and of women's condition of entrapment inside those myths and inside their own bodies. *The Edible Woman* belongs to a specific moment in the history of North American postwar feminism, which registered the first signs of the contemporary women's movement in its resistance to social myths of femininity. This is the territory charted by Betty Friedan in *The Feminine Mystique* (1963),[1] a study that Atwood herself read 'behind closed doors' like many other young women at the time, and I propose to read *The Edible Woman* in that context of early 'second wave' feminism. Atwood and Friedan highlight the same area of socio-political concern, and the thematic issues in *The Edible Woman* could even be classified under the chapter headings in Friedan's book.

However, the very title of Atwood's novel signals significant differences, with its dimensions of fantasy and metaphorical thinking which are absent from Friedan's sociological treatise, for *The Edible Woman* is an imaginative transformation of a social problem into comic satire as one young woman rebels against her feminine destiny. Whereas *The Feminine Mystique* documents the anxieties and frustrations felt by a whole generation of young white middle-class women in America in the 1950s and early 1960s, *The Edible Woman* goes beyond women's anger and bewilderment in its exploitation of the power of laughter to reveal the absurdities within social conventions. This is a subversive rather than a confrontational novel, which engages obliquely with social problems, adopting the form of a parodic revision of a traditional comedy of manners with its fixation on the marriage theme. Here Atwood mixes those earlier conventions with the language of 1960s advertising and cookery books, adding a dash of popular Freudianism and a few of the Jungian archetypes so fashionable in literary criticism of the 1950s and 1960s, to produce a satirical exposure of women's continuing conditions of entrapment within their own bodies and within social myths. The novel mounts its attack on social and gender ideology very wittily, though it bears the mark of its historical period with its deprecatingly feminine glance back over the shoulder when one of the characters comments, 'I don't want you to think that all this means anything.' [2] It is part of Atwood's playful ambiguity that the speaker here is male. That same speaker, a young graduate student in English literature, happens to be the novel's most vigorous critic of gender stereotypes, of advertising and of the consumerist ethic. Under a series of comic masks, Atwood's novel explores the relation between consumerism and the feminine mystique, where one young woman's resistance to consuming and to being consumed hints at a wider condition of social malaise which the new feminist movement was just beginning to address.

It would be fair to say that when *The Feminine Mystique* burst upon the popular market in 1963 it signalled the beginning of feminism as a political force in postwar North America. It had such a revolutionary impact for two reasons: first, because it was a 'scientific' response to a widely recognised phenomenon, and secondly, because it gave a name to that widespread malaise. Suddenly, 'The Problem That Has No Name' was named and became a public issue rather than something confined to the area of women's private discontents:

There was a strange discrepancy between the reality of our lives as women and the image to which we were trying to conform, the image which I came to call the feminine mystique. I wondered if other women faced this schizophrenic split, and what it meant. (*The Feminine Mystique*, p. 9)

The Feminine Mystique, whose brilliant title derives I suspect from Simone de Beauvoir's phrase the 'Myth of Femininity', exposes the dimensions of mystification and inauthenticity within current concepts of femininity, which gave dissenting women a platform for social protest as a new interest group. Friedan described the mystique of feminine fulfilment as 'the cherished and self-perpetuating core of contemporary American culture' (p. 18), then subjected it to a devastating socio-economic analysis, prying behind that 'pretty picture of the American suburban housewife-mother' to reveal the dimensions of women's loss of independence after the Second World War, which were concealed by an image of happy domesticity:

> The end of the road...is the disappearance of the heroine altogether, as a separate self and the subject of her own story. The end of the road is togetherness, where the woman has no independent self to hide even in guilt; she exists only for and through her husband and children.   (p. 47)

Friedan signals the personal dimensions of a social problem in chapter titles such as 'The Crisis in Woman's Identity' and 'The Forfeited Self', while as a sociologist she explores the link between myths of femininity, advertising and postwar North American consumerism. As she presented the situation in the 1960s, women were the victims not only of American business interests but also of sociologists and educators, and she roundly condemned the pieties of social science, Freudian psychology and anthropology, all of which championed the value of women's 'adjustment' to cultural definitions of femininity:

> At a time of great change for women, at a time when education, science, and social science should have helped women bridge the change, functionalism transformed 'what is' for women, or 'what was,' to 'what should be'... [and] so closed the door of the future on women.   (p. 135)

Some of her most vigorous condemnation is directed toward the anthropologist Margaret Mead, whose work on gender differences in primitive societies was popularly interpreted as a glorification of the female role, defined according to the biological function of childbearing. Friedan points the finger of criticism directly at Mead's study of men and women in primitive societies, *Male and Female* (1955), as the 'book which became the cornerstone of the feminine mystique'. What she criticises most is the inauthenticity of the return to 'primitive earth-mother maternity' in modern Western society, where that image of the 'natural' could only be maintained by an educated woman's negation of many of her own acknowledged capacities. Atwood's dramatisation of the contradictions within the concept of femininity provides some of the best comedy in *The Edible Woman* in her two parodic versions of earth-mothers, one a passive victim of the feminine mystique and one (a former psychology student and evidently a devotee of Margaret Mead) whose relentless pursuit of a father for her child 'bore a chilling resemblance to a general plotting a major campaign' (*The Edible Woman*, p. 85).

In North American society of the late 1950s and 1960s, where 'adjustment' for a woman meant accepting a dependent 'feminine' role, it was, as Friedan says, 'very hard for a human being to sustain such an inner split – conforming outwardly to one reality, while trying to maintain inwardly the values it denies' (*The Feminine Mystique*, p. 308). In a chapter whose full title is 'Progressive Dehumanization: the Comfortable Concentration Camp', Friedan glances at the territory of female neurosis which Atwood's novel explores with such imaginative insight:

> If the human organism has an innate urge to grow, to expand and become all it can be, it is not surprising that the bodies and the minds of healthy women begin to rebel as they try to adjust to a role that does not permit this growth.   (p. 292)

Friedan cites case histories of women suffering from fatigue, heart attacks and psychotic breakdowns, a catalogue of female hysterical illness induced by women's attempts to conform to the artificial codes of the feminine mystique. It is precisely in that speculative area of pathology so 'puzzling to doctors and analysts' that the nervous eating disorder of Atwood's heroine is located, where the female body becomes the site of victimisation, internal conflict and rebellion.

The Feminine Mystique helps to contextualise *The Edible Woman* as social commentary, for the latter is a 1960s story of a young woman's identity crisis provoked by pressures against which she finds herself seriously at odds. Marian MacAlpin is a Toronto university graduate in her twenties with an independent income, living in Toronto and sharing an apartment with another young woman, Ainsley Tewce. She also has a boyfriend, to whom she becomes engaged, Peter Wollander, an ambitious young lawyer with a passionate interest in guns and cameras. The narrative traces the stages of Marian's rebellion against social conformity as she becomes increasingly disillusioned with her job and her fiancé to the point where her inner conflict finds its outward expression in an eating disorder whose symptoms resemble anorexia nervosa. While the novel hints at the connection between social institutions and personal relations, which would become the central theme in Atwood's collection of poems *Power Politics* (1971), it cannot easily be classified as a realist text for it insistently challenges the conventions of realism by its excursions into fantasy and its flights of metaphorical inventiveness. *The Edible Woman* is a comedy of resistance and survival which subverts social definitions from within, as is shown by the way Marian finally wins her independence from the feminine mystique through her traditionally feminine gesture of making a cake, which she offers to the two men in her life. Her fiancé refuses it; her strange changeling mentor and guide, Duncan, a graduate student in English, helps her to eat it all up. Clearly, an iced cake in the shape of a woman is the central metaphor for Marian's perception of woman's condition and fate as decreed by the feminine mystique, so that her cake-baking is both a gesture of complicity in the domestic myth and also a critique of it. Atwood described the tea ritual as 'symbolic cannibalism', with the cake as simulacrum of the socialised feminine image which Marian rejects; but it is also of course a party game, with Duncan as the 'child' and Marian as the 'mother' once again in control. Eating the cake is an act of celebration that marks the decisive moment of Marian's recovery from an hysterical illness and her return to the social order. Once again she becomes a 'consumer', for it is difficult if not impossible to reconstruct one's identity outside the symbolic and social order, and individual survival is likely to mean compromises with society. As Atwood remarked, baking that cake is 'an action, a preposterous one in a way, as all pieces of symbolism in a realistic context are, but what she is obviously making is a subsitute for herself'.[3]

The originality of *The Edible Woman* lies in its exposure of the 'sexual sell' promoted by the feminine mystique, for the narrative reveals how social paradigms of femininity may distort women's perceptions of their sexuality in the interests of creating childlike or doll-like fantasy figures. A young woman like Marian, sensitised as she is to the social script of gender relations and feminine expectations, seems to have little consciousness of her own body either in its maternal urges or in its erotic pleasures. Female bodies and biological processes like pregnancy, childbirth and menstruation figure in the novel, but they are treated with a measure of comic detachment. When viewed through Marian's eyes, sexually mature female bodies become grotesque and rather disgusting, whether it is her friend Clara's pregnant body or the fat, ageing bodies of her fellow office workers at the Christmas party, or the fiasco of the coast-to-coast market research survey on sanitary napkins, where some of the questionnaires 'obviously went out to men' ('Here's one with "Tee Hee" written on it, from a Mr. Leslie Andrewes,' p. 110).

In contrast to Marian, her friends Clara and Ainsley celebrate women's biological destiny, though their different approaches to motherhood turn them into parodic images of the maternal principle. Clara, who enters the narrative heavily pregnant with her third child, looks to Marian 'like a boa-constrictor that has swallowed a watermelon' (p. 31). Marian sees her as one of the casualties of the female life, a representation of the duplicities of the feminine mystique, which could transform a girl who was 'everyone's ideal of translucent perfume-advertisement femininity' (p. 36) into a kind of female monster, the helpless victim of her own biology:

> She simply stood helpless while the tide of dirt rose round her, unable to stop it or evade it. The babies were like that too; her own body seemed somehow beyond her, going its own way without reference to any directions of hers.   (p. 37)

There are several ironies here, not least a foreshadowing of Marian's own bodily insurrection, but the most obvious is that Clara's own attitude to motherhood is quite savagely unmaternal: 'Her metaphors for her children included barnacles encrusting a ship and limpets clinging to a rock' (p. 36). Yet when Clara's baby is born, she describes the process to Marian with a kind of rapture: 'Oh marvellous; really marvellous. I watched the whole thing, it's messy, all that blood and junk, but I've got to admit it's sort of fascinating' (p. 128). Marian's response is not one of sympathy but of alarm at possibly being implicated by her age and her gender, and she escapes from the maternity hospital 'as if from a culvert or cave. She was glad she wasn't Clara' (p. 132).

If Clara represents woman's passive fulfilment of her biological destiny, then Ainsley represents a more intellectualised approach to maternity as she embarks on it as a social project with the aim of

becoming a single parent. (Ainsley's derogatory remarks about
men and fatherhood are amusingly similar to those of Offred's
mother in *The Handmaid's Tale*, written 20 years later.) Her pro-
gramme is entirely ideological and in a curious way academic and
theoretical:

> 'Every woman should have at least one baby.' She sounded like
> a voice on the radio saying that every woman should have at least
> one electric hair-dryer. 'It's even more important than sex. It
> fulfills your deepest femininity.' (pp. 40–1)

As an undergraduate Ainsley must have read Margaret Mead. Marian
mentions her fondness for paperbacks by anthropologists, about
primitive cultures, and Ainsley herself expounds on breast-feeding
habits in South America. In her quest to fulfil an anthropological
concept of female 'wholeness' Ainsley displays all the contradictions
between 'nature' and 'culture' identified by Friedan in her critique
of Mead's theories when they are put into practice by university-
educated North American women. Ainsley's pursuit of Marian's
friend Leonard Slank, a notorious womaniser with a penchant for
inexperienced young girls, works as a comic reversal of the traditional seduction plot, exposing the dynamics of the sexual game in
all its duplicity. Ainsley's artful imitation of youthful innocence ('it
was necessary for her mind to appear as vacant as her face', p. 119)
and Leonard's pose of world-weary drunken lecher are equally
false, as is revealed when she triumphantly announces to him that
she is pregnant. He collapses in a crisis of Freudian horror:

> 'Now I'm going to be all mentally tangled up in Birth. Fecundity.
> Gestation. Don't you realize what that will do to me? It's obscene,
> that horrible oozy...'
>   'Don't be idiotic,' Ainsley said. '...You're displaying the classic
> symptoms of uterus envy.' (p. 159)

It is Leonard who is the casualty in this battle between the sexes.
However, as part of the comic deconstruction of stereotypes here,
the most passionate advocate for the maternal principle is a male
Jungian literary critic, the graduate student Fischer Smythe, who is
obsessed with archetypal womb symbols and who in turn becomes
fascinated with the pregnant Ainsley as an Earth Mother figure just

as Leonard Slank recoils from her 'goddamn fertility-worship' (p. 214). Indeed, it is the male characters who display far more interest in female biology than the women and whose language rises to heights of eloquence or abuse in their fantasy representations of the female body. By contrast, Marian refuses to get involved either with Ainsley's 'fraud' or with Clara's domestic chaos.

Not only does Marian feel threatened by childbearing but she also feels alienated from her body in other ways as well. At the office Christmas party, surrounded by the fat and ageing bodies of her colleagues, Marian's perspective shifts from a kind of anthropological detachment to a sudden shocked recognition that she too shares this mysterious female condition:

> What peculiar creatures they were; and the continual flux between the outside and the inside, taking things in, giving them out...she was one of them, her body the same, identical, merged with that other flesh that choked the air in the flowered room with its sweet organic scent; she felt suffocated by this thick sargasso-sea of femininity. (p. 167)

We begin to understand that Marian does not wish to turn into any of the models of adult women offered by society, and that behind her conventional femininity lies a horror of the body which relates to her fear of growing up, signalled by either marriage, maternity or the office pension plan. She wants none of these futures, and it is in this context of challenge to the discourses of both femininity and adulthood that her hysterical eating disorder needs to be interpreted.

Marian's inability to eat may look like anorexia nervosa, but the etiology of her disease actually differs quite markedly from the clinical diagnoses as summarised by Noelle Caskey in her historical account 'Interpreting Anorexia Nervosa'.[4] Though Marian suffers from the visual and cognitive distortions that characterise semi-starvation, most of the usual symptoms of anorexia are absent. Hers is a pathological condition of self-division, which Dennis Cooley has identified in *Power Politics*:

> We find in *Power Politics* what we find in so many Atwood books of the 1970s especially (I include the novels): namely, a division of head and body at the neck. The neck figures as pinched conduit between faculties (mind/body) whose schism is disastrous.[5]

With Marian this division signals two powers of agency within herself, will and instinct acting in opposition to each other in a pattern which becomes the main line of narrative action:

> Whatever it was that had been making these decisions, not her mind certainly, rejected anything that had an indication of bone or tendon or fibre.   (p. 152)

Though she sees this as a malignant, possibly life-threatening condition, she is powerless to control it. At the peak of her disease she reaches the point where she cannot eat or drink anything at all:

> It had finally happened at last then. Her body had cut itself off. The food circle had dwindled to a point, a black dot, closing everything outside.   (p. 257)

Of all the diagnoses of anorexia, the one closest to Marian's case would appear to be what Susan Bordo calls 'a gender-related and historically localised disorder',[6] where the body's refusal to eat forms part of a discourse of hysterical protest. In this early feminist text the personal is fused with the political as Marian's body speaks its language of rebellion against the socialised feminine identity that she appears to have already accepted.[7] Marian can quote the received 1960s wisdom about the influence of the subconscious on behaviour, 'It was my subconscious getting ahead of my conscious self, and the subconscious has its own logic' (p. 101), though it is typical of her lack of self-knowledge that she should so disastrously misinterpret its messages in her own case. Marian's hysteria is a mode of metaphorical discourse popularised first by Freudian psychoanalysis as the language of the subconscious and of dreams, and then appropriated by feminist writers and critics as a distinguishing mark of female subjectivity, where the feminine 'imaginary' disrupts the logic of a masculine 'symbolic' order.[8] Marian's rebellion occurs at a level below consciousness and then manifests itself in hallucinations and body language. As Freud has shown, the body evades the repression of conscious will by speaking out in the language of metaphor, so that Marian's anxiety at the prospect of her 'erasure' as an independent social being through marriage to Peter is externalised first in images of metamorphosis, where she identifies with animal victims, and then even more overtly by her body's panic protest in its refusal to ingest food or drink. The social system 'makes her sick'. It is not insignificant that Peter represents the law-giver and the hunter in Marian's scenarios of violence, whereas she is the escape artist, identified with the spaces of the wilderness. The pattern is signalled in her first attempt at flight, when she runs away from the Park Plaza Hotel and the talk of her male companions, Peter, and Leonard Slank, about cameras and hunting. That attempt is fuelled by Marian's subconscious identification with the disembowelled rabbit in Peter's story, and then confirmed by the description of her recapture:

> I felt myself caught, set down and shaken. It was Peter, who must have stalked me and waited there on the side-street, knowing I would come over the wall. 'What the hell got into you?' he said. (p. 74)

Of course, she is accused by the two men of emotional instability: 'Didn't think you were the hysterical type,' though Marian's own silent response offers a different interpretation of 'hysteria' as an unconscious gesture of resistance.

The hunting imagery is continued in the narrative, for the trap is sprung with Peter's marriage proposal that same night. Though Marian makes every effort to adjust herself to the socially acceptable image of adoring female partner, her eating disorder is clearly a continuation of this pattern of psychic resistance, a metaphorical expression of panic at the idea of marriage. It is Marian's imagination which is the subversive force, the place where food is metamorphosed into living flesh and blood:

> She looked down at her own half-eaten steak and suddenly saw it as a hunk of muscle. Blood red. Part of a real cow that once moved and ate and was killed...and she had been devouring it. (pp. 151–2)

The cannibalism motif, which carries through to the end with the cake, is a sign of hallucinatory displacement, where metaphor inscribes Marian's unconscious fears of becoming an object of consumption herself. As her marriage gets closer, so her disorder gets worse and the list of 'forbidden foods' gets longer, until the point where she can eat nothing at all.

However, this is to leap ahead, neglecting the circumstances that produced Marian's rebellion in the first place. On the surface she would seem to be content with her destiny – with her job in a marketing firm which promotes sexual stereotyping, and then her forthcoming marriage and entry into domesticity. Reading back from her crisis, however, there are early warning signs of Marian's dissent in her antipathy to the maternal projects of Clara and Ainsley and her futile escape attempts from Peter. Even the marriage proposal itself, made unexpectedly in the midst of a furious argument and with an electric storm raging, is a parodic version of the female romance plot:

'When do you want to get married?' he asked, almost gruffly.

My first impulse was to answer, with the evasive flippancy I'd always used before when he'd asked me serious questions about myself, 'What about Groundhog Day?' But instead I heard a soft flannelly voice I barely recognized, saying, 'I'd rather have you decide that. I'd rather leave the big decisions up to you.' (p. 90)

This puppet voice imitates Friedan's helplessly dependent women, 'who wanted the men to make the major decisions' (*The Feminine Mystique*, p. 18). By the end of the Part 1, Marian's submission to the feminine mystique is almost complete as she throws away her university textbooks and prepares to think about what a 'well-organized marriage' (*The Edible Woman*, p. 102) might mean.

There is only one disruptive element in her scenario of social conformity. This is represented by the oddly childlike figure of Duncan, the young man who alone had challenged the rhetoric of Marian's Moose Beer questionnaires:

'First, what about "Deep-down manly flavour?"'

He threw his head back and closed his eyes. 'Sweat,' he said, considering. 'Canvas gym shoes. Underground locker-rooms and jock-straps.' (p. 52)

He is also the man in the laundromat who stares at the washing machines in their endlessly repetitive cycles and with whom Marian feels an inexplicable affinity. Though 'he has nothing at all to do with Peter' (p. 103), Duncan is the unaccommodated remainder, whose role is to unsettle the whole structure of Marian's expectations by revealing its lack.

The design of the narrative with its radical shift from the first-person narration in Part 1 to the third person in Part 2 underlines Marian's loss of an independent sense of self; it is also Part 2 which signals the onset and crisis of her nervous disease. As the bride to be, she has already opted out of the professional world and has nothing to do but wait passively for her wedding: 'She was floating, letting the current hold her up' (p. 115). Under the spell of the feminine mystique, she is merely biding her time, yet there are signals that this is for Marian what Friedan would call 'The Mistaken Choice'. Though an apparently willing victim, Marian is troubled by her strange eating disorder and by inexplicable intimations of 'sodden formless unhappiness'. Perhaps the best gloss on her condition is provided by the American poet Adrienne Rich, who writes about her own state of mind in the late 1950s using strikingly similar images: 'What frightened me most was the sense of drift, of being pulled along on a current which called itself my destiny, but in which I seemed to be losing touch with whoever I had been, with the girl who had experienced her own will and energy almost ecstatically at times, walking around a city or riding a train or typing in a student room.'[9] It is that concept of freedom which Duncan represents, enhanced in his case by a Peter Pan pose of childlike irresponsibility as he refashions the world according to his own wishes and so fantasises an alternative reality. He challenges all Marian's traditional ideas of masculinity, romantic love and parent–child relations, while his 'family' of two other male graduate students, Trevor and Fish, forms a gaily subversive trio who transgress traditional gender roles, dedicated as they are to the domestic arts of washing and ironing, cooking and parenting. Caught between this playful student world and the world of social conformity, Marian loses any sense of herself as a unified subject, beginning to hallucinate her emotional conflict in images of bodily dissolution and haunted by hallucinations of fragmentation. Lying in the bath on the evening of the first party which she and Peter are giving as an engaged couple, she begins to believe that her body is 'coming apart layer by layer like a piece of cardboard in a gutter puddle' (p. 218).

That party, to which all the main characters in the novel are invited, represents the climax of Atwood's 'anti-comedy':

I think in your standard 18th-century comedy you have a young couple who is faced with difficulty in the form of somebody who embodies the restrictive forces of society and they trick or overcome this difficulty and end up getting married. The same thing happens in *The Edible Woman* except the wrong person gets married. . . . The comedy solution would be a tragic solution for Marian.[10]

Atwood's fictional method revises a traditional genre in order to highlight the artifice of literary conventions and the social myths they inscribe. There are other divergences from traditional comic patterns here as well. Not only is the artifice of femininity exposed ('You didn't tell me it was a masquerade,' says Duncan, looking at Marian's lacquered hair and her slinky red dress) but the party provides the first occasion when the male protagonists speak about femininity from their own perspective, revealing a surprisingly high level of masculine anxiety about this topic. The most devastating analysis comes from Clara's husband Joe, the philosophy lecturer, who earnestly challenges such mythologising, making a political statement from his personal point of view as a husband and a teacher:

> she's hollow, she doesn't know who she is any more; her core has been destroyed. . . . I can see it happening with my own female students. But it would be futile to warn them.   (p. 236)

There is also a confrontation between the glowingly pregnant Ainsley and Leonard Slank, whose masculinity is revealed to be a fragile structure. When she makes her public announcement of his paternity he collapses in a drunken heap, only to be cast aside as Ainsley finds a new father figure for her unborn child in the scholarly Fischer Smythe. That Jungian enthusiast sees her as the living embodiment of the mythic feminine and he pats her belly tenderly, 'his voice heavy with symbolic meaning' (p. 241).

Such comedy co-exists with a more serious crisis of realisation for Marian, who looks into her vision of the feminine mystique only to find that she has disappeared from her own story:

> There was Peter, forty-five and balding but still recognizable as Peter, standing in bright sunlight beside a barbecue with a long fork. . . . She looked carefully for herself in the garden, but she wasn't there and the discovery chilled her.   (p. 243)

That self-obliteration in fantasy prefigures Marian's disappearance from the party for it combines with the traumatic moment when Peter tries to take her photograph, and Marian flees like a hunted animal:

She could not let him catch her this time. Once he pulled the trigger she would be stopped, fixed indissolubly in that gesture, that single stance, unable to move or change.   (p. 245)

At last Marian knows what she does not want, and so she escapes from the social script to her unscripted meeting in the laundromat with Duncan and into their brief liaison in a sleazy hotel. Though it begins as a parody of lovemaking, with Duncan's complaint that there is 'altogether too much flesh around here' (p. 253), it ends rather differently with him gently stroking her 'almost as though he was ironing her'. There is also a suggestion of their wilderness affinity as Duncan's face nudges into her flesh, 'like the muzzle of an animal, curious, and only slightly friendly' (p. 254), and it is in the wilderness of a Toronto ravine to which he guides her that Marian's undramatised clarification of mind occurs. Duncan's action in leaving her alone there is exactly what Friedan might have prescribed for bewildered dissenters from the feminine mystique, 'for that last and most important battle *can* be fought in the mind and spirit of woman herself' (*The Feminine Mystique*, p. 369).

By following her own line of metaphorical thinking, Marian discovers a way to solve what for her is an ontological problem, 'Some way she could know what was real: a test, simple and direct as litmus-paper' (*The Edible Woman*, p. 267). The test is of course the cake that she bakes and then ices in the shape of a woman, a transformation of science into domestic ritual. Gazing at the cake lady and thinking of her destiny she says, 'You look delicious.... And that's what will happen to you; that's what you get for being food' (p. 270). However, when offered the cake Peter flees, either from Marian's literalised metaphor or from her undisguised hostility, probably into the arms of Lucy, one of Marian's office friends with 'her delicious dresses and confectionery eyes' (p. 112). Maybe Marian was right and an 'edible woman' was what Peter had really wanted all along. It is as if a spell has been broken: Marian's confusion falls away, and recognising that 'The cake after all was only a cake' (pp. 271–2), she starts to eat it. Only Ainsley, ever alive to symbolic implications, bothers to translate the significance of Marian's cake eating, ironically echoing Peter's earlier accusations. '"Marian!" she exclaimed at last, with horror. "You're rejecting your femininity!"' (p. 272). This interpretation is confirmed by Marian, who 'plunged her fork into the carcass, neatly severing the body from the head' (p. 273). That violent gesture with its parody of vampire-slaying carries a further implication that the feminine image has been draining Marian's life blood but will have the power to do so no more.

Part 3, with its energetic return to a first-person narrative, 'I was cleaning up the apartment' (p. 277), is devoted to tidying up the plot in a comic *dénouement* where it is significant that the three women protagonists survive better than the men: Peter has left and Marian is once again independent; Leonard Slank has had a nervous breakdown and is being cared for by Clara like another of her numerous children, while Ainsley has fulfilled her biological mission while managing to conform neatly to social convention by marrying Fischer Smythe and going off to Niagara Falls for their honeymoon. Marian's house-cleaning works as another domestic analogy for her own rehabilitation, as her response to Duncan's phone call suggests: 'Now that I was thinking of myself in the first person singular again I found my own situation much more interesting than his' (p. 278). Their tea is a replay of Peter's visit, though with the important differences that Duncan eats the cake (described by Marian as 'the remains of the cadaver') and that they talk together in a way that she and Peter did not manage to do. It is a curious conversation in which Duncan casually offers five possible interpretations of the preceding narrative action as if he were commenting on a literary text in a graduate seminar. The one reading he categorically rejects is Marian's assertion that Peter was trying to destroy her: 'That's just something you made up' (p. 280). Instead, he multiplies the possibilities around the question: Who has been trying to destroy whom? Duncan's irony (like his ironing) represents a deliberate distancing from Marian's personal problems in a general comment on human behaviour. Such a device with its opening up of multiple perspectives shifts any reading of this novel beyond a single feminist focus, implying that the politics of gender is only one example of the power struggles in any relationship. It is Duncan who has the last word, transforming this into a comedy of good manners as he finishes cleaning up the cake: ' "Thank you," he said, licking his lips. "It was delicious" ' (p. 281). He is the good child who says thank you, as Marian the mother regards him with a smile. Yet the ending is not quite the sentimental resolution it may look at first glance, for Duncan remains an enigma,[11] and on a psychological level his eating of the cake resembles nothing so much as the activity of a psychotherapist.

The domestic scenario raises one last point which relates to the important question of female creativity. It is significant that Marian has chosen to make her protest through a traditionally feminine mode which bypasses language: 'What she needed was something that avoided words, she didn't want to get tangled up in a discussion' (p. 267). She thinks that she has accomplished her purpose, though as any reader in the twenty-first century would notice, none of the three young women – Marian, Ainsley nor Clara – has escaped from their culturally defined gender roles; they are still producing cakes and babies. This leaves unresolved the issue of women's attempts to establish themselves as independent subjects working creatively through writing or painting, though this first novel opens the way to Atwood's 'topical topic', to which she will return again and again from *Surfacing* to *The Blind Assassin*.

SUGGESTIONS FOR FURTHER READING

Gibson, Graeme (ed.), *Eleven Canadian Novelists* (Toronto: Anansi, 1973), pp. 1–31. Repr. in *Margaret Atwood: Conversations*, ed. Earl G. Ingersoll (London: Virago, 1992), pp. 3–19.

Keith, W. J., *Introducing Margaret Atwood's 'The Edible Woman': A Reader's Guide*, Canadian Fiction Series 3 (Toronto: ECW Press, 1989).

Mycak, Sonia, *In Search of the Split Subject: Psychoanalysis, Phenomenology, and the Novels of Margaret Atwood* (Toronto: ECW Press, 1996), pp. 47–69.

3
Surfacing and *Survival*

As far as I'm concerned, life begins with geology, and with geography ... look at a map of Canada.

(*Conversations*, p. 131)

Margaret Atwood's novel *Surfacing* and her literary history *Survival: A Thematic Guide to Canadian Literature* were both published in 1972 at the beginning of her career, when she first put Canadian literature on the map internationally by distinguishing it from British and American literature, 'with which it is often compared or confused'.[1] In *Survival* she refers to a distinctive 'Canadian signature', which would encode the signs of Canadian history, geography, and cultural attitudes in a literary work, and for the young Atwood that signature was represented by the trope of 'wilderness'. My emphasis in this chapter is on the distinctive ways in which the wilderness is used in these two early texts, though I shall also suggest some of the shifts in Atwood's writing of the wilderness that are visible in her later fiction. Writers are rooted in a particular place and Atwood's place is Canada:

> You come out of something, and you can then branch out in all kinds of different directions, but that doesn't mean cutting yourself off from your roots and from your earth.   (*Conversations*, p. 143)

The organic image of the tree and the emphasis on location point directly towards that significant element in Atwood's construction of Canadian identity, the concept of wilderness. Wilderness has multiple functions – as geographical location marker, as spatial metaphor, and as English Canada's most popular cultural myth. In its endless refigurings in her work, we may trace the ongoing narrative of Atwood's responses to shifts in Canadian social attitudes and ideology. In the 1970s with *The Journals of Susanna Moodie*, *Surfacing* and *Survival*, Atwood began by representing wilderness to Canadians as their own distinctive national space; in the 1990s with the short-story collection *Wilderness Tips*, the emphasis shifts to a much bleaker scenario where wilderness as geographical place is under threat from pollution and the spread of urbanisation, while as cultural myth of national identity it has clearly become an anachronism in multicultural Canada. At the beginning of the twenty-first century, *Surfacing* and *Survival* may be assessed as the products of 1970s English-Canadian cultural nationalism, taking their place in the history of continuing debates about postcolonialism in Canada, though we need to pay attention to Atwood's early wilderness texts in order to understand her importance as the major mythographer of modern Canada.[2]

Geographically, wilderness is defined as wild uncultivated land, which in Canada includes vast tracts of forest with innumerable lakes, and also the Arctic North. The important question for any narrative of Canadian identity is the way in which, and by whom, these unexplored spaces have been appropriated as popular cultural myth. The myth of wilderness as empty space is of course a white myth, for the wilderness was not really empty; it was only indecipherable to Europeans, who came to the New World as explorers, traders, soldiers, missionaries and settlers. Within colonial discourse, wilderness was presented as a space outside civilised social order and Christian moral laws, the place of mysterious and threatening otherness. In this sense only could it be construed as blank, for of course there were traces all through the forests of the indigenous inhabitants and the tracks of wild animals. Inevitably this construction of wilderness produced ambivalent not to say contradictory responses: on the one hand, it was construed by most Europeans as a place where one could get lost or killed; while on the other, it would be seen as the space of freedom from social constraints. Atwood's double vision entertains both these possibilities, while recognising a third possibility, that wilderness might be interpreted very differently from a Native perspective. The discourse of wilderness is now under revision, thanks to the increasing intervention of voices from the First Nations since the 1980s, which intermesh with popular contemporary ecological awareness about the dangers of environmental degradation.

For Atwood wilderness was already a cultural myth when she inherited it in the 1940s, and her fiction is full of references to the English-Canadian literary tradition of explorers' narratives, animal stories, woodcraft and survival manuals which she read as a child, and to representations of wilderness by the most famous school of early twentieth-century Canadian painters, the Group of Seven.

Atwood spent a great deal of her childhood in the forests of northern Ontario and Quebec, and then attended summer camps as a teenager in the 1950s; this is the territory to which she keeps returning in her fiction. There is a vivid representation of the wilderness in her ghost story 'Death by Landscape' done in the pictorial idiom of the Group of Seven, where the forest is presented as silent territory empty of any human figures, though their traces are there:

> They are pictures of convoluted tree trunks on an island of pink wave-smoothed stone, with more islands behind; of a lake with rough, bright, sparsely wooded cliffs; of a vivid river shore with a tangle of bush and two beached canoes, one red, one grey; of a yellow autumn woods with the ice-blue gleam of a pond half-seen through the interlaced branches.[3]

Out of the dual context of lived experience and cultural tradition Atwood has constructed her changing versions of wilderness as she writes and rewrites her distinctively Canadian signature.

Atwood's first complete figuring of wilderness occurs in the early poetic sequence *The Journals of Susanna Moodie* (1970), though there are earlier versions in her unfinished novel *The Nature Hut* (*c*.1966) and her unpublished story 'Transfigured Landscape' described by Atwood as 'the first, very first bit of *Surfacing* to emerge, Winter 64–5?'[4] *Susanna Moodie* is Atwood's chronicle of a nineteenth-century Englishwoman's response to the landscape of eastern Canada. Moodie had published her own autobiographical accounts in *Roughing It in the Bush* (1852) and *Life in the Clearings* (1856), and these poems reinvent that pioneer woman through whom Atwood articulates the 'inescapable doubleness of vision' which she sees as a peculiar historical characteristic of the Canadian psyche:

> We are all immigrants to this place, even if we were born here: the country is too big for anyone to inhabit completely, and in the parts unknown to us we move in fear, exiles and invaders.[5]

Initially wilderness is presented as an alien landscape that threatens to erase Susanna Moodie's sense of her identity as a Victorian lady, yet as the sequence develops it becomes the place of mysterious transformations. 'Crept in upon by green', Moodie begins to perceive her surroundings in a new way, no longer as a threat but as harmonious natural order. In this process of shifting subjective perceptions

Atwood sketches a feminised reading of wilderness in the relation between woman and the natural world, so that although Susanna Moodie leaves the bush before she learns its secret language, a hundred years later her ghost appears as a witness to the presence of the past in 1960s Toronto:

> Turn, look down:
> There is no city;
> This is the centre of a forest
> Your place is empty.
>
> ('A Bus along St Clair: December',
> *The Journals of Susanna Moodie*, p. 61)

As Atwood comments, 'Susanna Moodie has finally turned herself inside out, and has become the spirit of the land she once hated' (p. 64), while it is the modern city which has become an unexplored, threatening wilderness. With characteristic doubleness Atwood reinvents white English-Canadian constructions of identity, charting a distinctive New World positioning in relation to history, geography and culture suggestive of a continuity between immigration narratives and a contemporary awareness of psychic dislocation. This paradoxical position is emblematised in *Surfacing* by the narrator's comment: 'Now we're on my home ground, foreign territory',[6] as borders blur between 'home' and 'exile' in a wilderness place which may be buried under the city pavements of Toronto, but is still there in collective memory and myth.

Atwood uses this wilderness sign of distinctive national heritage when she addresses Canadian readers in *Surfacing* and *Survival*. Those texts arguably exist in a symbiotic relationship for although the novel was written first, it was through writing it that Atwood realised certain common themes that her fiction shared with other Canadian writing, and *Survival* in turn shows Atwood creating the critical context in which to read her own fiction. Beginning with the question, 'What's Canadian about Canadian literature?' (*Survival*, p. 14), her project is clearly related to raising her readers' cultural and national self-consciousness. In *Survival* she describes key patterns of plot, theme and imagery which are 'like the field markings in bird-books: they will help you distinguish this species from all others' (*Survival*, p. 13). Significantly, her definition of Canadianness hinges on concepts of wilderness and survival in the tradition of nineteenth- and early twentieth-century woodcraft manuals:

What a lost person needs is a map of the territory.... Our literature is one such map, if we can learn to read it as *our* literature, as the product of who and where we have been. We need such a map desperately, we need to know about here, because here is where we live. For members of a country or a culture, shared knowledge of their place, their here, is not a luxury but a necessity. Without that knowledge we will not survive.   (pp. 18–19)

Having traced a Canadian literary tradition which is dominantly anglophone from the early nineteenth century to the 1970s, Atwood moves at the end of *Survival* beyond literary history to wider questions of cultural politics, urging her fellow Canadians to rehabilitate themselves in a postcolonial context, resisting both their European 'mother countries' and the United States by taking control of their own country:

control our own space, physical as well as cultural. But that space must be controlled with love or it will be the control typical of a tyranny: there will not be that much difference between Canadian ownership and the absentee-landlord draining of the land we already live under.   (p. 244)

Atwood speaks out against exploitation and destruction of the forests, urging the need to pay attention to ecological principles in a way that the highly developed American technological society was not doing, in order to preserve the environment for future generations. That same anxiety would be expressed with increasing urgency in *The Handmaid's Tale* (1985), again in the stories and fables of *Wilderness Tips* (1991) and *Good Bones* (1992), and most apocalyptically in *Oryx and Crake* (2003).

Surfacing begins and ends with the forest, for just as wilderness is significant in Atwood's version of literary history, so is it in the story of one woman's quest to find an appropriate language in which to write about her changing perceptions of her own identity as Canadian and female. This novel can be approached from many different directions, and it has already received a great deal of critical attention.[7] All I can hope to do here is to indicate some of the main lines of inquiry as I focus my discussion on the topics of wilderness, language and narrative form. One of the first Canadian reviews signalled the emblematic status of the novel when it described *Surfacing* as 'a Canadian fable in which the current obsessions of Canadians become symbols in a drama of personal survival: nationalism, feminism, death, culture, art, nature, pollution'.[8] This catalogue also illustrates the parallels between *Surfacing* and *Survival*, and though it is not thematics which I wish to highlight here, it is worth noting how the novel actually offers one revisionary reading of a 'Canadian signature' as recommended in *Survival*. Explorers' journeys are refigured in contemporary Canada as individual quests for spiritual survival; victims (either Canadian or female) are urged to take responsibility for their situation and to assume power, thereby ceasing to see themselves as victims; perceptions of wilderness are reshaped so that Canada no longer figures as 'exile' but is transformed into 'home ground'.

The novel begins like a detective story, where the unnamed narrator goes back to the place of her childhood in the Quebec bush to search for her lost father, who, as we later learn, has already drowned in the lake while looking for Indian rock paintings. Gradually she discovers that what she is really searching for is her own past. She is looking for those lost bits of herself buried in her repressed memories, and it is only in the wilderness that she finds a way to heal the split within her own psyche, thereby restoring her emotional and spiritual health. The story traces the multilayered process of reintegration by which a dislocated and damaged woman manages to come to terms with her past, while recognising that the past cannot ever be retrieved, though it may be partially reconstructed through memory and fantasy. By the end, the narrator's perceptions of her relation to the world have changed, so that she is ready to leave the wilderness to return to society. Now the only map she possesses is the network of trails on her own hand, her 'lifeline' as she calls it.

This very human-centred position is one that Atwood character-istically adopts ('This above all, to refuse to be a victim'), where reverence for life, a commitment to love and trust and to moral responsibility, are asserted as primary values. Such a diagrammatic account of the novel leaves out many things – not only the crucial lie at its centre, which is revealed in Chapter 17 when the narrator dives down into the lake, but also the visionary episodes which chart the stages of her rehabilitation in the wilderness. These will be discussed, but I have tried to emphasise here the ways in which this text works simultaneously on two levels. There is the outer world of landscape and society and there is the inner world of the narrator's own mind, where borders blur between realism and fantasy as the language shifts between realistic description and metaphors of psychological space.

Of course, the site of this border-blur is in wilderness territory, for wilderness is not only 'geography and geology' but is also discursively located within the text as the site of dynamic transformations. It also functions as metaphor for the lost place of origin with its traces of Amerindian precolonial history in the submerged rock paintings and its forgotten Indian sacred sites. It is this spiritualised sense of place which is a significant component in *Surfacing*, for as Atwood tried to explain in an early interview:

> The only sort of good, authentic kind of a thing to have is something that comes out of the place where you are, or shall we put it another way and say the reality of your life.... Christianity in this country is imported religion. The assumption of the book, if there is one, is that there are gods that do exist here, but nobody knows about them.... The authentic religion that was here has been destroyed; you have to discover it in some other way. How that fits in with the book I don't know, but I'm sure it has something to do with it.[9]

Atwood is here sketching the metaphysical and historical dimensions of her cultural nationalism. Yet her novel begins from 'the place where you are', and one of the great strengths of *Surfacing* is its sense of specific location. The area where the novel is set has been identified as that forested part of the Canadian Shield north-west of North Bay near Lake Kipawa on the borders between Ontario and Quebec.[10] As the critic George Woodcock wrote in 1990, 'The environment is the great theme of *Surfacing*,'[11] and the opening paragraph of the novel presents a realistic description of a journey by car from a city which must be Toronto out into the wilderness:

> I can't believe I'm on this road again, twisting along past the lake where the white birches are dying, the disease is spreading up from the south, and I notice they now have sea-planes for hire. (*Surfacing*, p. 7)

The wilderness of the early 1970s is evidently no longer the wilderness of Canadian pastoral myth. Instead, it is a territory already suffering the effects of civilisation, where the trees are dying of acid rain blowing up from the United States and the area is invaded by tourist roads bringing week-end fishermen and hunters. As the highway signs show with their 'mélange of demands and languages' (English English, American English and French), this is cottage country on the border between two provinces and two cultures, and the district already has a history of European colonisation that goes back at least as far as the narrator's childhood memories of a paper mill and a dam built sixty years ago to 'control' the lake. The marks of a socialised nature are already there in the signs of human habitation and exploitation, the disappearance of the Native population ('The government had put them somewhere else, corralled them', p. 85), and the small community beside the lake, which represents a hybridised colonial culture. Yet though damaged, the forest landscape is still capable of regenerating itself and of offering its traditional protective cover: 'The peninsula is where I left it, pushing out from the island shore with the house not even showing through the trees' (p. 32).

Coming home is to enter not only another place but another time, as the narrator tracks back into an almost forgotten past that stretches beyond personal memory to the local history of the district and even further back into prehistory:

> In the cool green among the trees, new trees and stumps, the stumps with charcoal crusts on them, scabby and crippled, survivors of an old disaster. Sight flowing ahead of me over the ground, eyes filtering the shapes, the names of things fading but their forms and uses remaining, the animals learned what to eat without nouns.... Beneath it the invisible part, threadlike underground network. (pp. 149–50)

The living forest still bears traces of the past in the present, functioning like a text in another language. This, as the narrator comes to understand, is a language of changing natural forms, for the forest is the place of dynamic transformations within a delicately balanced ecological system:

> Out of the leaf nests the flowers rise, pure white, flesh of gnats and midges, petals now, metamorphosis... energy of decay turning to growth, green fire. I remember the heron; by now it will be insects, frogs, other herons. My body also changes, the creature in me, plant–animal, sends out filaments in me. (pp. 167–8)

The imagery encodes not only analogy but also harmony between human and non-human at the basic level of life processes, where the female biological cycle has its parallels in the life cycle of the forest. Susanna Moodie left the wilderness knowing there was something she had not learned, but the narrator of *Surfacing*, while ignorant of Native traditions, reinvents 'new meanings' alone on her island, immersing herself in 'the other language' of the wilderness and the 'multilingual water' of the lake.

Indeed, *Surfacing* might be read not only as a psychological and spiritual quest but also as the record of a gendered quest for a new language which is more responsive to an organic conceptualisation of reality. Some of the most interesting questions the novel raises are arguably linguistic ones and Atwood gave a hint of what these might be in an interview in 1986:

> How do we know 'reality'? How do you encounter the piece of granite? How do you know it directly? Is there such a thing as knowing it directly without language?   (*Conversations*, p. 209)

Returning to *Surfacing* with these questions in mind, it is evident that initially the narrator has a deep distrust of words, seeing them as instruments of deception and domination rather than of communication. As a woman she feels 'trapped in a language that wasn't mine' (p. 106), placed in the position of victim in male power games of love and war; as an anglophone in Quebec she has to confront problems of translation 'when people could say words that would go into my ears meaning nothing' (p. 11); as a Canadian she feels compromised by American cultural influences:

> If you look like them and talk like them and think like them then you are them, I was saying, you speak their language, a language is everything you do.   (p. 129)

So her quest for self-rehabilitation is also a quest to find her own 'dialect' amidst all the languages available to her: 'It was there in me, the evidence, only needing to be deciphered' (p. 76).

Her quest proceeds through a series of clearly marked stages to which the narrative structure draws our attention, for the novel is arranged in three sections, with the whole of Part 2 (Chapters 9–19) enclosed in a curious way by the image of the narrator's clenched fist:

From where I am now it seems as if I've always known, everything, time is compressed like the fist I close on my knee in the
darkening bedroom. I hold inside it the clues and solutions and
the power for what I must do now.   (p. 76)

That fist only uncloses after the series of discoveries at the centre of
the novel: first the discovery of her father's drawings of the Indian
rock paintings, then her dive into the lake, and finally the public
announcement that her father's drowned body has been found.
Only at this point does the narrative return to the present tense, and
we realise that the whole of the second section (which, we may also
notice for the first time, has been told in the past tense) has been
a reconstruction from memory and that the narrator has not moved
from her marginalised position in the bedroom of her father's cabin
while the others are playing cards in the sitting room:

> I unclose my fist, releasing, it becomes a hand again, palm a network
> of trails, lifeline, past present and future, the break in it closing
> together as I purse my fingers....I should be in mourning [for
> father]. But nothing has died, everything is alive, everything is
> waiting to become alive.   (p. 159)

Her most crucial discovery occurs when she dives down into the
lake, looking for the Indian rock paintings recorded in her father's
drawings. She does not find them; instead, she sees a strange
blurred image which may or may not be her father's drowned body,
but for her that image figures something else which has not so
far been revealed in the story. There are, however, hints from the
beginning of the narrative's self-division, in the 'funny break' in the
lines of her palm which her friend Anna observes, and in her own
observations about the break between the head and the body
because of the neck, which allows her to feel nothing. What she has
so assiduously repressed is the memory of her aborted child and this
is the revelation of the lie at the centre of the novel. There had never
been a marriage or a child as she had told her family and friends, but
only an affair with a married man and an abortion: 'I couldn't accept
it, that mutilation, ruin I'd made, I needed a different version' (p. 143),
as the narrator finally confesses. There is a long, detailed description
of how the narrator dives deep into the lake with the pale green
water darkening around her; yet only with that revelation does the
reader realise that the physical description has been shadowed by

another dimension. Looking beyond the printed text and back to the manuscript, we find the clue to that other dimension in a scribbled marginal note: the scribbled word is 'anaesthetic'.[12] Within the novel the hint is displaced to a different occasion entirely, for this text enacts the treasure hunt that the narrator is playing with her dead father, and all the clues are there for the reader to decipher:

> They slipped the needle into the vein and I was falling down, it was like diving, sinking from one layer of darkness to a deeper, deepest; when I rose up through the anaesthetic, pale green and then daylight, I could remember nothing. (p. 111)

Diving into the lake works both as a realistic description and as a metaphor for descent into the territory of the subconscious:

> It was there but it wasn't a painting, it wasn't on the rock. It was below me, drifting towards me from the furthest level where there was no life, a dark oval trailing limbs. It was blurred but it had eyes, they were open, it was something I knew about, a dead thing, it was dead. (p. 142)

As that blurred image surfaces into the narrator's consciousness it signals the beginning of her recovery process ('Feeling was beginning to seep back into me. I tingled like a foot that's been asleep,' p. 146). No other passage in Atwood has been so extensively interpreted and reinterpreted, so I shall merely add the comment that the redemption of her personal past is presented as a sacralised response to the wilderness itself in a tentative recognition of Native spiritual beliefs which have now been lost:

> These gods, here on the shore or in the water, unacknowledged or forgotten, were the only ones who had given me anything I needed; and freely. (p. 145)

That same night the narrator, whom from now on I shall call the 'surfacer',[13] insists that she and her partner go outside to make love, in a strange ritualistic encounter that she describes in language which has strong associations with her diving experience: 'He trembles and then I can feel my lost child surfacing within me, forgiving me, rising from the lake where it has been prisoned for so long...it buds, it sends out fronds' (pp. 161–2). The wilderness is for her a place of regeneration, and later when she is left alone on the island she has a series of wilderness encounters, which have been likened to shamanistic initiation rituals.[14] Certainly she undergoes a visionary education, where psycho-spiritual experience and sensory perceptions are presented as parallel modes of heightened awareness which lead to re-vision and insight. Atwood, in an interview, has commented on the relation her female characters have to landscape, contrasting it with some of her early poems about male explorers:

> The only way the [male] speaker could actually get into the landscape was by dying. In *Surfacing* it's a visionary experience in which language is transformed. There was some Indian influence on *Surfacing* at that point.   (*Conversations*, p. 114)

As the surfacer begins her invented 'initiation rites' she crosses another border, this time into the territory of hallucination and visionary experience. Suffering from exposure and near-starvation and having eaten nothing but some wrinkled yellow mushrooms, she has a series of visions. Significantly her first vision is of the lost Amerindian world of primeval forest, which looms up with the clarity of hallucination:

> The forest leaps upward, enormous, the way it was before they cut it, columns of sunlight frozen; the boulders float, melt, everything is made of water, even the rocks. In one of the languages there are no nouns, only verbs held for a longer moment.
>   The animals have no need for speech, why talk when you are a word
>   I lean against a tree, I am a tree leaning...
>   I am not an animal or a tree, I am the thing in which the trees and animals move and grow, I am a place.   (p. 181)

In this mythic world of dynamic process, reality consists of an uninterrupted flow of energy in perpetual metamorphosis. The surfacer experiences that process in imagination as her body boundaries dissolve and she has a vision of becoming vitally connected to the earth as a component of the wilderness landscape. However, to become part of that wilderness world would mean the loss of her individual identity as a human being, and she instinctively draws away from that merging, which is the way of mysticism or madness. Irremediably human, she has to 'break surface', to 'stand' separate again, marking her difference from trees and earth. This need for separation is confirmed in the surfacer's encounter with her father's ghost as wilderness monster, standing like a terrible warning against the abolition of borders: 'He wants the forest to flow back into the places his mind cleared' (p. 186). Immediately after this vision comes the crucial moment of recovery, where at the sight of a fish jumping on the lake the surfacer undergoes a series of radical shifts in perception till her vision settles back into a frame of normalcy:

> From the lake a fish jumps
> An idea of a fish jumps
> A fish jumps, carved wooden fish with dots painted on the sides, no, antlered fish thing drawn in red on cliffstone, protecting spirit. It hangs in the air suspended, flesh turned to icon, he has changed again, returned to the water. How many shapes can he take.
>   I watch it for an hour or so; then it drops and softens, the circles widen, it becomes an ordinary fish again.   (p. 187)

This is an exceptionally detailed record of how subjective perceptions of an object alter it, so that a real fish becomes first a visual image, then a word and an idea in the mind of the perceiver, changing into the wooden trophy seen earlier in the village bar, then into the antlered fish in the copy of the Indian rock paintings, then into the shadow of the dead father's body, till it finally becomes a fish again, dropping into the water. These multiple transformations are effected through subjective vision and registered in language that is closer to poetry than to prose. As the surfacer begins to see clearly again, she also 'sees' that the quest for her lost father has been at the same time the quest for herself, a realisation confirmed when she returns to what she thinks are the footprints of her father's ghost: 'I place my feet in them and find that they are my own' (p. 187).

The surfacer is at last able to tell her life story and to offer another model for remembering when she realises that her story, like the image of the fish, is always multiple and subject to changing perceptions. Having heard the other language of the wilderness, she has also realised that words are a human necessity, for to be alienated from words is to be alienated from one's fellow human beings. The final chapter is a curious blend of definition and indeterminacy. It begins with an assertion: 'This above all, to refuse to be a victim. . . . The word games, the winning and losing games are finished' (p. 191).

Incidentally, that statement parallels the 'creative non-victim' position which Atwood sketches in her famous 'Basic Victim Positions' in *Survival* (p. 38), a further illustration of the close connections between these two texts. However, a new language still has to be invented, and the surfacer is caught between new and old. As she contemplates the possibility of returning to her lover Joe, she faces the double possibility of love and trust but also of compromise and failure 'through the intercession of words' (p. 192). Her story ends tentatively as she stands hidden among the trees watching Joe, who has come back to find her and who is calling her name. Poised to step forward, she has not yet moved. However, the ending is optimistic for as the surfacer realises, 'withdrawing is no longer possible and the alternative is death' (p. 191). She no longer hears the voice of the wilderness but only Joe's voice as he comes like a mediator offering her 'something', whereas the wilderness has become silent again. The novel ends, 'The lake is quiet, the trees surround me, asking and giving nothing' (p. 192).

The narrator has surfaced through patriarchal language with its definitions of 'woman' and 'victim' and she has found an appropriate form for her own story of survival within a quest narrative that mixes realism and fantasy. Yet this is a quest which is markedly incomplete and it is worth turning back now to examine the significance of the novel's title. 'Surfacing' is a gerund (a noun made out of a verb), indicating process and activity (like the fish jumping) rather than a completed action. *Surfacing* charts a change in the narrator's subjective perceptions of reality, as she shifts from a position of alienation and victimhood to a new sense of the vital relationship between herself as human and the land which she inhabits, though it also signals a further stage that she has to face in coming to terms with human beings in the modern world. That is literally her next step forward. Atwood commented on the changes registered in the novel in an interview shortly after it was published:

> You can define yourself as innocent and get killed, or you can define yourself as a killer and kill others. I think there has to be a third thing again: the ideal would be somebody who would neither be a killer or a victim, who could achieve some kind of harmony with the world....Now in neither book [*Surfacing* or *Survival*] is that actualized, but in both it's seen as a possibility finally, whereas initially it is not.[15]

Surfacing ends with an emphasis on survival and the regenerative powers of the wilderness, while *Survival* ends with two questions:

> Have we survived?
> If so, what happens *after* Survival?　　(p. 246)

Twenty years later Atwood provides a sequel in *Wilderness Tips*, addressed not only to Canadians but to her international readership as well. The word 'wilderness' is there again, acknowledging the English-Canadian tradition out of which Atwood writes, but by 1991 there is a marked shift away from the optimism of the 1970s towards visions of loss and disempowerment in a late modern world where the grand narratives of history and national myth are collapsing and the survival of the human race is shadowed by threats of global warming and environmental degradation.[16] In this later collection there are several wilderness stories, notably 'Death by Landscape', 'True Trash' and also the title story, but their narrative dislocations suggest a shift in Atwood's attitudes towards the wilderness myth. To consider briefly the two most 'traditional' stories in the collection, 'Death by Landscape' and 'Wilderness Tips', is to notice how they question the wilderness framework and so position themselves as postmodern fictions that challenge the very traditions to which they allude. In fact they offer different and opposing versions of the wilderness, with 'Death by Landscape' referring to representations of wilderness in the paintings of the Group of Seven and 'Wilderness Tips' referring to the 'indigenous' tradition of English-Canadian wilderness writing and stories of heroic survival that date back to male writing of the nineteenth century. These stories, however, are told not from the traditional male point of view but from the perspectives of two contemporary women and one postwar Hungarian immigrant, thereby questioning the authority of the 'master narratives' projected through painting and literature. When viewed from the margins, the wilderness myth begins to look like a white, male, imperialist fantasy not unlike the American myth of the Wild West, whether it be a heroic survival story or a story of disaster – what Atwood called the 'Death by Nature' syndrome, in *Survival* (pp. 54–5). By putting both versions in circulation, Atwood destabilises any absolute 'truth' about wilderness narratives, for these stories offer alternative interpretations and suggest that national myths are open to revision at different times in a nation's history and when viewed from different perspectives.

In the time since *Surfacing* and *Survival* were published there has been, as Atwood records in *Wilderness Tips*, 'a slippage in the bedrock' of English-Canadian definitions of national identity and a national culture. The traditional assumptions of the 1970s cultural nationalists have come under increasing pressure from a range of different interest groups within English Canada – women, immigrants, First Nations – who claim their right to participate in a new discourse of nationhood which more adequately represents cultural difference and interaction in contemporary multicultural Canada. 'Survival' is still the keystone, or maybe 'Surfacing', but no longer 'wilderness', as the basis for any singular definition of Canadianness. And yet, the final paradox may be that though the Canadian wilderness is in danger of disappearing from the earth and receding into myth, yet it is in the very power of mythmakers like Atwood to imaginatively transform perceptions that hopes of regeneration and survival may lie.

SUGGESTIONS FOR FURTHER READING

Atwood, Margaret, 'Dissecting the Way a Writer Works: Interview with Graeme Gibson', in *Margaret Atwood: Conversations*, ed. Earl G. Ingersoll (London: Virago, 1992), pp. 3–19.

Barzilai, Shuli, 'Who is He? The Missing Persons Behind the Pronoun in Atwood's *Surfacing*', *Canadian Literature*, 164 (Spring 2000): 57–79.

Hatch, Ronald B., 'Margaret Atwood, the Land and Ecology', in R. Nischik (ed.), *Margaret Atwood: Works and Impact* (New York: Camden House, 2000), pp. 180–201.

Humm, Maggie, *Border Traffic: Strategies of Contemporary Women Writers* (Manchester and New York: Manchester University Press, 1991).

Quartermaine, Peter, 'Margaret Atwood's *Surfacing*: Strange Familiarity', in Colin Nicholson (ed.), *Margaret Atwood: Writing and Subjectivity* (Basingstoke: Macmillan, and New York: St Martin's Press, 1994), pp. 119–32.

Van Spanckeren, Kathryn, 'Shamanism in the Works of Margaret Atwood', in K. van Spanckeren and Jan Garden Castro (eds), *Margaret Atwood: Vision and Forms* (Carbondale, IL: Southern Illinois University Press, 1988), pp. 183–204.

Woodcock, George, *Introducing Margaret Atwood's 'Surfacing'* (Toronto: ECW Press, 1990).

4
Lady Oracle

Atwoodian Gothic is both sinister and jokey, rather like the scary party game which Atwood describes in her prose poem *Murder in the Dark*, a game about murderers, victims and detectives played with the lights off. The only other thing the reader needs to know is that the victim is always silent and that the murderer always lies:

> In any case, that's me in the dark. I have designs on you, I'm plotting my sinister crime, my hands are reaching for your neck or perhaps, by mistake, your thigh. You can hear my footsteps approaching, I wear boots and carry a knife, or maybe it's a pearl-handled revolver, in any case I wear boots with very soft soles, you can see the cinematic glow of my cigarette, waxing and waning in the fog of the room, the street, the room, even though I don't smoke. Just remember this, when the scream at last has ended and you've turned on the lights: by the rules of the game, I must always lie.[1]

This game is emblematic of Atwoodian Gothic; its aim is to scare, yet it is a sort of fabricated fright; there are rules and conventions and as readers we enter into a kind of complicity because we want to be frightened. Atwood suggests, 'You can say: the murderer is the writer' (*Murder in the Dark*, p. 49), and then either the book or the reader would be the victim, which makes an interesting identification between Gothic storyteller and murderer, trickster, liar. We could take that one stage further with Atwood's female Gothic storytellers, beginning with Joan Foster in *Lady Oracle*, and continuing in a long line through the protagonists in *The Robber Bride*, *Alias Grace*, *The Blind Assassin*, and Atwood herself, identified as sybils, witches, supreme plotters all ('I have designs on you').

So, what is Gothic? At the core of the Gothic sensibility is fear – fear of ghosts, women's fear of men, fear of the dark, fear of what is hidden but might leap out unexpectedly, fear of something floating around loose which lurks behind the everyday. The emblematic fear within Gothic fantasy is that something that seemed to be dead and buried might not be dead at all. Hence the Gothic outbreaks of terror and violence as things cross forbidden barriers between dream and waking, life and death. It is easy to recognise a Gothic novel, for it is characterised by a specific collection of motifs and themes, many of which come through folklore, fairy tale, myth and nightmare.[2] Gothic motifs might be summed up as figuring 'the unspeakable' and 'live burial',[3] imaging something that is 'deeply familiar but which has become alienated through repression'.[4] It is this uncanny quality of Gothic which is embodied in its obsession with the transgression of boundaries and with transformations – 'change from one state into another, change from one thing into another' (*Conversations*, p. 45). On the level of the supernatural, there is the phenomenon of ghosts crossing boundaries between life and death, while on the psychological level there is the erosion of boundaries between the self and the monstrous Other. (What does a Gothic protagonist see or fear to see when she looks in the mirror?) In the borderline territory between conscious and unconscious, a space is opened up for doubles and split selves, which are not total opposites but dependent on each other and linked by a kind of unacknowledged complicity, like Dr Frankenstein and his monster. To return to that game in *Murder in the Dark*, Atwood reminds players that they may take turns to be murderer or victim, for one role does not preclude the other. Gothic finds a language for representing areas of the self (like fears, anxieties, forbidden desires) which are unspeakable in terms of social conventions. In relation to fiction the major point to consider is how these transgressions are expressed through narrative, most obviously in the shifts between realism and fantasy. There is also the difficulty any Gothic story has in getting itself told at all: Gothic plots are characterised by enigmas, multiple stories embedded in the main story, dark doubles and mixed genres, where fairy tale and nightmare may blur into history or autobiography.

Not surprisingly, Gothic romance has been a favourite genre for women novelists, and Atwood writes in a tradition that goes back to the late eighteenth century with Ann Radcliffe's *The Mysteries of Udolpho* (1794), Mary Shelley's *Frankenstein* (1818), the Brontës' *Wuthering Heights* and *Jane Eyre* (1840s), through to Daphne du Maurier's *Rebecca* (1938) and the contemporary fiction of Angela Carter, Beryl Bainbridge, and mass-market paperback Gothics. In a novel like *Lady Oracle* it is easy to see the old stories surviving, updated but still retaining their original charge of menace and mystery, which for Atwood in the 1970s centred on the theme of sexual politics. Commenting on her novelist heroine in *Lady Oracle*, Atwood said:

> She's someone who is attempting to act out a romantic myth we're all handed as women in a non-romantic world. I'm interested in the Gothic novel because it's very much a woman's form. Why is there such a wide readership for books that essentially say 'Your husband is trying to kill you'?...They connect with something real in people's lives. (*Conversations*, p. 107)

However, the feature that makes *Lady Oracle* distinctively neo-Gothic is its dimension of ironic humour as her realistic novel collides with Gothic conventions. Opening with a voice speaking from beyond the grave, *Lady Oracle* would at first appear to be a traditional Gothic text, though as we read the first paragraph it transforms itself into a Gothic parody. We discover that the speaker is not dead after all:

> I planned my death carefully; unlike my life, which meandered along from one thing to another, despite my feeble attempts to control it. My life had a tendency to spread, to get flabby, to scroll and festoon....I wanted my death, by contrast, to be neat and simple...the trick was to disappear without a trace, leaving behind me the shadow of a corpse, a shadow everyone would mistake for solid reality. At first I thought I'd managed it.[5]

This is a fictive autobiography told by a woman called Joan Foster, who is a novelist and a poet, suggesting shadowy parallels with Atwood herself early in the 1970s when she was becoming a cultural icon in Canada. More to the point, because this is not autobiography but an autobiographical fiction, she tells her life story in different versions under different names, and her stories never quite fit together. Who is Joan Foster, who writes popular Gothic romances under the pseudonym Louisa K. Delacourt? What is the significance of Lady Oracle, Joan's other pseudonym when she writes poetry? The one thing the reader can be sure about with Joan is that she is a fantasist and a trickster: 'All my life I'd been hooked on plots' (p. 310). As critic Sharon R. Wilson comments, 'Joan sets the pattern for all of Atwood's tricksters. She plays at being a Delphic oracle and sybil, manufactures her own labyrinths and minotaurs, and enacts a *Red Shoes* script.'[6]

Lady Oracle is a story about storytelling, both the stories themselves and the writing process, for Joan offers us multiple narratives, figuring and refiguring herself through different fictional conventions. The novel is structured through a series of interlocking frames. First, there is the story of Joan's real life in the present, set in Italy where she has escaped after her fake suicide in Toronto, Canada. Enclosed within this is her private memory narrative of a traumatic childhood filled with shame, pain and defiance centring on her relationship with her mother, of an adolescence when she escapes to London and becomes a writer of popular Gothics and mistress to a Polish count, her marriage to a Canadian, her celebrity as a poet, followed by the threat of blackmail and her second escape from Canada to Italy. Embedded within this narrative are snippets from Joan's Gothic romances ('Bodice Rippers' as she calls them), which provide more glamorous plots than everyday life in Toronto during the late 1960s and early 1970s. Then there is a fourth narrative thread, the curiously mythic 'Lady Oracle' poems, produced as Joan believes by automatic writing when she looks into a dark mirror in her bedroom in Toronto. These shifting frames generate a series of comic collisions, confrontations and escape attempts, but there are no clear boundaries between them as borders blur between present and past, art and life. Joan's fantasies of escape are always duplicitous and riddled with holes, so that one story infiltrates another and fantasy is under continual barrage from the claims of real life. Joan may adopt multiple disguises in the form of fancy costumes, wigs, different names and different personas, but 'it was no good; I couldn't stop time, I could shut nothing out' (p. 277). Through this shimmer of different figures, the reader wonders if there is any chance of getting beyond the veils to the centre of the plot or to the enigma of Joan Foster herself. Do we ever get beyond the distorting funhouse mirrors? Joan is nothing if not a self-caricaturist as well as a parodist of Gothic romance conventions, as she switches roles in a continual process of double coding.

Not only does Joan write popular Gothic romances, but she also tries quite disastrously to construct her real life like a Gothic plot, with herself as the female victim. Indeed, the novel opens in Italy, the classic territory of Radcliffean Gothic romance, though sitting alone in her apartment in Terremoto, Joan realises that the other side of a heroine's escape fantasy is isolation:

The Other Side was no paradise, it was only a limbo. Now I knew why the dead came back to watch over the living: the Other Side was boring. There was no one to talk to and nothing to do.   (p. 309)

Haunted by memories of her visit to this same Italian village the previous year with her husband, Joan is now filled with longing for him to come to rescue her from her own perfect plot, which begins to look 'less like a Fellini movie than that Walt Disney film I saw when I was eight, about a whale who wanted to sing at the Metropolitan Opera...but the sailors harpooned him' (p. 9). Critics have been rather fond of saying that Joan's real-life narrative and the Gothic novel she is writing in Italy start off separate and gradually become entwined, till at the end of the narrative borders blur and Joan enters the Gothic maze in *Stalked by Love*.[7] However, borders are blurred from the very beginning as Joan continually slides from the embarrassments of the present into fantasy scenarios and back again, for she is an escape artist who is beset by one inconvenient insight, 'Why did every one of my fantasies turn into a trap?' (p. 334).

Before going any further into Joan's Gothic plotting, it is advisable to look at the title, *Lady Oracle*, in order to see what it signifies about Joan as a woman writer who faces the challenging questions: How do you find a voice to speak for yourself, and what do you say when you do? The most significant thing about an Oracle is that it is a voice which comes out of a woman's body and is associated with hidden dangerous knowledge, but that it is not her own voice. The voice of the Delphic Oracle was the voice of the god Apollo, or earlier the voice of the Earth Goddess. Atwood's research notes for her novel contain a significant amount of material on oracles, on Pythia the priestess of Apollo at Delphi, and on the Sybil of Cumae, all of whom are described as 'possessed' and as speaking 'in a convulsive state'.[8] The role of prophetess is here in danger of being reduced to the role of the hysteric. Joan Foster presents herself as uncomfortably close to this model – not only in the automatic writing of her Lady Oracle poems but also in her costume Gothics. They too are a form of automatic writing, for Joan is writing through Gothic romance formulas and she types with her eyes closed. The very name 'Lady Oracle' is not her own choice but is chosen for her by her male publishers: 'You write, you leave it to us to sell it' (p. 234). When she becomes a celebrity, Joan even begins to feel a certain paranoia about her media persona:

> It was as if someone with my name were out there in the real world, impersonating me...doing things for which I had to take the consequences: my dark twin....She wanted to kill me and

take my place, and by the time she did this no one would notice the difference because the media were in on the plot, they were helping her. (pp. 250–1)

In other words, Joan starts to feel like one of the victims in her Gothic romances. This double identity may be a threat, but it also provides her with a kind of escape, for she cannot be defined by any statement made in her name, and her names are always changing. Is she Lady Oracle, the poet? Is she Louisa Delacourt, the Gothic novelist? She is also Joan Foster, but whether she was named after Saint Joan or the American film actress Joan Crawford she is not sure. Her assumed names, which can be put on and off like costumes, constitute nothing less than a set of aliases for a woman who has a very insecure sense of her own identity.

Jean is a very slippery subject who offers her readers multiple versions of the truth about herself, cultivating duplicity with an energy that suggests the forces of repression behind her performances:

It was true I had two lives, but on off days I felt that neither of them was competely real.... If I brought the separate parts of my life together (like uranium, like plutonium, harmless to the naked eye, but charged with lethal energies) surely there would be an explosion. (pp. 216–17)

Indeed, Joan never does take the consequences for the minor explosion she participates in when she and her lover, the 'Royal Porcupine' (whose less picturesque real name is Chuck Brewer), stage an absurdly sixties happening in a snowy park using the sticks of dynamite that Joan is supposed to be carrying around Toronto for a crazy Canadian nationalist plot to blow up the Peace Bridge at Niagara Falls. She even uses those explosives as the basis for another of her fantastical plots, her fake suicide, which is transformed in her absence into a real-life murder mystery.

Joan assumes no responsibility for what she writes and yet through this pose she tells us a great deal about herself – her fears and ambitions and her forbidden feelings. It is through her memory narrative of a postwar middle-class Toronto childhood (that 'can of worms' as she calls it) that Joan reveals the sequence of humiliations and betrayals against which she has constructed her parade of defensive personas. Her life story is a tale of grotesques and monsters for Joan is an only child, the unwanted product of an unhappy wartime marriage, who cannot please her neurotic mother and who in a rage of adolescent defiance overeats till she looks like 'a beluga whale':

> I ate to defy her, but I also ate from panic. Sometimes I was afraid I wasn't really there, I was an accident; I'd heard her call me an accident. Did I want to become solid, solid as a stone so she wouldn't be able to get rid of me? (p. 78)

For Joan, everyone is shadowed by their opposites. The most important and duplicitous figure is her mother, who 'puts on her face' with its larger-than-life lipsticked mouth (p. 68); her small daughter really believes she is a 'triple headed monster', and that mother returns to haunt her throughout her adult life. Joan's father, the benevolent anaesthetist, also had a double career as a French-speaking Canadian who had been an assassin for the Resistance during the war, a fact that causes his daughter as much bewilderment as the flasher in the ravines who might also have been the Daffodil Man who rescued Joan when she was tied up and left behind by her girl friends after Brownies. There is also her fat fairy godmother Aunt Lou, who leaves Joan enough money in her will to escape from home, but only on condition that she loses weight. Through past experience, Joan suspects everybody of having a secret life, and sees herself too as a 'duplicitous monster' whose only means of expression is through disguise. Joan learns the value of this double coding when she becomes a self-parodist at the age of seven in a ballet recital, where instead of being a fairy in a pink tulle tutu, the fat little girl is tricked into being a mothball in a furry suit. Her 'dance of rage and destruction' is interpreted by the watching parents as a comic entertainment to be applauded, while behind the performance Joan's anguished childhood self remains hidden. It is no wonder that as an adult Joan cannot bring herself to tell her raw-boned idealist husband that she writes costume Gothics, for 'He wouldn't have understood' and she is afraid of losing his affection and respect. Indeed, Joan's primary motivating force is fear – fear of the past, fear of blackmail, fear of the loss of Arthur's love, and above all, fear of being found out. After all, 'when it came to fantasy lives I was a professional' (p. 216).

In such a context Joan's insistence on the automatic writing of her poems begins to look like a psychological necessity, though Atwood's own comments on such a method of production are sceptical: 'In my experience, writing is not like having dreams.... It's much more deliberate.... You can shape your material into a coherent pattern' (*Conversations*, p. 48). An examination of the *Lady Oracle* manuscript materials bears out this conscious construction, for in the Atwood Papers there is a letter to her research assistant in which Atwood asks for a map of Italy; an English–Italian dictionary; details of the water fountains in the Villa d'Este at Tivoli, 'especially the sphinxes with water squirting out their tits and the statue of Diana of Ephesus which is covered with breasts'; an Italian *photoromanze*; and a copy of *Jane Eyre*. 'Later, I'll tell you what all this is for.'[9]

The connections between *Jane Eyre* and Joan's popular Gothic romances are plain (she even calls one of her heroines Charlotte), though we may question why anyone would write them and why so many women read them. Joan's short answer would be, 'The pure quintessential need of my readers for escape, a thing I myself understood only too well' (p. 34). Joan justifies her project to herself: 'The truth was that I dealt in hope, I offered a vision of a better world, however preposterous. Was that so terrible?' (p. 35). However, the fact remains that there is more anguish than pleasure in these Gothic tales with titles like *Escape from Love*, *Love My Ransom*, and *Stalked by Love*. Janice Radway in *Reading the Romance* would seem to agree with Atwood when she argues that the appeal of popular romance fiction relates less to escapism than to women's fears about the loss of independence, male indifference and male violence. These issues are recuperated under the happy endings of romance, though women know such endings to be illusory.[10] Possibly women read these novels out of lack and dissatisfaction, which is why they need to keep on reading them – or, in Joan's case, to keep on writing them.

Joan attempts to figure out her life through her Gothic plots, which are as grotesquely distorted as the fantasy of the discarded sodden clothes which come back to haunt her dreams in Italy, or the Fat Pink Lady fantasy of her childhood. This last is an extraordinarily interesting fantasy, which is both reflection and sublimation for Joan, a grotesque fairytale image of 'The Biggest Modern Woman in the World', who walks across Canada on a tightrope, much to everyone's amazement, but who in real life is nothing but a circus freak. As Joan insists, it's all a trick, but like her other more sinister Gothic narrative tricks, 'it's still not so simple' (p. 203). The Charlottes, Felicias and Penelopes are all partial figurings of her fantasies of desirable femininity, while their persecutions are displacements of her own sense of inadequacy and dread. These costume Gothics also allow Joan to indulge her naively Canadian fascination with Europe – its history, its decaying aristocracy, and its words for outmoded female fashions like 'fichu', 'paletot' and 'pelisse'. It is no accident that her first lover was a Polish count who rescued Joan when she fell off a bus in London, nor that it was he who encouraged her to write costume Gothics while he indulged his own fantasies by writing Nurse novels under the pseudonym 'Mavis Quilp', a name he had found in Dickens. The titles of Paul's Nurse novels are as formulaic in that genre as Joan's Gothics: *Janet Holmes, Student Nurse, Helen Curtis, Senior Nurse* – and after he emigrates to Canada, *Nurse of the High Arctic*. It is also symptomatic of Joan's romantic transformations of real life that she would fall in love with Arthur Foster, a graduate student from the Maritimes, not in their native Canada but in Hyde Park, London, when she happened to bump into him while he was distributing leaflets for 'Ban the Bomb' and she was walking the course for one of her novels. This chance encounter gives Arthur a Byronic tinge which is entirely imaginary:

> I looked at him more closely. He was wearing a black crew-neck sweater, which I found quite dashing. A melancholy fighter for almost-lost causes, idealistic and doomed, sort of like Lord Byron, whose biography I had just been skimming. We finished collecting the pamphlets, I fell in love.   (p. 165)

Joan spells out her Gothic formula when she is looking over the proofs for her *Lady Oracle* poems:

> On re-reading, the book seemed quite peculiar. In fact, except for the diction, it seemed a lot like one of my standard Costume Gothics, but a Gothic gone wrong. It was upside-down somehow. There were the sufferings, the hero in the mask of a villain, the villain in the mask of a hero, the flights, the looming death, the sense of being imprisoned, but there was no happy ending, no true love. The recognition of this half-likeness made me uncomfortable. Perhaps I should have taken it to a psychiatrist instead of a publisher...and no one would understand about the Automatic Writing.   (p. 232)

Joan does not understand it herself but Atwood does. There is a passage in an essay Atwood wrote in 1965 on Rider Haggard's exotic nineteenth-century African novel *She*, which casts light on her attitude to Joan's psychological riddle. Haggard claimed that he had written his novel in a trance, and Atwood quotes one of his biographers as saying, 'Haggard was writing deep, as though hypnotized.' However, Atwood's wry comment is worth noting: 'Haggard may have been writing "deep, as though hypnotized"; but if so the unconscious experience he was drawing upon was the creation of his [five] previous books.'[11]

Atwood's emphasis on intertextuality points to the location of Joan's sources of reference within her own real-life experience and her reading. Of special significance is her relationship with her mother, one of those terrible War Bride mothers, who turns up again, tripled, as three mothers in *The Robber Bride*, who are responsible for generating their daughter's insecurities and escape fantasies. The Gothic images of the 'Lady Oracle' title poem, deriving from *She*, Tennyson's 'The Lady of Shalott', Khalil Gibran, Leonard Cohen, and obscure modernist poetry, display an excess of signification that hints at complex energies incompletely understood by Joan herself for most of the novel. Her tormented relationship with her mother forms the 'unspeakable' subtext throughout her real-life narrative, for even after she leaves home (when her mother in a fit of rage and frustration has plunged a kitchen knife into Joan's arm) she is haunted by her mother's 'astral body' and her mother's face remembered from childhood, 'crying soundlessly, horribly; mascara was running from her eyes in black tears' (p. 173). Her 'Lady Oracle' poem adopts traditional symbolism which both veils and reveals Joan's repressed memories of her mother, whose ghost she had failed to recognise as the figure standing behind her when she looked into the dark mirror during her experiments with automatic writing:

> She is one and three
> The dark lady   the redgold lady
> the blank lady   oracle of blood,
> she who must be
> obeyed   forever
>
> (p. 226)

Though the words of this poem cry out for interpretation, they are sufficiently vague for Joan to be able to repress any recognition of the dark figure, who 'certainly had nothing to do with me' (p. 222). Only near the end of the novel when her mother's ghost appears in a dream does she realise that her mother is the most important of her shadowy doubles, for as Susanne Becker explains, that ambivalent relationship of love, desire and guilt between mother and daughter is the mainspring of Joan's powers as a female creative artist:

> It had been she standing behind me in the mirror....My mother was a vortex, a dark vacuum, I would never be able to make her happy. Or anyone else. Maybe it was time for me to stop trying. (p. 329)[12]

That revelation occurs at the same time as Joan's growing unease with her Gothic plots, in real life and in fiction. Whereas up to this time *Stalked by Love* had been progressing according to its set Gothic formula while her real-life narrative spiralled and twisted, now Joan's novel also swings out of control when she finds that she is identifying with the villainess rather than with the heroine. As she becomes increasingly bewildered, the only thing Joan knows for certain is that she is going to have to let her heroine go into the maze in *Stalked by Love*. This is a classic piece of Gothic plotting, where 'the horrors of the labyrinth and its confusion of fears and desires lies in its utter separation from all social rules and complete transgression of all conventional limits'[13] – or as Atwood describes it, 'the maze I use is a descent into the underworld' (*Conversations*, p. 47). We are reminded of the winding passages that Joan encountered in her walk into the dark mirror of her unconscious, the territory from which both her poetry and her novels are generated. And who is Joan's double on her latest Gothic walk – Charlotte the heroine or Felicia the villainess? Is Joan an innocent victim or is she a witch, as the Italian villagers believe her to be? Faithful to habit, Joan closes her eyes and follows Charlotte into the Gothic maze, but much to her surprise, this time the plot does not conform to stereotype: 'I'd taken a wrong turn somewhere' (p. 333). Later, when Joan resumes her storytelling, she discovers that she is following the villainess and not the heroine – another case of split identities: 'Suddenly she found herself in the central plot.' That plot is both the centre of the labyrinth and a narrative location that makes Joan's book look less like a Gothic romance than like a Fellini film, for Felicia finds herself confronting four ghostly women all of whom claim to be 'Lady Redmond', her own doubles. There is no way out for Felicia – or for Joan – except through a door which looks the same from both sides. When this opens to reveal Redmond the Gothic hero–villain standing on the threshold, Felicia addresses him as 'Arthur', which is the name of

Joan's husband. The climax of the plot reminds us of Atwood's game of 'Murder in the Dark', as Redmond–Arthur, the demon lover, reaches for Felicia's throat. He undergoes a dazzling series of transformations, which shadow all the men with whom Joan has ever been involved: her father, her lovers, her husband, and most oddly in this conventionally European Gothic scenario, the figure of the cannibalistic Wendigo with its 'burning eyes and icicle teeth', straight out of Native Canadian folklore.

Romantic fantasy, violence and death are fused together but nothing is resolved, for Joan is interrupted by the sound of footsteps coming down the path. Does she think it is Arthur or does she think it is the figure of death? And are they the same? (Why do women see their husbands as 'potential murderers'?) Once translated into the realistic genre, such terror becomes comic, for the man Joan fears has come for her life is a newspaper reporter has in fact come for her life story, which we realise is the novel we have just been reading: 'I guess it will make a pretty weird story...and the odd thing is that I didn't tell any lies. Well, not very many' (p. 344). Like *Northanger Abbey* this novel is about the perils of Gothic thinking, just as it is also about the heroine's moral education: 'Joan's gotten as far as saying, I am who I am – take it or leave it' (*Conversations*, p. 66). However, again like Jane Austen, Atwood gives her plot a mischievous twist at the end: Joan confesses that she has not yet returned to Toronto; she is still in Rome looking after the intrusive reporter, whom she knocked on the head with an empty Cinzano bottle: 'I've begun to feel that he's the only person who knows anything about me' (p. 345). She has also decided to give up writing Costume Gothics and to write science fiction instead, exchanging one narrative game for another. After all, 'the future is better for you' – or so Joan hopes.

SUGGESTIONS FOR FURTHER READING

Becker, Susanne, *Gothic Forms of Feminine Fictions* (Manchester: Manchester University Press, 1999).

Botting, Fred, *Gothic* (London and New York: Routledge, 1996).

Fee, Margery, *The Fat Lady Dances: Margaret Atwood's 'Lady Oracle'* (Toronto: ECW Press, 1993).

5

Life Before Man

An Albertosauras, or – the name Lesje prefers – a Gorgosaurus, pushes through the north wall of the Colonnade and stands there uncertainly, sniffing the unfamiliar smell of human flesh, balancing on its powerful hind legs, its dwarfed front legs with their razor claws held in close to its chest. In a minute William Wasp and Lesje Litvak will be two lumps of gristle. The Gorgosaurus wants, wants. It's a stomach on legs, it would swallow the world if it could. Lesje, who has brought it here, regards it with friendly objectivity.

(Margaret Atwood, *Life Before Man*)[1]

This is a strange passage to find in a novel that is generally regarded as Atwood's most depressingly realist fiction.[2] Clearly it belongs to another genre altogether, that of science fiction fantasy, for the dinosaur that pushes into the Toronto coffee house on Saturday, 30 October 1976, summoned up by a young woman's imagination, is one of those contingent presences which interrupt the discourses of everyday life and threaten to collapse the conventions of realism. Of course this is Lesje's fantasy, which at some level relates to her sense of otherness, coded into the racial slurs of 'William Wasp' and 'Lesje Litvak' in this first Atwood novel to signal Toronto's multiculturalism. Yet the appearance of this monster with its ravenous desires intruding into the modern world from the margins of prehistory introduces a principle of radical discontinuity into this novel. Not only is *Life Before Man* a multivoiced text told from the different perspectives of the three main characters (of whom Lesje is one), but within this structure there is a wide range of individual gestures of resistance and survival, which fracture its social surfaces. We may well ask what kind of story Atwood is telling us, in a novel that looks backward to prehistory and forward to the future. The promise of doubleness is kept throughout in the unsettling shifts between realism and fantasy that characterise the discourse of the narrating characters, just as the evolutionary theme suggested by the title balances threats of the extinction of species against evidence of individual survival.

From this perspective, claims about the realism of *Life Before Man* may seem strange indeed. Yet Atwood regards this as her most domestic novel, with its triangular plot where a wife takes a lover and later that lover commits suicide, the marriage breaks up, and her husband goes to live with another woman. Atwood is credited with saying that she wrote *Life Before Man* as a homage to George Eliot's *Middlemarch*, which is generally acknowledged to be the classic Victorian realist novel. In response to an interviewer's request to discuss that claim, she replied:

> In *Middlemarch* everything is middle – it's the middle of the nineteenth century, it's middle class, it's the middle of England.... It's about life as lived by the middle and that's what *Life Before Man* is. It's the middle of Toronto, it's somewhat the middle of the twentieth century, the people are middle-aged. (*Conversations*, p. 226)

Before trying to sort out the puzzles about realism and the relation between Atwood's novel and George Eliot's, we might remember that Atwood also refers to *Middlemarch* when speaking about the novel form and 'changing the rules'. It is in the double context of conventions of realism and 'ways of moving beyond the conventions to include things not considered includable' (*Conversations*, p. 194) that connections between *Life Before Man* and *Middlemarch* might be profitably explored.

Conventions of realism assume that the text is a representation of everyday life, giving the illusion of referentiality through what Roland Barthes called 'solidity of specification'. The action of *Life Before Man* is set at a particular historical moment in a socially and geographically specific location and the characters act in ways with which most readers can readily relate. This is Atwood's 'life as lived by the middle', or as Janice Kulyk Keefer describes it, 'Atwood has taken for her subject matter the near-terminal impoverishment of the human, and therefore moral, imagination as applied to contemporary urban life, and she has attempted to situate this impoverishment in its proper devastating context.'[3] A realist text would seem to be a 'closed' text, and in the case of *Middlemarch* such closure has been associated with the authority of an omniscient narrator's voice, which controls and interprets all the proliferating discourses within the novel. Certainly that is the view of *Middlemarch* as a 'classic realist text' which David Lodge argued against in an influential essay of the early 1980s, where he described George Eliot's methods of evading such reductiveness of meaning.[4] Interestingly, many of the criticisms of *Life Before Man* have tended to treat it as a 'classic realist text' despite the fact that Atwood's novel lacks an omniscient narrative voice, presenting instead the shifting perspectives of the three main characters themselves. Against charges of realism we could argue that *Life Before Man* draws attention to the fact that words are not transparent windows on the world, but that for these characters words become the means of escaping the restrictions of real life. *Life Before Man* begins to look like a very slippery text indeed, composed of multiple discourses, some of which conform to realism but many of which do not.

Yet in some ways that homage to *Middlemarch* does frame our reading of *Life Before Man*, and I would like to pursue those questions of similarity further. As far as realism goes, both *Life Before Man* and *Middlemarch* are social chronicles tracing a web of invented lives, so that the role of the novelist is close to the role of social historian. But there is another dimension to both these novels which makes the comparison more interesting, and that relates to the way in which Atwood and Eliot employ discourses of science – in particular the Darwinian theory of evolution. Charles Darwin's *On the Origin of Species by means of Natural Selection* (1859) and *The Descent of Man* (1871) revolutionised representations of humanity's place and significance in the natural world and raised fundamental questions about the nature and habits of the human species. George Eliot was standing very close to this radical reassessment for she read *On the Origin of Species* when it appeared, and *Middlemarch* is her novelistic response to evolutionary theories. While she accepted the gradualism of Darwin, which she incorporated into her ideas of social progress, she resisted the amoral patterns of determinism in his biological model, arguing instead for the unpredictability of individual human lives. Atwood's project a hundred years later looks like a very similar enterprise, less wide-ranging in its social samplings but vaster in its time projections backwards to prehistory. (It is worth remembering that the early working titles for *Life Before Man* were *Notes on the Mesozoic*, and then *Notes from the Lost World*.) Both novels set their inquiry in relation to scientific and social doctrines of evolution, just as they both resist any mechanistic concept of determinism. Atwood's scientific frames of reference are natural history, geology and astronomy, with the principal setting for the novel being the Royal Ontario Museum in Toronto where both the female protagonists work. (Lesje is a paleontologist and Elizabeth is in charge of Special Projects and publicity, so that both women are engaged in translating science into popular language for the general public.) It must be said that Atwood's scientific narrative is rather more violent than Eliot's, combining evolution with its correlatives of extinction and catastrophe ('Cosmic Disasters' is the name of the show which Elizabeth goes to see at the Planetarium), no doubt in response to late twentieth-century anxieties about the destruction of the human race. However, like Eliot's narrative, Atwood's works against the vast impersonality of the natural world, setting the forces of human intelligence, emotion and imagination within a narrative of social relationships.

Atwood's emphasis falls differently from Eliot's, for she focuses on two awkward concepts within evolutionary theory: the struggle for survival and the extinction of the dinosaurs. However, this is balanced against the more optimistic principle of survival through adaptation to environment, and it is this biological concept that Atwood translates into the psychological and moral parameters of her novel. Seen from this perspective, *Life Before Man* might actually be read as an argument *for* evolution, though for evolution of a different kind from Darwin's as Atwood sets out possibilities for the moral and social evolution of human beings, an attitude which resonates with Eliot's argument for progress through social interdependence. All three major characters have survived by the end of the novel, and their perceptions as well as their circumstances have changed. As Atwood says of Elizabeth:

> The last scene in the Museum looking at the Chinese art show, indicates that Elizabeth is able to formulate a vision beyond the personal (which has obsessed her till now) and though she may not believe in the existence of this vision (a social world in which true interaction and support is possible) the fact that she is able to think of this at all indicates a possible direction for her ... outwards, if not upwards. She's come to the end of merely personal and sexual concerns.[5]

Similar shifts are experienced by the other two main characters, as I shall show. Of course there are no cataclysmic changes in life, for only death is associated with cataclysm in this novel.

It is perhaps worth pointing out a few other similarities and differences between *Middlemarch* and *Life Before Man* in their use of scientific discourse. The opening of *Middlemarch* is clearly a response to Victorian scientific method, for Eliot presents her fiction as a series of 'experiments' designed to study the 'history of man, and how the mysterious mixture behaves under the varying experiments of Time'.[6] While this signals her resistance to deterministic conclusions, it also emphasises the gap between mechanical processes of natural law and individual human responses. *Middlemarch* presents no single key or unified meaning but suggests infinite possibilities for variation within the web of social circumstance. Certainly there are parallels between *Middlemarch* and *Life Before Man* for they both construct a fabric of multiple discourses through dynamic images of lives in process. There are, however, differences in their uses of science, which might be summarised by the contrast between Eliot's use of the microscope and Atwood's use of the telescope. The first section of *Life Before Man* opens out into the vast spaces of the universe, while the third section sweeps back via Lesje's imagination into the primeval forests, occupying dimensions of fantasy not envisaged by Eliot's narrative.

Both novels offer versions of determinism which are challenged by the indeterminacy of individual narrative perspectives. It is perhaps a case of there being no new stories to tell, for any story is a repetition of other stories, told according to different generic conventions. Atwood's novel combines the story of evolution with the story of a domestic triangle and the fabulous story of discovering an unknown world. (This story too has already been written, by Sir Arthur Conan Doyle, as Lesje's references to *The Lost World* amply acknowledge.) The novelistic awareness that every story is a recycling of existing narrative elements parallels the scientific assertion that all the molecules now in circulation were already present at the creation of the earth, a view expressed by Lesje as she sits in the kitchen of her married lover's house at the beginning of their affair:

> These molecular materials have merely combined, disintegrated, recombined. Although a few molecules and atoms have escaped into space, nothing has been added.
> Lesje contemplates this fact, which she finds soothing. (p. 169)

Against that background the problem is to tell any story which will sound new. As Atwood asked on one occasion, 'How am I to know what kind of stories you wish to hear?'[7] I would argue that against the background of prehistory and the extinction of species this complex social narrative contains three different narratives of survival. The limits of mortality are recognised by all of them but they resist those limits in order to go on living in the present. Taken in simple biological terms, the novel may be seen to be writing against death, with the evidence of a forward movement there in the plot: it begins with the report of a suicide and ends with the anticipation of a birth.

Before pursuing the private plots of individual characters, it is worth looking at the overall narrative design of the novel. Whereas *Middlemarch* was a Victorian multiplot novel, *Life Before Man* is a late twentieth-century multivoiced novel, though both are constructed on similar principles with parallel interrelated plots narrated from the perspectives of characters who are equivalent centres of consciousness, thus giving a panoramic representation of lives over a period of time. With *Life Before Man*, the time period is nearly two years, though there are frequent flashbacks of memory and the crucial event of the suicide of Chris Beecham, Elizabeth's lover, has happened one week before the narrative action begins. Arching over all is the evolutionary narrative as a reminder of a 'transcendent' dimension, while on a social scale but outside the characters' consciousness, the narrative itself constructs significant patterns of correspondence which break down difference in favour of a shared human condition. The scope of the narrative enterprise is signalled in the two epigraphs, the first referring to a fossil as it opens out into the spaces of prehistory, and the second referring to life, or at least to spectral presences:

> Look, I'm smiling at you, I'm smiling in you, I'm smiling through you. How can I be dead if I breathe in every quiver of your hand?   (Abram Tertz [Andrei Sinyavsky], *The Icicle*)

The temporal and spatial documentation is very specific, giving details of date, location and speaker for every section, rather like the form of a diary, and for the first couple of days there is a tight pattern of triple voices per day, where the three protagonists are named: Elizabeth Schoenhof, her husband Nate, and Lesje Green (whose first name encodes her ethnic origins though her 'unlikely' surname obscures these traces). Though by the third day the rigid structure begins to break down, the narrative follows a consistently forward movement over almost two years, from 29 October 1976 to 18 August 1978, during which time, circumstances change for all the characters. By the end the domestic plots of Elizabeth and Nate and of Lesje and William have re-formed into different patterns: Nate and Lesje are now living together and Elizabeth is alone in the family home, no longer a wife but a divorced mother with her two young daughters. The novel is characterised by unsettling shifts of focus, with radical changes of perspective within every section as a character's attention moves between intense preoccupation with present issues and the wider spaces of memory, world atrocities or prehistory. Under such pressures the identifiable Toronto world seems to disperse into a variety of other worlds as strange as Maple White Land in *The Lost World*. Toronto is represented as the site of heterogeneous discourses, where remoteness and alienation are precariously balanced against human efforts to imagine better alternatives to the present.

In order to demonstrate how this contradictory motion works, I shall look closely at the first three chapters, all ostensibly occupying the same time slot in 1976 and the same Toronto location, two of the characters being inside the same house. The novel opens with Elizabeth's interior monologue:

> I don't know how I should live. I don't know how anyone should live. All I know is how I do live. I live like a peeled snail. And that's no way to make money.   (p. 11)

With this desperate outcry of a subject at odds with the world, the human dimension is given priority over the vastness of prehistory signalled in the title. For Elizabeth, as we quickly discover, real time has ceased to exist; everything is construed as being merely *after* Chris's suicide. This is the focal point of her attention, though the narrative perspective slides disconcertingly between Elizabeth's inner state and external description, suggestive of her own split consciousness. Elizabeth's state of suspension is close to that form of daydreaming which has been described not as an 'alternative' to the real world but as a 'supplement' to it, occupying a problematical space on the borders of the rational, and contiguous with perceptual reality but also discontinuous with it, 'near but different'.[8] It is within such a discontinuous scenario that Elizabeth can 'see' the cracks in the ceiling and at the same time 'know' the 'vacuum on the other side, which is not the same as the third floor where the tenants live' (p. 12). The space that she 'knows' to be there is the space of absence, as figured in the 'black holes' which later appear (invisibly) on the screen at the Planetarium of the Royal Ontario Museum. This is Elizabeth's inner-space scenario, imaged as the abyss into which she steadfastly resists falling though sucked towards it by the shock of Chris's suicide. Its menace continues to co-exist in her mind with the rituals of domestic life as she listens through her half-open door to her daughters innocently preparing for Hallowe'en and hears her husband bringing her a cup of tea. The two worlds are contiguous but for Elizabeth there is no way of crossing between them.

Nate's narrative on the same day is bound to his wife's by the echo of his own word 'love', though he no longer knows what that word means. It is nothing more than an empty ritual left over from what he nostalgically calls 'the olden days' before Chris, when their marriage appeared to have some stability. Nate is floundering around in domestic wreckage, shut out from Elizabeth's bedroom as he is shut out from her life, fixated like her on Chris's death, which looms in his memory in grisly detail. Nate is as trapped by that suicide as Elizabeth, and though not given to flights of fantasy he comes to feel himself and Chris to be doubles: 'Nate's other body, joined to him by that tenuous connection, that hole in space controlled by Elizabeth' (pp. 16–17). He is always in restless motion – running in circles as he jogs around Queen's Park, cycling furiously between houses owned by the four women in his life (his wife, his former mistress, his mother, and his lover) while not belonging in any of these houses himself, switching between jobs as he moves from his work in Legal Aid at a Toronto lawyer's office to become a toymaker, then back to the law firm again. Nate seems engaged in a continuous process of reinventing himself, shaving off his beard so that he looks like another person ('His hands have decided it's time for him to be someone else', p. 43), as he occupies multiple identities as husband and father, lover, son, and finally father to Lesje's child without knowing it. Nate does not completely fit into any of these social identities, and while there is a dimension of unsatisfactoriness about his position it must be said that he is a resisting subject who remains open to new possibilities. Atwood described him as a political idealist and somewhat of an optimist, also as a man facing a moral dilemma about 'whether to leave the kids because the marriage is rotten, or whether to stay with the marriage for the sake of the kids...he's actually the nicest person in the book' (*Conversations*, p. 145). Whether we agree with this authorial assessment or not, the language of his narrative suggests some measure of progress and a cautious optimism, for the final words of his last entry suggest an end to his wandering.

As he thinks about meeting Lesje after work on the steps of the
Museum, something he did for years with Elizabeth, Nate considers:
'They will either go for a drink or not. In any case, they will go
home' (p. 314).

To return to the opening trilogy, the third voice is Lesje's, asocial
and isolated, for her imagination inhabits the wide spaces of the
Upper Jurassic period, where dinosaurs roam free:

> Lesje is wandering in prehistory. Under a sun more orange than
> her own has ever been, in the middle of a swampy plain lush with
> thick-stalked plants and oversized ferns, a group of bony-plated
> stegosaurs is grazing.   (p. 18)

Lesje's position up in the top of a tree and watching through binoculars
is one of 'blissful uninvolvement'; her otherness is so incomprehen-
sible to the dinosaurs that they will not even notice her, which 'is the
next best thing to being invisible'. Of course such fantasising is
escapist but it is also creative and recreational, opening up spaces
where she feels at home in a way she never does in the real world.
Like the 'delicate camptosaurs' Lesje too is 'cautious, nervous, and
sensitive to danger', for she is a casualty of her multicultural
upbringing across three cultures – those of her Ukrainian and Jewish
grandmothers and the Canadian culture of her birth. Marked by her
ethnicity and her scientific interests as irremediably 'other' in
Toronto, Lesje in early childhood discovered her 'true nationality' in
the Royal Ontario Museum, to which she was regularly taken by
one or other of her grandmothers. Not surprisingly, she chose to
become a paleontologist and to work in that museum: 'This is the
only membership she values' (p. 307). Lesje's fantasy is that of a professional scientist whose job is to classify fossils and to educate the
public 'on matters pertaining to Vertebrate Paleontology', though
her passion for her subject is so intense that she has dreams of
reversing the course of history to make the dinosaurs live: 'strange
flesh would grow again, cover the bones, the badlands would
flower' (pp. 80–1). Like Elizabeth's black holes, this imagined territory
is the place where she negotiates the gaps between real life and
desire, though like any supplementary state it remains in constant
dialogue with the voice of reason. Lesje knows that her dinosaur
scenario is a regressive fantasy, but 'thinking about men has become
too unrewarding', by which she means her relationship with William,
a young environmental engineer. This is the first signal that their

domestic plot has no future, or as Lesje phrases it, 'what they have in common is an interest in extinction. She confines it to dinosaurs, however. William applies it to everything' (p. 126). Whereas Lesje exists with confidence in her imagined world, it is the everyday world whose social codes she cannot fathom. She jumps every time the telephone rings and at work she commits the *faux pas* of mentioning a series of silent phone calls she has been receiving, only to discover when Elizabeth Schoenhof walks out that her lover had been doing the same thing to her for a month before he committed suicide – something Lesje would have known if she had ever listened to office gossip. In this oblique fashion the first significant connection in the plot is made, for Lesje's mysterious caller, as we discover later, was Elizabeth's husband Nate, whose behaviour pattern is a repetition of Chris's as Nate acts through his 'other body' with its speaking silences.

Certainly Lesje's self-division is no more strange than Nate's or indeed Elizabeth's but her fantasies are more exotic. How the pre-historic jungle offers her a place of refuge from the embarassments of social life is amply demonstrated at the dinner party to which Elizabeth invites her and William, for Elizabeth already suspects that her husband is falling in love with Lesje. Awkward and ill at ease, Lesje knocks over her coffee cup and flees to the bathroom, where she escapes to her wilderness:

> Is she really this graceless, this worthless? From her treetop she watches an Ornithomimus, large-eyed, birdlike, run through the scrub, chasing a small protomammal.... Surely these things are important.   (p. 157)

As a subject Lesje is under continual threat of erasure, preferring to be invisible and certainly sexless as she runs through the Upper Jurassic out of the living room, 'wearing her Adidas and a navy-blue sweatshirt' (p. 264). If fantasy suggests the trajectory of a character's consciousness then we can trace the subterranean shifts in Lesje's internal dialogue through the changing scenarios of her lost worlds. Just as her antagonism to William projected the image of the ravenous Gorgosaurus, so, at the lowest ebb in her relationship with Nate, all her fantasies become visions of extinction:

> Such visions are still possible, but they don't last long. Inevitably she sees a later phase: the stench of dying seas, dead fish on the

mud-covered shores, the huge flocks dwindling, stranded, their
time done. All of a sudden, Utah.   (p. 238)

This fantasy is, incidentally, an echo of Nate's similar anxieties about
their relationship, suggesting the poetic language of image clusters
which binds this novel together: 'It's this, this desert, this growing
fiasco, that has driven him, finally, into Elizabeth's mushroom-
colored parlor' (p. 258). In her state of desperation, Lesje finally
perceives an affinity between herself and Elizabeth's dead lover in
their comparable roles. She even thinks of following his example but
suddenly rejects this and switches plots: 'If children were the key,
if having them were the only way she could stop being invisible,
then she would goddamn well have some herself' (p. 293).

As a 'pregnant paleontologist' in the final section, Lesje discovers that
not only has her perspective on life changed but also her perspective
on prehistory, though she is still capable of wryly looking at her own
act of vengeful conception from an objective, scientific point of
view: 'And what will Nate do, what will she do?...Though the past
is the sediment from such acts, billions, trillions of them' (p. 308).
Instead of an absence, Lesje's plot now has a centre; at last she has
become significant to herself and suddenly visible to her dinosaurs.
With that knowledge comes the destruction of her fantasy as she
realises not only that they are long since dead but that if they were
alive, 'they'd run away or tear her apart'. Even her favourite fantasy
of the dinosaurs dancing down the steps of the Museum fades as the
biological narrative of her own pregnancy takes priority: 'In the
foreground, pushing in whether she wants it to or not, is what
Marianne would call her life' (p. 311). With the intrusion of real life
comes a new quality of compassion less familiar to Lesje than her
dinosaurs but opening out her narrative onto hitherto undreamed
of emotions: 'Forgiveness....She would prefer instead to forgive,
someone, somehow, for something; but she isn't sure where to begin'
(p. 311). Like Atwood's other female protagonists, Lesje finds that
her perceptions have changed, and she is left facing tentatively
towards the future.

To double back briefly into Lesje's Jurassic Park fantasy, we should
note that this country of the mind is not only the product of her
scientific imagination. Its topography has already been laid out by
Sir Arthur Conan Doyle in *The Lost World* (1912), his scientific
romance about an exciting mission to an uncharted South American
plateau where Darwinian evolution has failed to happen. This is

Lesje's favourite novel, which she first read as a schoolgirl at the age of ten: 'She can't remember which came first, her passion for fossils or this book; she thinks it was the book' (p. 45). With many narratives of origin the original cannot be traced, though here the Ur-text is readily available. Her heroic exploring adventures, the wilderness landscape with its lake (Conan Doyle's Lake Gladys and his Maple White Land, renamed by her as 'Lesjeland') and the behaviour of the prehistoric creatures themselves all derive from *The Lost World* – even to the dinosaurs' dance out into the modern city, which is already written in Conan Doyle's account of a pterodactyl which escaped from Professor Challenger's scientific lecture in the Albert Hall and flew away over Edwardian London. We are also reminded of Joan Foster's words at the end of *Lady Oracle*. 'Maybe I'll try some science fiction. The future doesn't appeal as much to me as the past, but I'm sure it's better for you' (p. 345). In *Life Before Man*, Atwood writes a pastiche of science fiction while also suggesting that the future may possibly be better for you, but only if science fiction is abandoned. Incidentally, David Ketterer in his masterly study of Canadian science fiction cites two Canadian examples of the scientific romance dealing with the long evolutionary perspective exploited by Conan Doyle: Sir Charles G. D. Roberts's *In the Morning of Time* (1919) and E. J. Pratt's *The Great Feud (A Dream of the Pliocene Armageddon)* (1926), remarking that 'prehistoric creatures occur with sufficient regularity in early Canadian SF to constitute a trend'.[9] The first chapter of Roberts's novel is entitled 'The World Without Man', which conforms to Lesje's version of Life Before Man, so maybe once again the story of origins blurs with the possibility that *Life Before Man* is also the inheritor of its Canadian precursors.

To add a further twist, there are revisionary elements in Lesje's fantasy which might be interpreted as a resistance to Conan Doyle's imperialist values, where the challenge of the unknown for his white, British, all-male exploring party was as much cultural as scientific, and where the confrontation involved dinosaurs and also ape men and cave dwellers in an emblematic representation of the whole Darwinian evolutionary scale. Needless to say, 'civilised' values prevail after a bloody combat where the white men have all the rifles, and the territory is marked down as ripe for colonial exploitation. Lesje's relation to the Lost World ('Lesjeland', Herland) is quite different. Not only is she an observer rather than an invader in an unpeopled land, but the distinction between 'civilised' and 'savage' blurs when her prehistoric fantasy brushes up against real life.

Given the behaviour of William and Elizabeth, not to mention the atrocities documented in Nate's mother's Amnesty International bulletins, primitive violence is not alien to late twentieth-century human beings and Lesje's opinion of the human race is low:

> Does she care whether the human race survives or not? She doesn't know. The dinosaurs didn't survive and it wasn't the end of the world. In her bleaker moments, of which, she realizes, this is one, she feels the human race has it coming.   (p. 27)

Her fantasy, far from being merely escapist or recreational, is a reminder of the savagery latent within the conventions of civilised life. The evolutionary story gives as much evidence of instability and regression as it does of progress, so that Lesje's narrative with its juxtaposition of prehistory and the present might be read as illustrative of a continuity of irrationality and violence rather than of the moral evolution of the human race.

However, hers is only one voice in this multivoiced novel and this bleakness does not characterise Lesje's mood at the end, nor Nate's as he faces their shared future with a shadowed optimism. Neither is it an adequate description of Elizabeth's mood in the final section as she stands in the empty museum after closing time, looking at the Chinese Peasant Art exhibition which she has been responsible for arranging. In the struggle for social and psychological survival that has been narrated she too has succeeded, though not in the ways she had hoped. Hers is not the dominating discourse but only one among three in a structure of mutually responsive and frequently antagonistic discourses. Within her roles of wife, lover, mother and niece, she has survived Chris's suicide, separation and divorce from Nate, and the death of her Auntie Muriel. She has come very close to being sucked into the black vacuum by her ghosts and witches, where her collapse at her aunt's funeral is represented through an image of falling into the abyss of outer space – though at the same time it is ironically interpreted as appropriate social behaviour. Elizabeth returns from her dark fantasy world while remaining aware that those forces rage just beyond the borders of sanity: 'She has no difficulty seeing the visible world as a transparent veil and a whirlwind. The miracle is to make it solid' (p. 302). Elizabeth's vocabulary may be different from Lesje's but she shares with her a similar apprehension about borderlines. Such sharing, however, is known only to the reader.

The final view is of Elizabeth looking at one of the Chinese paintings, which presents an idyllic view of farm labour, '*A Fine Crop of Eggplants*, the caption says, in Chinese, English and French' (p. 315). That picture represents an imagined space outside the limits of the everyday, offering her an image of otherness which is quite separate from the 'black holes' and strikes a correspondence with the spaces of contemplation contained by Kayo's bowls in her living room ('empty bowls, pure grace', p. 302). These paintings occupy the same dimensions of Oriental space as the bowls though with the difference that the space is no longer empty but filled with images:

> China is not paradise; paradise does not exist. Even the Chinese know it, they must know it, they live there. Like cavemen, they paint not what they see but what they want. (p. 316)

This perception of Elizabeth's is not unlike Atwood's comment on the task of the novelist: 'What kind of world shall you describe for your readers? The one you can see around you, or the better one you can imagine? It is only by the better world we imagine that we judge the world we have.'[10] Though she returns to her domestic responsibilities, remembering that she has to go to the supermarket on the way home, yet Elizabeth has her vision of a better place elsewhere within the impossible space opened up by the picture on the wall: 'China does not exist. Nevertheless she longs to be there' (p. 317). So the novel ends with Elizabeth poised on the borderline between realism and fantasy in the knowledge that the paintings represent optimistic illusions and that such illusions are necessary for survival. Her moment of suspension is one we have come to recognise as characteristic of Atwood's endings, where a way forward is 'seen as a possibility finally, whereas initially it is not'.[11] This was Atwood's description of the endings of *Survival* and of *Surfacing*, and 'survival' is still a key word in her thematic vocabulary.

Elizabeth's story, like Nate's and Lesje's, is remarkably resistant to closure although it does not ignore the threat of extinction:

> ALAN TWIGG: What's radical about *Life Before Man* is that it's the first Canadian novel I know of that seriously conveys an awareness that the human race can become extinct. Was that a conscious theme while writing the book?
>
> ATWOOD: Yes. It's why the novel is set in the Royal Ontario Museum. And why Lesje is a paleontologist who studies dinosaurs.
>
> (*Conversations*, p. 121)

Certainly the arguments from prehistory are no more reassuring about the survival of species than the arguments from contemporary history, but we should not forget that the Chinese art exhibit as well as the dinosaur skeletons are housed in the Royal Ontario Museum. Both Lesje's and Elizabeth's narratives end there as well, opening out into spaces of the imaginary which exceed the actual dimensions of the museum, just as the novel exceeds the limits of the classic realist text. This multivoiced narrative contains many more voices than three if we include the discourses of social realism and science as well as of science fiction, fantasy and moral idealism. Similarly, the Royal Ontario Museum itself shimmers with multiple meanings and its definite outlines tend to blur when viewed from the inside:

> Sometimes she thinks of the Museum as a repository of knowledge, the resort of scholars, a palace built in the pursuit of truth.... At other times it's a bandits' cave: the past has been vandalized and this is where the loot is stored. (p. 308)

Like everything else in the novel, the Royal Ontario Museum has a double existence, a solid edifice that may at any moment disappear into fantasy scenarios of Jurassic swamps or idealised Chinese landscapes. Such slippages open the way out of the museum and beyond the deterministic narratives of prehistory so that we may hear the heterogeneous voices of human survivors in the present – in 'mid-history' as Atwood described it (*Conversations*, p. 123) – as the 'before' of the title reverses its direction to point not backwards to the distant past but forwards to the future.

SUGGESTIONS FOR FURTHER READING

Margaret Atwood: Conversations, ed. Earl E. Ingersoll (London: Virago, 1992), pp. 121–30, 141–5.

Kulyk Keefer, Janice, 'Hope against Hopelessness: Margaret Atwood's *Life Before Man*', in Colin Nicholson (ed.), *Margaret Atwood: Writing and Subjectivity* (Basingstoke: Macmillan; New York: St Martin's Press, 1994), pp. 153–76.

6

Bodily Harm

What art does is, it takes what society deals out and makes it visible, right? So you can see it.

(Margaret Atwood, *Bodily Harm*, p. 208)[1]

This comment by a male porn artist in *Bodily Harm* connects with Atwood's own comments on the social function of the novel, made in an interview five years later:

I do see the novel as a vehicle for looking at society – an interface between language and what we choose to call reality, although even that is a very malleable substance. (*Conversations*, p. 246)

Atwood's formulation is more sophisticated than her visual artist's, taking in both the space of fictional representation and the social myths and fantasies through which people construct their images of reality – all of which might serve as a warning against reading *Bodily Harm* as straight realistic fiction. On the contrary, *Bodily Harm* is another version of Atwoodian Gothic, full of sinister games like Murder in the Dark; here it is the detective game of Cluedo, where every player can be a possible murder suspect or murder victim and their positions keep changing. Again Atwood 'does it with mirrors' – in this case mirror sunglasses, for this is Gothic in the tropics – and the narrative, which moves between Toronto and the Caribbean, is populated by characters who keep splitting into their doubles or shadow selves in a series of endless substitutions and replications. The Gothic genre with its elements of fear and menace combines here with other popular genres like the detective novel, the female romance and the spy thriller ('I was writing a spy story from the point of view of one of the ignorant peripherally involved women'[2]) so that the novel becomes an exercise in deciphering clues, not only for the protagonist Rennie Wilford, a Toronto journalist, but for the reader as well, for Rennie's activity is mirrored in our own attempts to make sense of this fragmented narrative. Reality is a very malleable substance here. When it is refracted through Rennie's perspective it becomes a melodrama or an 'exceptionally tacky movie' (p. 159) from which there is no exit. But is reality inside or outside the protagonist, and how far is external reality reshaped through the subjectivity of the viewer? *Bodily Harm* is another version of writing the female body, this time from the point of view of a woman whose own body is already damaged by cancer and a mastectomy. From this 'post-operative' angle she scrutinises social myths of femininity, medical discourse on breast cancer and, most significantly, the rhetoric of pornography; this novel is emphatically not about bodily pleasures but about bodily harm.

As a journalist, Rennie is another of Atwood's women writers like the novelist and poet Joan Foster in *Lady Oracle*, Antonia Fremont the female historian in *The Robber Bride*, or Iris Chase Griffin in *The Blind Assassin*, so this novel also explores the question of the woman writer's task and possible subjects for women's writing. Rennie is forced to move beyond female romance plots and her 'lifestyle' journalism in Toronto when her escape fantasy to a tropical island opens out into a scenario of political violence in a newly independent Caribbean republic. In many ways this novel may appear to be the least Canadian of Atwood's fictions, but this is true only in the most literal, geographical sense; actually it is very much concerned with Canadian attitudes to international relations in its satire on the dangerous naivety of the 'sweet Canadians':

> I wanted to take somebody [like Rennie] from our society where the forefront preoccupations are your appearance, your furniture, your job, your boyfriend, your health, and the rest of the world is quite a lot further back. . . . I wanted to take somebody from our society and put her into *that*, cause a resonance there. (*Conversations*, p. 227)

Through the web of connections established by the narrative, Rennie is forced to see how the personal and the political cannot be separated. This is emblematised in the phrase 'massive involvement', where the meaning shifts from a specific medical terminology about cancer to become a description of Rennie's moral position as a socially responsible member of the body politic:

> In any case she is a subversive. She was not one once but now she is. A reporter. She will pick her time; then she will report. For the first time in her life, she can't think of a title. (*Bodily Harm*, p. 301)

Rennie has finally found 'something legitimate to say' (p. 66), though the irony is that trapped in her present situation inside the prison of a revolutionary regime, her political commentary is in danger of remaining confined to the private spaces of her imagination. *Bodily Harm* is such a complex and enigmatic structure that I am tempted to adopt the approach of the female historian in *The Robber Bride* who decides to 'pick any strand and snip, and history comes unravelled' (p. 3). I shall begin my unravelling attempt as literary critic by referring back to the fascinating mass of manuscript materials for this novel in the Atwood Collection at the University of Toronto Library[3] and in particular to the wide range of epigraphs through which Atwood evidently rehearsed different emphases for her narrative. In the first holograph version (Box 33:1), entitled 'The Robber Bridegroom', there are no epigraphs at all, though the draft typescripts, with titles varying from 'The Robber Bridegroom' to 'Rope Quartet' to 'Bodily Harm', play with a range of sixteen different prefatory quotations arranged in six patterns. Given the original title, it is not surprising that the first quotation from *Grimms' Fairy Tales* occurs three times:

Then said the bridegroom to the bride, 'Come, my darling, do you know nothing? Relate something to us like the rest.' She replied, 'Then I will relate a dream.'   (33:2, 33:4, 33:6)

This initial emphasis on female storytelling with its revelations of men's crimes against women occurs as frequently as the quotation from John Berger's *Ways of Seeing*, which is the only epigraph to appear in the published version:

A man's presence suggests what he is capable of doing to you or for you. By contrast, a woman's presence ... defines what can and cannot be done to her.   (33:2, 33:4, 33:6)

This statement with its focus on sexual power politics and female experience indicates what is probably the major focus of the narrative.[4] Yet it is not the exclusive focus, as is proved by the many quotations emphasising the role of fiction as social and moral witness that occur among the epigraphs. Some of them emphasise the uncompromising nature of storytelling:

This story is horrifying; if you have suffered from it, forgive me, but I'm not sorry.   (Pablo Neruda, *The Heroes*, 33:2)

Other epigraphs pay more attention to reader response, arguing the need for stories when all public access to truth fails:

> What do I do when I am told a lie about events that have happened in my lifetime? I listen for stories.   (Miguel Algarin, 33:4)

The epigraphs fan out from this awareness of the power of narrative to suggest a comprehensive view of power politics ranging from state brutality to the insidious domination of social conventions and late twentieth-century consumerism. There are also several epigraphs which hint at Rennie's mastectomy, though they point not towards the theme of bodily harm but to the contradictory nature of the surgeon's art:

> To search for some meaning in the ritual of surgery, which is at once murderous, painful, healing, and full of love.   (Richard Selzer, *Mortal Lessons*, 33:4)

Just as the mystery of healing serves to undermine the coercive discourses of power politics, so there is another strand in the epigraphs, which points to Atwood's insistent inquiry into the mysteries of male–female relations:

> Men and women are two locked caskets, each bearing within it the key to the other.   (Isak Dinesen, 33:4, 33:6)

While recognising sexual difference, such a perception dissolves any politics of domination and invites a more subtly inflected view than the discourses of pornography and violence within the novel.

To examine these epigraphs, which appear and disappear in the typescript, is rather like studying a palimpsest where one word or passage of text is written over another. These multiple layers and revisions not only suggest the range of Atwood's thematic preoccupations and the shifting emphases of the writing process but also set up resonances behind the single Berger quotation which was her final choice. However, such drafts are only 'raw material' and all they do is to indicate possible directions for the narrative while it is being made. They are not explicit about many of its distinctive features, like the discourse of pornography (though we may see it as being implicit in the Berger epigraph), nor the topic of postcolonial violence (though again the many comments on abuses of power might seem to suggest this). Moreover, the epigraphs do not give any indication of the fragmented structure of this novel nor of the dislocated female subject through whom the story is focused. They merely serve as another set of clues, outlining the range of discourses through which reality might be reconstructed as narrative.

The novel opens with the promise of a very specific location and a distinctive narrative voice: 'This is how I got here, says Rennie' (p. 11), who proceeds to tell her life story. It's a story that begins with a crisis and an enigma, for she returns home to find two policemen sitting in her Toronto kitchen waiting to tell her that an intruder has broken into her flat and has left one sinister clue, a coiled rope lying on her bed. Taken together with the title, this could be the beginning of a detective novel, whose plot would be, 'Who is the faceless stranger?' and indeed Rennie thinks of the game of Cluedo. Is it 'Miss Wilford, in the bedroom, with a rope?' (p. 14) or should it be 'Mr X, in the bedroom, with a rope?' (p. 41). In a sense it is a detective story, but the narrative sequence soon begins to disintegrate as the focus shifts from 'I' to 'she' and time and space become dislocated with the introduction of numerous memory fragments and the protagonist's flight away from Toronto to the Caribbean as she tries to sidestep the problems of her real life. Instead she finds herself in a political situation where she is really in danger of physical violence. By the end we realise that this is in fact a prison narrative, but a sense of awkwardness and unease is there from the opening section. Sections are separated from one another by large graphic dots, which create the effect of a peculiarly fragmented text. Despite the shift from first to third person, a technique familiar from *The Edible Woman*, the reader soon becomes aware that this account is being focalised through Rennie's disturbed consciousness, for it is a subjective narration refracted through her dreams and memory flashbacks, distorted by her fears, and pervaded by her precarious sense of unreality. It is the 'Gothic chamber of horrors interior to the heroine's consciousness', which Judith McCombs identified in her essay on Atwood's poetic sequences at the beginning of the 1980s: 'The Gothic terror and the Gothic horror, so divided and redoubled, take place in a hall of mirrors, where reality is constantly evaded and yet reflected, distorted and yet magnified.'[5] Not only the reader but Rennie herself has difficulty in negotiating between what is going on inside and outside her own head as her narrative shifts from one crisis point to another, insistently trying to figure out connections yet baffled by the opacity of surfaces and threats of imminent collapse.

It is surely no accident that Rennie's story begins with the sinister image of the rope, for in its indeterminacy of meaning it provides the perfect connection between her fears of death from cancer and external physical violence, just as it also signals the perversion of sexual desire when the male erotic gaze becomes the hostile scrutiny of a rapist or a killer, a scenario to which Rennie is peculiarly vulnerable since her mastectomy and her break-up with Jake. There is a further dimension of which we become subsequently aware through Rennie's flashbacks to her childhood in the small Ontario town of Griswold, 'not so much a background as a subground... nothing you'd want to go into' (p. 18). Brought up by her lonely mother and her grandmother, Rennie knows about threadbare decency where women grow embittered and dream they have lost their hands – 'the ones they feel with' – and where retribution is bound to descend sooner or later: 'In Griswold everyone gets what they deserve. In Griswold everyone deserves the worst' (p. 18). Despite her acquired urban sophistication, Rennie remains a small-town girl, haunted by those moral codes so that the man with the rope, like her breast cancer, would seem to emerge from the shadows of her past.

From Rennie's perspective, she is always the victim – of her own body and of external circumstances. The diagnosis of breast cancer and her subsequent mastectomy are the central trauma of her life:

> The body, sinister twin, taking its revenge for whatever crimes the mind was supposed to have committed on it. Nothing had prepared her for her own outrage.   (p. 82)

In her first shock at the news, Rennie's concept of her body changes, for she no longer sees it as a unified whole but as something being undermined from within as the blood cells 'whisper and divide in darkness' (p. 100). Yet she fears the operation almost as much as she fears death from cancer, for she has a horror of the violence of surgery and of her body being dismembered. When she wakens after the operation, 'She did not want to look down, see how much of herself was missing' (p. 32). In her discussion of Rennie's traumatised condition Sonia Mycak describes the cancer as 'threatening the borders between the inside of Rennie's existence and what is usually positioned as being outside her and other', referring to Julia Kristeva's psychoanalytical concept of 'abjection' to explain the processes of Rennie's dislocation and decentring.[6] Rennie no longer trusts herself inside her own skin, as her imaginary representations of her body would suggest. At times she fears that her scar will come unzipped like a purse, whose contents will spill out all over the place, and sometimes she fears that her body is 'infested':

> The creature looks far too much like the kind of thing she's been having bad dreams about: the scar on her breast splits open like a diseased fruit and something like this crawls out.   (p. 60)

It is this irrational fear of collapsing boundaries between inside and outside which haunts Rennie in her dreams and in her waking life, transforming even the sight of Lora's bitten fingernails into a site of psychological horror:

> She wouldn't want to touch this gnawed hand, or have it touch her. She doesn't like the sight of ravage, damage, the edge between inside and outside blurred like that.   (p. 86)

Rennie's disgust at her own damaged body inevitably affects her account of her relationships with men in the novel. Jake the Toronto interior designer, Daniel the Finnish-Canadian surgeon and Paul the American drug dealer and gun-runner in the Caribbean (described by Rennie both as 'the X factor' and as 'the connection') are all her lovers at different times in her painful progress through the failure of the old romance plots to which she clings. As a further twist, one of the draft titles, 'Rope Quartet', suggests a more sinister connection between these three and the 'faceless stranger' within the scenarios of Rennie's psychodrama about female victims and male power games. In her highly subjectivised account it is difficult to see these men as individuals, for each of them occupies a shifting series of roles – as lovers, rescuers, tormentors and betrayers. The stories of all three overlap as they appear and disappear at different stages of the narrative, almost as functions of Rennie's desire and need, though of course they have all vanished by the time Rennie tells this story. Oddly, Jake's existence is first signalled by his absence ('It was the day after Jake left,' p. 11), and their love affair is recapitulated through a series of vividly remembered fragments – Jake's rape fantasies, his soft-porn art photographs and his 'lunchtime quickies'. These are now recalled with a pained sense of severance from the past, for their relationship was one of the casualties of her mastectomy. Trapped inside her victim scenario Rennie cannot acknowledge that Jake left because she had rejected him and that neither of them is capable of imagining a new structure for a loving relationship.

Rennie's failures of imagination are again evident in her brief affairs with Daniel and Paul, both of whom she tries to coerce into her fantasy scripts of romance, though the plots switch in ways for which she is not prepared. As she admits, it is difficult to have an affair with her doctor: 'It would be unethical, he said. I'd be taking advantage of you. You're in an emotional state' (p. 143). When she finally does persuade him to go to bed with her however, what she discovers is that they have switched roles:

> The fact was that he had needed something from her, which she could neither believe nor forgive. She'd been counting on him not to: she was supposed to be the needy one, but it was the other way around.... She felt like a straw that had been clutched.... She felt raped.   (p. 238)

Paul, the enigmatic American, would seem to provide the ideal holiday romance, 'the biggest cliché in the book', though it is through her affair with him that Rennie finds herself involved in a revolutionary coup and thrown into prison. Yet she feels grateful to Paul, for it is he who restores her lost confidence in her sexuality – by his gaze as much as by his lovemaking. Her scar when looked at by him ceases to be a disfigurement and becomes simply a mark of human mortality, for Rennie knows that 'he's seen people a lot deader than her':

> He reaches out his hands and Rennie can't remember ever having been touched before. Nobody lives forever, who said you could? This much will have to do, this much is enough. She's open now, she's been opened, she's being drawn back down, she enters her body again and there's a moment of pain, incarnation...she's grateful, he's touching her, she can still be touched.   (p. 204)

The lyricism of this passage is echoed in the illicit affair between Offred and Nick in *The Handmaid's Tale*, while the painful restoration of feeling harks back through Rennie's memory of her operation all the way to *Surfacing*, when the unnamed narrator feels her body

tingling 'like a foot that's been asleep' (*Surfacing*, p. 146). It is one of
the ironies of *Bodily Harm* that Rennie is rescued only in time to be
thrown into prison, and that Paul disappears, 'which could mean
anything' (p. 283).

In prison Rennie summons her three ghosts, all of whom appear
to be dismembered and far away: she can hardly remember what
Jake looks like, whereas 'Of Paul, only the too-blue eyes remain'
(p. 283), and Daniel moves through the day at an immense distance
from her, 'enclosed in a glass bubble' like a mirage. Rennie is back in
her private Gothic chamber of horrors as these figures slip in and
out of her dreams in an endless series of shifting identities in which
she also is implicated:

> Rennie is dreaming about the man with the rope, again, again. He
> is the only man who is with her now, he's followed her, he was
> here all along, he was waiting for her. Sometimes she thinks it's
> Jake...sometimes she thinks it's Daniel....But it's not either of
> them, it's not Paul...he's only a shadow, anonymous, familiar,
> with silver eyes that twin and reflect her own.   (p. 287)

Rennie's subjective reconstruction of reality shapes the narrative,
but her story is always breaking down as she is forced to take into
account unexpected events and other discourses that represent reality
from perspectives other than her own. As a woman writer who
specialises in lifestyle journalism, inventing fake fashion trends and
doing pieces on personality makeovers and fast food outlets, Rennie
has chosen a carefully calculated apolitical stance where her social
comment is confined to the trivial: 'I see into the present, that's all.
Surfaces. There's not a whole lot to it' (p. 26). Yet from this deliberately
marginalised position the novel shifts to a passionately committed
moral stance towards political issues relating to gender and colonial
oppression, which is epitomised in the title *Bodily Harm*. Searching
for clues to this mysterious change, I would suggest that the crisis
point for Rennie is the article she is asked to write on pornography
for the men's magazine *Visor*, which she researches but then refuses
to write. This episode provides an interesting crux for a woman's
novel of the early 1980s written in the wake of American feminist
anti-pornography campaigns which began in the late 1970s. I want
to trace this issue of pornography in *Bodily Harm*, focusing on Rennie's
responses but casting my net more widely as an inquiry into Atwood's
position on the politics of fiction at that time. Indeed, I would assert

that though Rennie cannot write the article on pornography from the woman's angle, Atwood's narrative does it for her, so that the ground of my inquiry becomes the way in which Atwood uses the rhetoric of pornography to explore the connections between discourses of sexuality on the one hand and discourses of political power on the other.

Rennie's journalistic assignment to write about pornography as an art form is contextualised in two ways: first in relation to Jake's rape fantasies and his dangerous games ('Danger turns you on, he said. Admit it', p. 207) and then in the context of feminist debate. Both Jake and her editor emphasise the playfulness of sexual fantasy, though as Rennie points out, this is a very male perspective: 'Rennie said she thought the subject might have more to do with men's fantasy lives, but Keith said he wanted the woman's angle' (p. 207). Her research leads Rennie first to the studio of a male porn artist who makes chairs and tables out of female mannequins locked into attitudes of submission, and whose comment on art as parodic social critique I quoted at the beginning of this chapter. Like her friend Jocasta, proprietor of the retro dress shop called Ripped Off, he is an exponent of camp culture: 'Of course it's gross, said Jocasta. But so's the world, you know what I mean? Me, I'm relaxed' (p. 24). As long as she can stay in this world of 'lifestyles' and playful surfaces Rennie can survive, but as Lorna Irvine remarks in her sociological analysis of Atwood's novels, 'Atwood insists on depth in a superficial post-modern landscape.'[7] The breaking point comes when Rennie has to confront the unmediated evidence of hard-core pornography, known in the trade as the 'raw material'. Rennie's visit with Jocasta to the Metropolitan Police Department's pornography collection reveals terrifying visual evidence of male sadistic fantasies: there are images of female bodies bound and mutilated and, most shocking of all, the film clip of a black woman's pelvis with a live rat poking its head out of her vagina (p. 210). The peculiar horror of this racialised image of a victimised female body lies in its double representation of female fears of violation, which work in counterpoint to male fantasies of violence. Luce Irigaray's formulation of woman's position in the male 'dominant scopic economy' spells out the connection: 'Her sex organ represents the horror of *nothing to see*,'[8] a challenge that may only be met by dismemberment or violation of the female body.

After watching the film clip Rennie is immediately sick all over the policeman's shoes and withdraws from the assignment. To recall the words of Mary Ann Caws in this context, 'How could we possibly think that a seeing woman writing about women [and pornography] would have an "objective" point of view?...She, we are bound to think and say, is implicated heavily.'[9] Neither Jocasta nor Jake will contemplate the implications of this image for even a moment; Jocasta angrily upbraids the policeman with the remark, 'You need your head repaired' (p. 211), and when Rennie tells Jake he replies, 'Come on, don't confuse me with that sick stuff (p. 212). Yet their reasons for refusing to look are different from Rennie's, for where they resist taking up any moral position, she cannot separate fantasy from moral issues in this way – any more easily than she can say 'fuck' unselfconsciously. Troubled as she is by glimmerings of a connection between rape games and male violence against women, she can no longer take pleasure in playing the victim in Jake's fantasies as soon as she starts thinking of herself as 'raw material' (p. 212).

Within the iconography of porn as presented in this novel there is an underlying rhetoric of representation that relates directly to discourses of patriarchal power. None of the images Rennie has seen pay any attention to women as subjects; they project them only as objects of male fantasies of desire and domination. Female bodies are all passive, distorted or dismembered, witnesses to the sexual power politics of the Berger epigraph. To define pornography as 'a coincidence of sexual phantasy, genre and culture in an erotic organisation of visibility', as film critic Beverley Brown did in 1981,[10] is to describe a cultural phenomenon which is crucial to Atwood's analysis of a power politics of sexual domination. As I have already suggested, *Bodily Harm* begins with a very crude representation of sexual power politics, the rope on the bed and Jake's rape fantasies being very close to the feminist anti-pornography position adopted in texts like Andrea Dworkin's *Pornography: Men Possessing Women* (1979), which asserted strong links between pornography as misogynist power fantasy and male violence against women. ('Pornography is the theory and rape is the practice.') The fundamental issue is always power, and pain and fear are its visible proofs: 'With lovers like men, who needs torturers?'[11] Within such an interpretation of pornographic culture women like Rennie, Jocasta and Lora would all be seen as collaborators and willing victims.

However – and it is one of Atwood's most skilful narrative manipulations – by the time Rennie is telling her story, her perspective and her situation have entirely changed. For all its illusion of pre-sentness, the whole novel is about the *past* and spoken from within her prison cell, all of which offers a subtly inflected view of the feminist scenario about pornography and violence. Rennie has learned that violence pervades the relations between the sexes at every level of social and aesthetic activity – in pornographic art and advertising, prostitution, child abuse and wife beating, the threat of the man with the rope in Toronto, all of which would endorse the feminist anti-porn position. Where Atwood dissents from that position is in her recognition that while pornography as patriarchal discourse may be focused on sexual difference, its rhetoric of domination extends into the wider political scenario that is displayed during the first general elections to be held in a former British Caribbean colony, now an independent republic.

Looking back, Rennie perceives that her escape to the Caribbean islands landed her in a truly unfamiliar place where everything seems threatening. Alighting from the plane at St Antoine, Rennie finds herself in a landscape full of oddly undecodable messages, like the airport advertisement, 'THE BIONIC COCK: IT GIVES YOU SPURS' (p. 38), or the woman whom Rennie assumes to be a religious maniac because she is wearing a T-shirt with the slogan 'PRINCE OF PEACE' on it – though she turns out to be the mother of one of the political candidates, whose name really is Prince. It is evident that Rennie's view of the Caribbean has all the superficiality of a white tourist's perspective, described by Paul as 'alien reaction paranoia' (p. 76). As Diana Brydon remarks in her critique of the novel, '*Bodily Harm* is neither counter-discursive nor cross-cultural, but it locates some gaps in the apparently seamless web of white cultural discourse.'[12]

Amid the confusion and danger of the revolt when the newly elected prime minister is shot in the back of the head, Rennie finds herself thrown into prison on charges of 'suspicion'. Although she has not been harmed herself, she has been forced to witness within her cell the brutal bashing up of her friend Lora, and through the window the naked exercise of police power in the prison yard. The violence is not against women this time but against other men, though the discourse partakes of the same sadistic performance elements as the representations of pornography:

> The courtyard is oddly silent, the noon beats down, everything is bright, the men's faces glisten with sweat, fear, the effort of keeping in the hatred, the policemen's faces glisten too, they're holding themselves back, they love this, it's a ceremony.... The man with the bayonet stuffs the handful of hair into the bag and wipes his

hand on his shirt. He's an addict, this is a hard drug. Soon he will need more. (p. 289)

Atwood has taken the rhetoric of pornography but drained out the sexual dimension, as Rennie's sudden flash of insight fuses the discourses of pornography and power politics together: 'She's afraid of men and it's simple, it's rational, she's afraid of men because men are frightening' (p. 290).

Though Atwood does not elide the sexual differences emphasised by pornography, she does point to the features that all male and female bodies share and to those ways in which both sexes can be abused and victimised. The narrative of bodily harm turns out to be infinitely more psychologically and socially complex than the simple slogans of the early 1980s feminists would allow, as Atwood turns the topic inside out till there is no longer 'a *here* and a *there*' and 'nobody is exempt from anything' (p. 290).

Rennie tells her story from the prison cell in St Antoine as she sits beside the brutally battered body of a dead woman, realising finally that she is powerless and alone. Spoken from that interior space, her narrative is a reconstruction and a reinterpretation as she laboriously tries to fit together the fragments of her life, seeking connections between Lora's damaged body and her own mastectomy, as between the overt violence that she has seen in the Caribbean and the hidden violence which she has not seen in Toronto but which she knows is there. The plot she constructs might be said to hinge on discovering the identity of the 'faceless stranger' at the end of the rope. Rennie thinks she has solved the riddle when she sees the brutality of the policemen in the prison yard ('She's seen the man with the rope', p. 290), but just as in the game of Cluedo, the players' positions change, so the identity of the faceless stranger turns out to be plural. Paul when she first meets him wearing his sunglasses is a faceless stranger 'without his eyes' (p. 99), and finally, the faceless stranger turns out to be someone else again. In an unfamiliar gesture of compassion Rennie reaches out her hand to touch Lora's face, now battered out of all recognition, and in the process learns another meaning for faceless stranger: 'It's the face of Lora after all, there's no such thing as a faceless stranger, every face is someone's, it has a name' (p. 299).

Rennie's effort to tell the story is, like her effort to save Lora, an exercise of the moral imagination, as she comes to see her own private pain from a wider human perspective:

She doesn't have much time left, for anything. But neither does anyone else. She's paying attention, that's all.   (p. 301)

At last she is ready to fulfil the requests of two of her ghosts, Lora and Dr Minnow, both of whom had urged her to 'tell somebody what happened' (p. 282). As she is a reporter she determines to 'report', offering her interpretation of contemporary lifestyles in two different countries but now with an edge of moral engagement as she takes up the now vacant position of the most fervently idealistic character in the novel:

> Dr Minnow pauses. . . . They cannot imagine things being different. It is my duty to imagine, and they know that for even one person to imagine is very dangerous to them, my friend. You understand?   (p. 229)

Rennie understands at last about the moral function of storytelling, which does more than 'take what society deals out and make it visible'. She has begun to imagine a future which will be different from the present, just as from her prison cell she manages to see herself at the end as 'overflowing with luck', and in flight: 'It's this luck holding her up' (p. 301).

SUGGESTIONS FOR FURTHER READING

Brydon, Diana, 'Atwood's Postcolonial Imagination: Rereading *Bodily Harm'*, in Lorraine M. York (ed.), *Various Atwoods: Essays on the Later Poems, Short Fictions and Novels* (Toronto: Anansi, 1995), pp. 89–116.

Irvine, Lorna, 'Recycling Culture: Kitsch, Camp, and Trash in Margaret Atwood's Fiction', in Reingard M. Nishcik (ed.), *Margaret Atwood: Works and Impact* (New York: Camden House, 2000), pp. 202–14.

Mycak, Sonia, *In Search of the Split Subject: Psychoanalysis, Phenomenology, and the Novels of Margaret Atwood* (Toronto: ECW Press, 1996).

7
The Handmaid's Tale

My room, then. There has to be some space, finally, that I claim as
mine, even in this time.
(Margaret Atwood, *The Handmaid's Tale*, p. 60)[1]

These words, spoken by Atwood's Handmaid, deprived of her
own name and citizenship and known simply by the patronymic
'Offred', might be taken as emblematic of a woman's survival
narrative told within the confines of a patriarchal system represented
by the dystopia known as Gilead. Restricted to private domestic
spaces and relegated to the margins of a political structure which
denies her existence as an individual, nevertheless Offred asserts
her right to tell her story. By doing so she reclaims her own private
spaces of memory and desire and manages to rehabilitate the traditionally 'feminine' space assigned to women in Gilead. Atwood's
narrative focuses on possibilities for constructing a form of discourse
in which to accommodate women's representations of their own
gendered identity while still acknowledging 'the power of the (male/
'universal') space in which they cannot avoid, to some extent,
operating'.[2] Like *Bodily Harm*, this is another eye-witness account
by an 'ignorant, peripherally involved woman', this time interpolated
within the grand patriarchal narratives of the Bible and of history,
just as Offred's tale is enclosed within an elaborate structure of
prefatory materials and concluding Historical Notes. However, her
treasonable act of speaking out in a society where women are
forbidden to read or write or to speak freely effects a significant
shift from 'history' to 'herstory'. Offred's tale claims a space, a large
autobiographical space, within the novel and so relegates the
grand narratives to the margins as mere framework for her story,
which is the main focus of interest. Storytelling is this woman's
only possible gesture of resistance to imprisonment in silence, just
as it becomes the primary means for her psychological survival. In the
process of reconstructing herself as an individual, Offred becomes
the most important historian of Gilead.

Since its publication in 1985, *The Handmaid's Tale* has become Atwood's most popular novel. It has been translated into more than thirty languages, made into a film by German director Volker Schlondorff and into an opera by Danish composer Poul Ruders. The novel that began as a satirical critique of religious and political trends in early 1980s North American society has slipped away from its historically specific context to become a political fable for our time, as if the present is rushing in to confirm Atwood's dire warnings about birth technologies, environmental pollution, human rights abuses, religious fanaticism, extreme right-wing political movements – and since 11 September 2001, international terrorism followed by the war in Iraq. In 2003, one reviewer of the opera commented on the novel's increasing relevance in today's world with its 'jostling theocracies and diminished civil liberties'.[3] A great deal of attention has been paid to it as dystopian science fiction and as a novel of feminist protest.[4] Certainly Atwood's abiding social and political concerns are evident here in her scrutiny of structures of oppression within public and private life, yet the novel exceeds its definition as feminist dystopia and it is not exactly science fiction,

> if by that you mean Martians, teleportation, or life on Venus. Nor is it a sort of travelogue of the future. It's the story of one woman under this regime, told in a very personal way, and part of the challenge for me was the creation of her voice and viewpoint.[5]

A critical reading which focuses attention on Offred as narrator, on her language and the structural features of her storytelling, might allow us to see how *The Handmaid's Tale* eludes classification, just as Offred's storytelling, allows her to escape the prescriptive definitions of Gilead.

Nevertheless, the political dimensions of the dystopian model need to be considered in order to gauge the purpose of the fiction, while bearing in mind Atwood's definition of what 'politics' means: 'What we mean is how people relate to a power structure and vice versa' (*Conversations*, p. 185). Set in a futuristic United States at the beginning of the twenty-first century after a military coup has wiped out the President and the Congress, Gilead is a totalitarian regime run on patriarchal lines derived from the Old Testament and seventeenth-century American Puritanism plus a strong infusion of the American New Right ideology of the 1980s. Individual freedom of choice has been outlawed and everyone has been drafted into the service of the state, classified according to prescribed roles: Commanders, Wives, Aunts, Handmaids, Eyes, down to Guardians and Econowives. There is strict censorship and border control, as Offred reminds us in her recurrent nightmare memory of her failed escape to Canada with her husband and daughter, which has resulted in her being conscripted as a Gileadean Handmaid. The novel is an exposure of power politics at their most basic: 'Who can do what to whom'. Women are worst off because they are valued only as child-breeders in a society threatened with extinction where, because of pollution, AIDS and natural disasters, the national birthrate has fallen to a catastrophically low level. This essentialist definition of women as 'two-legged wombs' works entirely in the interests of a patriarchal elite, denying women any freedom of sexual choice or of lifestyle. Atwood's feminist concerns are plain here but so too are her concerns for basic human rights. Most men are oppressed in this society: there are male bodies hanging every day on the Wall, while homosexuals, Roman Catholic priests and Quakers of both sexes are regularly executed, and male sexual activity is severely restricted as well. A more comprehensive reading of the novel would suggest that it is closer to the new feminist scholarship, which has moved beyond exclusively female concerns to a recognition of the complexities of social gender construction. Offred's tale challenges essentialist definitions, whether patriarchal or feminist, showing not only how state sexual regulation criminalises male violence against women and suppresses women's sexuality but how it also militates against basic human desires for intimacy and love. As Offred reminds her Commander, Gilead's policies of social engineering have left out one crucial factor:

Love, I said.
Love? said the Commander. What kind of love?
Falling in love, I said.   (pp. 231–2)

The novel represents Atwood's version of 'What If' in the most powerful democracy in the world. She describes her dystopian project precisely, in an unpublished essay:

It's set in the near future, in a United States which is in the hands of a power-hungry elite who have used their own brand of 'Bible-based' religion as an excuse for the suppression of the majority of the population. It's about what happens at the intersection of several trends, all of which are with us today: the rise of right-wing fundamentalism as a political force, the decline in the Caucasian birth rate in North America and northern Europe, and the rise in infertility and birth-defect rates, due, some say, to increased chemical-pollutant and radiation levels, as well as to sexually-transmitted diseases.[6]

When describing the origins of her book, Atwood has acknowledged a variety of influences both literary and historical, though always emphasising contemporary social issues and anxieties.[7] When she began thinking about the novel in the early 1980s she kept a clippings file (now in the Atwood Papers, University of Toronto Library) of items from newspapers and magazines which fed directly into her writing. These show her wide-ranging historical and humanitarian interests, where pamphlets from Friends of the Earth and Greenpeace sit beside Amnesty International reports of atrocities in Latin America, Iran and the Philippines, together with items of information on new reproductive technologies, surrogate motherhood, and forms of institutionalised birth control from Nazi Germany to Ceausescu's Romania. It is to be noted that Gilead has a specifically American location, for Offred lives in the heartland of Gilead in a city that was formerly Cambridge, Massachusetts, and Harvard Campus (where Atwood was herself a student) has become the site for the Rachel and Leah Women's Re-education Centre, the setting for public rituals like Prayvaganzas and Particicutions, and Gilead's Secret Service headquarters. When asked why she had not set her novel in Canada, Atwood replied: 'The States are more extreme in everything.... Canadians don't swing much to the left or the right, they stay safely in the middle.... It's also true that everyone watches the States to see what the country is doing and might be doing ten or fifteen years from now' (*Conversations*, p. 223).

When we consider that the American religious right, or the 'New Right' as it was called in the 1980s, is one of Atwood's prime satiric targets, the location takes on a particular significance. The clippings file contains a lot of material on the New Right with its warnings about the 'Birth Dearth', its anti-feminism, its anti-homosexuality, its racism and its strong religious underpinnings in the Bible Belt.[8] Perhaps by coincidence one of the best known New Right studies (also in the Atwood papers) is a collection of essays, *The New Right at Harvard* (1983) edited by Howard Phillips, which refer to the desirability of building a coalition, 'a small dedicated corps' to 'resist the Liberal democracy' with its 'libertarian positions'. Chillingly the militaristic rhetoric of Gilead could already be heard at Harvard three years before *The Handmaid's Tale*, set in and around that university, was published. It is possible to read the novel as an oblique form of Canada–US dialogue where a Canadian writer warns Americans about their possible future.

The Handmaid's Tale may be set in the future, but Gilead is a society haunted by the past, and there is continual tension between a collective social memory of life in late twentieth-century America, which has to be vilified and erased, and Gilead's new ideological reinterpretation of the nation's history. With its passion for 'traditional values' as a way of legitimating the repressive regime as thoroughly American, Gilead has adopted a peculiarly American version of religious fundamentalism which leans heavily on the country's Puritan inheritance. As Atwood explained, 'The mind-set of Gilead is really close to that of the seventeenth-century Puritans' (*Conversations*, p. 223). Atwood's interest in Puritan New England is signalled from the start in her dedication of the novel to Mary Webster and Perry Miller. Mary Webster was her own favourite ancestor, who was hanged as a witch in New England in 1683 but who survived her hanging and went free.[9] Professor Perry Miller, a great scholar of seventeenth-century Puritan history, was Atwood's Director of American Studies at Harvard. Much of the rhetoric and many of the cultural practices of Gilead are to be found in Miller's histories, such as the Founding Fathers' references to women as 'handmaids of the Lord' or Cotton Mather's description of a dissenting woman as 'an American Jezebel'. Gilead also employs many of the Puritan practices associated with childbirth, like the Birthing Stool, and the provision of refreshments at a birth which were known as 'groaning beer' and 'groaning cakes'.[10] While paying tribute to Miller's scholarship, Atwood shifts the emphasis from the seventeenth century to the twenty-first, showing how Gilead's attempt to reinvent Puritan history results in nothing better than antiquarianism and a grotesque parody of that history, and underlining the fundamentalist ideology of the regime.

Not only does Atwood satirise the New Right and its Puritan inheritance, but she also takes a critical look at North American feminism since the 1960s. As a feminist with a deep distrust of ideological hardlines, she refuses to simplify the gender debate or to swallow slogans whole, for slogans always run the risk of being taken over as instruments of oppression, like the late 1970s feminist phrase 'a women's culture', which Gilead has appropriated for its own purposes. It is significant that Gilead is a society 'in transition' where all the women are survivors of the time before, and their voices represent a range of feminine and feminist positions dating back to the Women's Liberation Movement of the late 1960s. Offred's mother belongs to that early activist group, with its campaigns for women's sexual freedom, their pro-abortion rallies, and their 'Take Back the Night' marches. Thanks to the feminist movement, in the United States women gained an enormously widened range of life choices when equal rights and legalised abortion were endorsed by Congress in the early 1970s, though in 1982 the Equal Rights Amendment failed to be ratified, owing to the opposition of Pro-Life campaigners and fundamentalist Christians. These voices are represented by the Commanders' Wives and the terrible Aunts. Among the Handmaids (who are women of childbearing age who grew up in the 1980s and early 1990s) positions are equally varied, ranging from the classic female victim figure of Janine (later Ofwarren), to radical feminists like Moira the lesbian separatist, to Offred herself, who highlights the paradoxes and dilemmas of contemporary feminism. Offred, aged 33 at the time she tells her story, must have been born in the early 1970s, a date which would fit with her mother's feminist activities and the film about the Nazi's mistress that she sees at the age of eight; she would have been at university with Moira in the late 1980s.[11] Just as there are many different kinds of women, so there is no simple gender division between masculine and feminine qualities: if men are capable of violence then so are women – even the Handmaids themselves at the Particicution – and Aunt Lydia with her coyly feminine manner is probably the most sadistic character in the novel. *The Handmaid's Tale* may be a critique of feminism but it is a double-edged one which rejects binary oppositions, just as Offred's double vision allows her to evaluate both Gilead and her own, lost, late twentieth-century America. It is she, the witty heterosexual woman who cares about men, about mother–daughter relationships, and about her female friends, whose storytelling voice survives long after Gilead has been relegated to past history.

Offred's narrative forms the bulk of this novel, refiguring the space she can claim as her own within the confines of Gilead. *The Handmaid's Tale* is inner-space fiction or perhaps space-time fiction, for it deals with the continuities of memory and those persistent traces of social history that survive to undermine the authority of even the most repressive regime. Though trapped within a system where there would seem to be no room for individual freedom, Offred claims her own private space by her refusals; she refuses to forget the past, she refuses to believe in the absolute authority of Gilead, just as she refuses to give up hope in her anguished version of the Lord's Prayer: 'Then there's Kingdom, power, and glory. It takes a lot to believe in those right now. But I'll try it anyway. *In Hope*, as they say on the gravestones...' (p. 205).

Crucially Offred refuses to be silenced, as she speaks out with the voice of late twentieth-century feminist individualism, resisting the cultural identity imposed on her. She manages to lay claim to a surprising number of things which the system forbids: 'my own time' (p. 47), 'my room' (p. 60), 'my own territory' (p. 83), and even 'my name' (p. 94). She guards her lost name as the secret sign of her own identity and as guarantee of her hopes for a different future:

> I keep the knowledge of this name like something hidden, some treasure I'll come back to dig up, one day. I think of this name as buried...the name floats there behind my eyes, not quite within reach, shining in the dark. (p. 94)

Incidentally, this name is one of the secrets Offred keeps from the reader, though she does trust her lover Nick with it, and at the end the name acts as promise of a future beyond Gilead. One Canadian critic argues that Offred's real name is hidden in the text, there to be deduced from one name in the whispered list of Handmaids' names at the end of the first chapter: 'Alma. Janine. Dolores. Moira. June' (p. 14).[12]

Offred's assertion about the 'space I claim as mine' (p. 60) directly addresses questions about the feminine subject's position within a rigidly patriarchal system and a woman's possible strategies of resistance. Appropriating her temporary room in the Commander's house as her own, Offred makes her surprising declaration of freedom as she transforms that prison cell into an escape route out into the spaces of private memory:

> I lie, then, inside the room...and step sideways out of my own time. Out of time. Though this is time, nor am I out of it.
>
> But the night is my time out. Where should I go? Somewhere good. (p. 47)

There is a surprising amount of mobility in this narrative as Offred in imagination moves out and away from Gilead. Her story induces a kind of double vision in the reader as well, for she is always facing both ways as she shifts between her present life and her past, or sometimes looks longingly towards the future.

In the face of state repression and domestic tyranny Offred manages to tell her wittily dissident tale about private lives, not only her own story but the stories of other women as well, all of them willing or unwilling victims of the Gileadean regime and so in some sense her own doubles. Appropriating their remembered turns of phrase, Offred's storytelling voice multiplies to become the voices of 'women' rather than the voice of a single narrator. There is the story of Moira the rebel, who spectacularly defies the power of the Aunts and escapes from the rehabilitation centre, only to reappear in the brothel scene at Jezebel's, where she satirises male sexual fantasies by looking totally ridiculous as a Bunny Girl with a floppy ear and a draggly tail. There is also the story of Ofglen, Offred's shopping partner and member of the secret Mayday resistance, who finally hangs herself, and Offred's unnamed predecessor at the Commander's house, who scratched a secret message in the wardrobe before hanging herself from the light fitting in the room Offred now occupies. The blank space where the fitting has been removed is seen by Offred as a 'wreath' or a 'frozen halo' (p. 17) as she comes to regard that absent woman as her own dark double. She also tells the stories of older women like her mother, the old-fashioned Women's Libber condemned by the Gileadean regime as an Unwoman and sent to the Colonies to die, but who refuses to stay dead. Instead she reappears to Offred and to Moira, preserved on film at the rehabilitation centre, and haunts her daughter's memory. By contrast, there is the story of the Commander's Wife, whom Offred remembers from the time before as 'Serena Joy', a popular gospel television show personality, now trapped within the New Right ideology that she had helped to promote: 'She stays in her home, but it doesn't seem to agree with her. How furious she must be, now that she's been taken at her word' (p. 56). Sitting in her beautiful enclosed garden in her blue gown, Serena appears to Offred like an ageing parody of the Virgin Mary, childless, arthritic and snipping vengefully at her flowers. All these women are casualties of the system though perhaps the saddest figure of all is Janine, a female victim in both her lives. Gang-raped in the time before Gilead, she becomes the Handmaid Ofwarren, who produces the required baby only to have it condemned to death as a 'shredder'. When Offred sees Janine for the last time, after the Particicution, she has become a madwoman, a 'woman in free fall' drifting around grasping a clump of the murdered man's bloodstained blond hair.

Combined with fragments of gossip overheard from the Wives and the Marthas, Offred's story presents a mosaic of alternative female worlds which undermine Gilead's patriarchal myth of women's submissiveness and silence, though it must be said that women's chances of survival are slim, and many of the stories remain unfinished so that we never know what happened to most of these women.

Offred describes her narrative as 'this limping and mutilated story', using that metaphor to refer both to its structure and to the violent social conditions out of which it is told:

> I'm sorry there is so much pain in this story. I'm sorry it's in frag-ments, like a body caught in crossfire or pulled apart by force. But there is nothing I can do to change it.   (p. 279)

Composed of isolated scenic units with gaps and blanks in between where the episodes drift free of present time, the fragmented narrative represents the mental processes of someone in Offred's isolated situation as her mind jumps between vividly realised present details and flashbacks to the past. Offred's narrative self-consciousness is also one of the identifiably postmodern features of her narrative, for she is continually drawing our attention to her storytelling process, commenting on the ways this telling shapes and changes real experience, giving reasons why she needs to tell her story at all, and reminding readers that she may not always be a reliable narrator as she recounts what happened in Gilead. At the time, she tells it in her head in order to survive by seeing beyond the present moment where she does not wish to be, and also because she needs to believe there is still someone outside Gilead who is listening to her: 'Because I'm telling you this story, I will your existence. I tell, therefore you are' (p. 279). Storytelling becomes a substitute for dialogue, though Offred also likens her narrative reconstruction to a letter addressed to 'Dear You ... You can mean thousands' (p. 50). It takes a couple of hundred years for her letter to be delivered, when it is presented (in a third reconstruction) at a Symposium on Gileadean Studies long after the regime has become ancient history. Through this radical dislocation the reader's own position in time becomes ambiguous, for we are reading in a fictive future that bears an uncomfortable resemblance to our present society.

Offred's story is incomplete and her account of life in Gilead is in danger of being overlaid by a male professor's academic reconstruction at the end, yet it is her voice, coming through the transcribed tapes, which gives the narrative its interest and continuity. This is history in the feminine gender, addressed directly to its listeners:

> I wish this story were different...I wish it were about love, or about sudden realizations important to one's life, or even: about sunsets, birds, rainstorms, or snow.
>
> Maybe it is about those things, in a sense; but in the meantime there is so much else getting in the way. (p. 279)

Though Offred may adopt a conventionally feminine tone here of wistful apology and sentimentality, she slips into an entirely different register when speaking about her own body in her challenge to Gilead's doctrines of biological essentialism. Her tale is as profoundly subversive as Hélène Cixous's feminist text of the mid-1970s, 'The Laugh of the Medusa', with which it has much in common as a project to inscribe the complex dimensions of female being.[13] Atwood's novel enacts in practice what Cixous's essay proposes as theory, for Offred is Cixous's woman 'confined to the narrow room' and 'given a deadly brainwashing' but who becomes the 'I-woman, escapee', 'breaking out of the snare of silence' to 'write herself'. (The vocabulary here is entirely taken from 'Medusa'.) Offred's situation might be read as a literal translation of Cixous's highly metaphorical text, except that Atwood is sceptical of any utopian vision of woman's glorious liberation from the shackles of patriarchy. Offred is not a revolutionary; she refuses to join the Mayday resistance movement in Gilead and she does not want to adopt Moira's separatist feminism, though she admires her friend's recklessness and swash-buckling heroism. Her own position is much closer to the traditionally feminine role of woman as social mediator, for though she resists the brutal imposition of male power in Gilead she also remembers the delights of heterosexual love and her story *is* about love, with a strong traditional female romance component. It is symptomatic of Offred's non-confrontational role that though she finally defeats the Commander's assurance of male superiority, she herself is not in a commanding position at the end (unlike the film version, where she murders the Commander and escapes). Led out of his house as a prisoner and feeling guilty at having let down the household, she has no idea whether she is going to her death or towards a new life of freedom when she steps up into the Black Van. Offred fails to make Cixous's 'shattering entry into history'; on the contrary, she never finishes her story and her voice is almost drowned out by the voice of a male historian.

However, Offred's story is a 'reconstruction' in more senses than one, for not only is it her narrative of memory but it is also the means by which she rehabilitates herself as an individual in Gilead. Though she begins her tale as a nameless woman traumatised by loss and whispering in the dark, Offred refuses to believe that she is nothing but a Handmaid, 'a two-legged womb': 'I am alive, I live, I breathe, I put my hand out, unfolded, into the sunlight' (p. 18). She insists on chronicling her subjective life from within her own skin, offering her own personal history of physical sensation and emotion, together with those imaginative transformations through which body space opens out into fantasy landscape. According to Cixous's prescription, 'By writing herself [or in Offred's case "speaking herself"] woman will return to the body which has been more than confiscated from her, which has been turned into the uncanny stranger on display' ('Medusa', p. 250). This is for Offred the uncanny shape of the red-robed Handmaid. Indeed, it is from within this role that Offred finds her strength to resist, for just as Gilead is obsessed with the female body and its reproductive system so Offred silently talks back to those patriarchal prescriptions in Atwood's version of *écriture féminine*. Cixous asserts that the 'dark continent' of the female body is neither dark nor unexplorable and Offred answers that challenge, using similar images of immense bodily territories, volcanic upheavals and the Medusa's own subversive laughter. On the evening of the monthly Ceremony of sexual intercourse with the Commander (a time when her body would seem least of all to be her own), Offred becomes the explorer of her own dark inner space:

I sink down into my body as into a swamp, fenland, where only I know the footing. Treacherous ground, my own territory. I become the earth I set my ear against, for rumours of the future.... Each month I watch for blood, fearfully, for when it comes it means failure. I have failed once again to fulfil the expectations of others, which have become my own. (p. 83)

With her minute attention to physical details, Offred chronicles her bodily awareness and her shifts of perspective under the influence of cultural doctrines which have effected a change in her imaginative conceptualisation of her self. No longer a 'solid object, one with me', her body has become a 'cloud' surrounding the dark inner space of her womb, whose dimensions expand till it becomes Cixous's 'immense astral space' or Atwood's cosmic wilderness, 'huge as the sky at night and dark and curved like that, though black-red, rather than black'. Her meditation offers a kind of imaginative transcendence though without Cixous's promise of erotic pleasure, for Offred knows that she is nothing more in Gilead than a breeding machine serving the state. What Offred experiences is a sense of dissolution within her body as every month its only issue is menstrual blood: 'To feel that empty again, again. I listen to my heart, wave upon wave, salty and red, continuing on and on, marking time' (p. 84). This is the hidden female space where time is kept by the body: 'I tell time by the moon. Lunar, not solar' (p. 209), though 'marking time' also reminds Offred that time is running out and she will be sent to the Colonies if she does not soon produce a child. Offred's condition is one of compromised resistance, where she regrets not becoming pregnant as the system requires of her ('*Give me children, or else I die*' has more than one meaning for a Handmaid, as she ironically remarks), while at the same time she steadily resists Gilead's imposition of control over her mind.

Yet it would be wrong to forget the comic dimension in this novel, for Offred's simmering humour bubbles up at the most inappropriate times, and she can hardly contain her laughter the first time the Commander invites her to play an illicit game of Scrabble with him. The game provides her with the welcome opportunity to play with words, and her image of the Scrabble counters as candies, which she would like to put into her mouth, makes a beautifully literal equivalent for Cixous's metaphor of women's seizing language 'to make it hers, containing it, taking it into her mouth' ('Medusa', p. 257).[14] As soon as she gets back to her room, we hear the muffled explosion of her own Medusa laughter:

> Then I hear something, inside my body. I've broken, something has cracked, that must be it. Noise is coming up, coming out, of the broken place, in my face.... My ribs hurt with holding back, I shake, I heave, seismic, volcanic, I'll burst. Red all over the cupboard, mirth rhymes with birth, oh to die of laughter.   (p. 156)

Her language at this point displays a disturbing mixture of merriment and hysteria, tinged with irony. She likens her laughter to an epileptic fit, and the images she uses are not simply about loss of control but also about bodily damage. Standing in the cupboard scrawled with her hanged predecessor's secret message, Offred is aware that she too, like that other Handmaid, is trapped: 'There's no way out of here.' Yet her irrepressible energy impels her towards life rather than death, as she listens to her heartbeat 'opening and closing, opening' (p. 156).

Offred keeps adapting Gilead's patriarchal script as she tells her autobiographical narrative, for like the flowers in the Commander's Wife's garden, her silent discourse of resistance is dynamic, lyrical, and as difficult to stop as a natural process:

> There is something subversive about this garden of Serena's, a sense of buried things bursting upwards, wordlessly, into the light, as if to point, to say: Whatever is silenced will clamour to be heard, though silently.   (p. 161)

The summer garden provides a sublimated image of Offred's own repressed desires, but more than that it becomes suddenly and over-whelmingly the space of romantic fantasy, a 'Tennyson garden, heavy with scent, languid; the return of the word *swoon*' (p. 161), where traditional images of femininity breathe through Offred's prose as the garden itself 'breathes, in the warmth, breathing itself in. To walk through it in these days, of peonies, of pinks and carnations, makes my head swim.' In this eroticised feminine space conjured by Offred's imagination, everything signifies romance, temptation and desire. For her it is a pagan garden of delights, presided over by goddesses and not by a faded version of the Virgin Mary like Serena, as she riots verbally in her rhapsody of the flesh. Of course it is characteristic of Offred's ironic self-awareness that she should see round her fantasy even while revelling in it, wryly recognising that such excess is at least in part a sublimation of her sexual frustrations, where longing generates its own scenarios. Yet it is the very intensity of her desire which allows Offred for a moment to transcend her human limits and to enter into the life of the pulsating organic world around her, 'as if I'm a melon on a stem, this liquid ripeness' (p. 162). Offred's language runs in harmony with Cixous's *écriture féminine*, where images of desire deriving from the human body and the natural world constitute a 'feminine' alternative language which resists Gilead's polluted technological nightmare and its compromised 'biblico-capitalist rhetoric' ('Medusa', p. 257).

Offred's text is truly self-seeking as she tries to win back 'her womanly being, her goods and her pleasures' ('Medusa', p. 250), which have been stolen from her. Appropriately enough, it is through her body that Offred finds her way to emotional survival, for in the unpropitious circumstances of Gilead she falls in love – not with the Commander, whose image is irretrievably tainted with patriarchal authority, but with Nick his chauffeur. She turns a situation of coercion into a love story during her secret meetings with Nick, which are arranged by the Commander's Wife solely for the purposes of making her pregnant. In a curious way, Offred's re-visioning of Gilead's dystopian plot looks like a cultural survival of 'the time before' when 'falling in love' was the fashion, for this forbidden love story follows a traditional romance plot, with its strong undercurrent of sexual magnetism leading the heroine into dangerous territory with a dark stranger who turns out to be her rescuing hero at the end. That Offred is aware of such conventionality is evident in the triple versions through which she tells the story of their illicit affair (p. 273), but there is no doubt that falling in love is for her an act of survival. This reawakening of sexual desire releases her into what Cixous has called 'the marvellous text of herself' as she allows Nick to read her body:

> He seems indifferent to most of what I have to say, alive only to the possibilities of my body, though he watches me while I'm speaking. He watches my face.   (p. 282)

By a double irony, that love relationship achieves precisely the goals which Gilead intended and that Offred has resisted for so long. She becomes pregnant and she is reconciled to staying where she is: 'The fact is that I no longer want to leave, escape, cross the border to freedom. I want to be here, with Nick, where I can get at him' (p. 283).

Offred may try to refashion the social rules of Gilead into a private utopia (though she knows that 'this is a delusion of course', p. 281) but dystopian conventions dominate the plot, and the love story is cut short through a series of violent events and discoveries which reaffirm Gilead's control over life and death. The romance plot is put to a crucial test when one day Nick bursts into Offred's room accompanied by a party of Eyes (secret police), to take her away in the dreaded Black Van reserved for dissidents. Is this a betrayal or a rescue? Offred does not have the faintest idea and she realises that she knows so little about Nick that 'trust' is, ironically, all that she is left with: 'Trust me, he says, which in itself has never been a talisman, carries no guarantee' (p. 306). Her narrative ends with Offred laying herself open to all risks and all possibilities as she departs from the Commander's house like a criminal under guard and climbs into the van:

> I have given myself over into the hands of strangers, because it can't be helped.
> And so I step up, into the darkness within; or else the light.
> (p. 307)

Offred's own story ends when she climbs into the Black Van, but the novel does not end here. There is also a supplement in the Historical Notes, told by a different narrator in a different place and at a different time, setting one woman's private autobiographical record in a wider historical context, and incidentally suggesting that she was indeed rescued by Nick. These Notes are a transcript of a lecture given by a Cambridge Professor, Darcy Pieixoto, at an academic symposium on Gileadean Studies held in the year 2195 at the University of Denay, Nunavit, in Arctic Canada, long after the regime has fallen and Offred is dead.[15] It is this professor who is responsible for the transcription of the story we have just finished reading, because it turns out that Offred's story was recorded on cassette tapes, which he has edited and entitled 'The Handmaid's Tale' in 'homage to the great Geoffrey Chaucer' (p. 312). Already the voice of the male historian threatens to drown out Offred's voice, for Pieixoto is not at all concerned with her as an individual but is preoccupied with establishing the authenticity of her tale and its value as objective historical evidence. His reconstruction effects a radical shift from 'herstory' to 'history' as he attempts to discredit Offred's narrative by accusing her of not paying attention to significant events. In response, the reader may feel that it is the professor who is paying attention to the wrong things, for the historical facts that Pieixoto selects as significant effectively erase Offred from the Gileadean narrative: of the twelve pages of his account a mere one and a half pages are devoted to her, and her fate 'remains obscure'. In fact, he does exactly what Offred feared history would do to the Handmaids: 'From the point of view of future history, we'll be invisible' (p. 240).[16]

The abrupt shift from Offred's voice to the historian's voice challenges the reader on questions of interpretation. We have to remember that *The Handmaid's Tale* was Offred's transcribed speech, reassembled and edited by a male historian and not by her. Her tale has been appropriated by an academic, who seems to forget that his reconstruction is open to questions of interpretation too. He is abusing Offred as Gilead abused her, removing her authority over her own life story and renaming it in a gesture that parallels Gilead's patriarchal suppression of a woman's identity in the Handmaid's role. No wonder the professor claims to have lost Offred, as like Eurydice's ghost 'she slips from our grasp and flees' (p. 324), though he is quite wrong to accuse her of not answering him, when he has refused to listen to what she has been saying. The challenge of interpretation is finally directed out to the readers, who have heard the story in its multiple reconstructions. Finally, I would suggest that just as Offred's story has shown up the limits of Gilead's autocratic power to control the subjective lives of at least two of its inhabitants, so it defies Pieixoto's appropriation two centuries later. This may look like a case of the 'disappearing author', though that is a postmodern position that Atwood vigorously resists ('Deny None of It') in the interests of our shared moral responsibility. By telling her story Offred has put herself 'into the world and into history', challenging readers to connect her world with our own in the present, in the hope of averting a nightmare like Gilead for our own future.

SUGGESTIONS FOR FURTHER READING

Atwood, Margaret, 'Witches', in *Second Words: Selected Critical Prose* (Toronto: Anansi, 1982; repr. 1996), pp. 329–33.

Cixous, Hélène, 'The Laugh of the Medusa', in *New French Feminisms: An Anthology*, ed. E. Marks and I. de Courtivron (Brighton: Harvester, 1981), pp. 245–54.

Dvorak, Marta, 'What's in a Name? Readers as both Pawns and Partners, or Margaret Atwood's Strategy of Control', in J.-M. Lacroix and J. Leclaire (eds), *Margaret Atwood: The Handmaid's Tale/Le Conte de la servante: The Power Game* (Paris: Presses de la Sorbonne Nouvelle, 1998), pp. 79–97.

Howells, Coral Ann, 'Transgressing Genre: a Generic Approach to Atwood's Novels', in Reingard M. Nischik (ed.), *Margaret Atwood: Works and Impact* (New York: Camden House, 2000), pp. 139–56.

Hunter, Lynette, '"That Will Never Do": Public History and Private Memory in *Nineteen Eighty-Four* and *The Handmaid's Tale*', in Marta Duorak (ed.), *The Handmaid's Tale: Margaret Atwood* (Paris: Ellipses, 1998), pp. 19–29.

Reynolds, Margaret and J. Noakes (eds), *Margaret Atwood: The Essential Guide* (London: Vintage, 2002).

Thompson, Lee Briscoe, *Scarlet Letters: The Handmaid's Tale* (Toronto: ECW Press, 1997).

8
Cat's Eye

What's the difference between vision and a vision? The former relates to something it's assumed you've seen, the latter to something it's assumed you haven't. Language is not always dependable either.
(Margaret Atwood, 'Instructions for the Third Eye')[1]

The light that we see from distant galaxies left them millions of years ago, and in the case of the most distant object that we have seen, the light left some 8,000 million years ago. Thus, when we look at the universe, we are seeing it as it was in the past.
(Stephen Hawking, *A Brief History of Time*)[2]

These two passages, one from a prose poem questioning the reliability of modes of visual perception and the other from a book of popular physics describing how we see back through the present to the distant past, might together serve as preface to *Cat's Eye*, for this is a novel which combines the discourses of fiction and autobiography, science and painting in its attempt to represent the female subject in the text. Arguably *Cat's Eye* could be read as Atwood's own retrospective glance back at the imaginative territory of her earlier fictions. There is a female artist here who is more successful than the nameless woman in *Surfacing* and the same parent and brother figures as in that novel; the same childhood tormentors and traumatic experiences in the Toronto ravine have appeared in *Lady Oracle* and in some of the poems in *The Circle Game*; 'the eyes of cats, fixed for the pounce' have been referred to in *The Handmaid's Tale*, to name but a few of the intertextual references here. There are figures and events and modes of imagery which chime with resonances from Atwood's earlier works, but I do not want to pursue those explorations here, fascinating as they are.[3] Instead I shall focus on the crucial importance of retrospective art in the female protagonist's construction of her self, for *Cat's Eye* is Atwood's most developed version of life-writing in the feminine, where her middle-aged protagonist Elaine Risley struggles to define herself through figuring out her life story in different versions, a process analogous to the narrative structuring of *Lady Oracle*, *The Robber Bride*, and *The Blind Assassin*. Who is Elaine Risley? And what is the significance of the 'Cat's Eye' of the title? Elaine is a painter; the story is littered with references to her pictures and culminates in her first retrospective exhibition, in Toronto. It is her return to her home town for this exhibition which provides the stimulus for her curiously doubled narrative with its 'discursive' memoir version and its 'figural' version presented through her paintings.[4] Indeed, it is this double figuration of the self, projected through the relationship between the discursive and the figural as forms of autobiography, that is the site of my inquiry. I shall pay particular attention to Elaine's paintings and the retrospective exhibition in order to highlight Atwood's distinctive contribution to the problematical construction of female subjectivity in fiction.[5]

The retrospective exhibition positioned near the end of the novel might be taken as Elaine's final statement, a *summa* of all the elements of her life already contained in the narrative. The exhibition is presented as a chronicle, with its brief views of earlier paintings and detailed descriptions of five later paintings (the last one with the promising title 'Unified Field Theory'), together with a few less-than-helpful interpretations from the catalogue supplemented by/contradicted by Elaine's comments. As readers we have the advantage over the compiler of the catalogue because we already know the private references that are coded into the paintings, whereas she does not. What we also know if we remember back 318 pages is that this retrospective statement is not an authoritative one, for Elaine has left the arrangement of the paintings to the gallery's director (p. 87). Her own position at the opening is that of a visitor:

> I walk slowly around the gallery, sipping at my glass of wine, permitting myself to look at the show, for the first time really. What is here, and what is not.   (p. 404)[6]

Actually the exhibition has the same kind of provisionality as *The Handmaid's Tale*, where Offred's narrative, transcribed from her tapes, is presented as the editor's version rather than as her own. In both cases, the recording subject remains elusive; she cannot be defined by the statements made on her behalf. Yet a retrospective exhibition (not the one described at the end) is the informing principle of the novel, for it has already been constructed on the Contents page, where the chapter titles are all given the names of paintings mentioned in the text. The only painting missing bears the title of the first chapter, 'Iron Lung', which Elaine cannot paint because she is still inside it for as long as she lives, 'being breathed' by time. In the Atwood papers there are two versions of the 'Iron Lung' painting, both deleted from the published novel, and both are striking for what the artist realises much later in time. One version is particularly interesting, for the exhibition catalogue entry suggests that the 'mandala-shaped object' reflects the 'influence of Op Art' on Risley's work, whereas the artist's own comment contradicts this: 'It isn't a mandala, or Op Art. The smaller points are rivets, the larger circle is an iron lung, as seen from the bottom end. I painted it that way because I didn't know whose head to put, sticking out the top end. I would know now.'[7] Throughout the narrative, individual paintings offer a disruptive commentary figuring events from a different angle from that of the memoir, so that it is only appropriate that they should be collected and shown in a gallery named 'Sub-Versions'. The doubled retrospective device[8] creates a complex patterning where painted surfaces present a riddling version of the truth. These visual artefacts, always of course mediated through language, represent the relation between 'vision' and 'a vision' (what it's assumed you've seen and what it's assumed you haven't), where socially accepted codes of seeing are challenged by the eye of the artist. As Elaine looks through the lens of the Cat's Eye, her Third Eye, the 'single eye that sees more than anyone else looking' (p. 327), she sees more because she sees differently.

However, for all her insight Elaine remains a slippery subject, difficult to get into focus. Even now at the age of nearly 50 she is a 'blur' to herself when she looks in the mirror:

> Even when I've got the distance adjusted, I vary. I am transitional; some days I look like a worn-out thirty-five, others like a sprightly fifty. So much depends on the light, and the way you squint.   (p. 5)

And again, 'There is never only one, of anyone' (p. 6). It is surely significant that the first and only complete picture of her face is the photograph on the poster near the gallery where her exhibition is to be held: 'The name is mine and so is the face, more or less. It's the photo I sent the gallery. Except that now I have a moustache' (p. 20). Her view of her own face 'defaced' is surrounded by images of multiple identities, disguises ('I could be a businesswoman…a bank manager… a housewife, a tourist, someone window-shopping,' p. 19), and by a reference to her double, Cordelia – all of which underline Elaine's indeterminacy and multiplicity as a subject. In order to 'read' Elaine's autobiography we could not do better than turn to the theoretical essay by Paul de Man, 'Autobiography as De-facement', which would seem to be signalled by the grotesque visual self-image on the poster. Atwood's project in this novel bears a fascinating resemblance to de Man's deconstructive critique:

> Are we so certain that autobiography depends on reference, as a photograph depends on its subject or a (realistic) picture on its model? We assume that life produces the autobiography as an act produces its consequences, but can we not suggest, with equal justice, that the autobiographical project may itself produce and determine the life and that whatever the writer *does* is in fact governed by the technical demands of self-portraiture and thus determined, in all its aspects, by the resources of his [her] medium?[9]

This construction of subjecthood would seem to be confirmed by Elaine's response to the poster, which may be, as she says, a feeling of wonder, but which also may be read as a self-reflexive comment on her autobiography: 'A public face, a face worth defacing. . . . I have made something of myself, something or other, after all' (p. 20). Elaine's confrontation with her own face defaced, like her return to Toronto, constitutes that 'specular moment' which de Man identifies as the autobiographical impulse, with its sudden alignment between present and past selves, that opens up multiple possibilities for 'mutual reflexive substitution', displacements and doublings. These are for him the 'defacements' endemic to the autobiographical project, which 'deals with the giving and taking away of faces, with face and deface, figure, figuration and disfiguration'.[10] *Cat's Eye* would seem to provide the perfect exemplars of such 'defacements' – wittily in the comic-book story of the two sisters, 'a pretty one and one who has a burn covering half her face' who comes back from the dead to get 'into the pretty one's body' (p. 211), and more seriously in Elaine's portrait of Cordelia, which is called *Half a Face* (p. 227). It is Cordelia, her childhood companion and tormentor, for whom Elaine searches incessantly on her return to Toronto, Cordelia who belongs to that city, which 'still has power; like a mirror that shows you only the ruined half of your face' (p. 410). Lacking her dark double trapped in an earlier period of time, Elaine remains unfixed, incomplete: 'We are like the twins in old fables, each of whom has been given half a key' (p. 411). Cordelia as the absent Other would also confirm de Man's theory of autobiography as a double project of self-representation, moving towards self-restoration at the same moment as it marks splits and divisions within the self.[11]

Returning for a moment to an earlier stage of de Man's critique, I should like to highlight his question about figures and figuration:

> Does the referent determine the figure, or is it the other way round: is the illusion of reference not a correlation of the structure of the figure, that is to say no longer clearly and simply a referent at all but something more akin to a fiction, which then, however, in its own turn, acquires a degree of referential productivity?[12]

The notion that it is the mode of representation which produces the referent is crucial to Atwood's subject-constructing project, where two kinds of figuration are used. While Elaine's discursive narrative remains incomplete, her paintings offer a different figuration, acting as a kind of corrective to the distortions and suppressions of memory and offering the possibility of theoretical solutions. Not that autobiography can ever attain completeness:

> The interest of autobiography, then, is not that it reveals reliable self-knowledge – it does not – but that it demonstrates in a striking way the impossibility of closure and totalization (that is the impossibility of coming into being) of all textual systems made up of tropological substitutions.[13]

Though de Man's discussion focuses exclusively on linguistic signifiers here, and Elaine's autobiography offers the variant of (verbalised) visual images, the result is the same. As seeing eye or discursive recorder, she tells her own private history, together with fragments of Cordelia's story, her brother Stephen's story, the stories of her parents and of Josef, Jon and Ben, the men in her life, and the story of Mrs Smeath. Arguably, Elaine succeeds in establishing her position as a speaking/painting subject, but she herself always exceeds her carefully constructed parameters of vision: 'I'm what's left over' (p. 409). Atwood also situates Elaine's private story in a wider social narrative, as she presents a historical documentary account of Toronto in the 1940s and 1950s from the perspective of an English-speaking Canadian girl, together with a cultural critique of feminism in Canada in the 1970s and 1980s. It is also possible to read Elaine's narrative from a national perspective, focusing on shifting definitions of Canadian identity in the postwar period through Elaine's relationship with the immigrant figures of Miss Lumley and Miss Stuart, Mr Banerji, Mrs Finestein and Josef Hrbik. That reading would be substantiated in Elaine's painting of her *Three Muses* (pp. 406–7).[14]

Atwood's novel adds one important dimension to de Man's theory of autobiography, and that is the dimension of time. Curiously, he neglects this, possibly because he is more interested in the opposition between life and death implied by life-writing, but Atwood does not. As she said in her *Cat's Eye* discussion at the National Theatre, London, in April 1989, 'The thing I sweated over in that novel was Time,' for Elaine's story covers a period of nearly fifty years, from the early 1940s to the late 1980s. This is a 'space–time' novel (a phrase with precise scientific connotations here), where the narrator tries to establish her position by using the three spatial co-ordinates plus the temporal co-ordinate, only to discover that when she is back in Toronto, though her space might be defined, she is living in at least two time dimensions at once as she remembers the past: 'There are, apparently, a great many more dimensions than four' (p. 332). Here Elaine transcribes the words of her dead brother Stephen, who grew up to become a theoretical physicist and was later killed by terrorists in an aircraft hijacking. As so often happens in life-writing, her story is also a memorial to the dead.

The narrative begins with a speculation on time: 'Time is not a line but a dimension, like the dimensions of space. . . . It was my brother Stephen who told me that' (p. 3). It is filled with echoes of Stephen's voice in allusions to his theories about space–time, curved space, the expanding universe, light, black holes, string theory and the uncertainty principle.[15] In significant ways Stephen's scientific enthusiasms have shaped Elaine's imagination, so that her paintings and his theories come to occupy the same area of speculation on the mysterious laws that govern the universe. They are both engaged in trying to reconstruct the past, he through physics and mathematics and she through memory and imaginative vision. His discourse from theoretical physics provides the conceptual framework for her paintings, for Elaine is 'painting time': 'These pictures of her, like everything else, are drenched in time' (p. 151), and finally at the retrospective, 'I walk the room, surrounded by the time I've made' (p. 409). Recording her brother's death, she recalls his anecdote about identical twins and the high-speed rocket, part of his youthful disquisitions on the theory of relativity and its effect on the behaviour of time:

What I thought about then was the space twin, the one who went on an interplanetary journey and returned in a week to find his brother ten years older.
Now I will get older, I thought. And he will not.	(p. 392)

Perhaps the most important single memorial to her brother's influence is her last painting, *Unified Field Theory*, to which I shall return in my discussion of the retrospective exhibition.

We should remember that Elaine trained not as a painter but as a biologist, like her father, producing slide drawings of planaria worms that looked like 'stained glass windows' under the microscope (p. 247), and that her instructor Dr Banerji appears in one of her late paintings dressed like a magus holding a round object figured with bright pink objects ('They are in fact spruce budworm eggs, in section; though I would not expect anyone but a biologist to recognize them', p. 406). The boundaries between science and art are dissolved here in what might be seen as an act of gendered transgression, where Elaine's paintings and drawings show one way in which a woman deals with the master discourse of science, transforming it through another medium or 'another mode of figuration'.

Whether as a trainee biologist or a painter or as the sister of a budding astronomer, Elaine's primary activity is 'seeing'. Eyes are important, but so are microscopes and telescopes and so are lenses, with their ability to magnify and to focus more powerfully than the naked eye. It is in this context that we might consider the significance of the Cat's Eye of the title. Certainly the cat's eye marble exists as a referential object in the text, introduced first in the childhood games in the schoolyard with 'puries', 'bowlies', and 'cat's eyes' (p. 62), where it is strongly associated with her brother's superior skill. It recurs many times in an almost casual way, as something to be fingered in Elaine's pocket as a secret defence against her tormentors when she is nine years old (p. 141); later, as something she has grown out of, like her red plastic purse (p. 203); and later still, as an object to be rediscovered among the debris in the cellar: 'I open it up and take out my blue cat's eye. . . . I look into it, and see my life entire' (p. 397–8). Suddenly the cat's eye marble is transformed into the lens of imaginative vision, becoming that Third Eye through which 'each brick, each leaf of each tree, your own body, will be glowing from within, lit up, so bright you can hardly look. You will reach out in any direction and you will touch the light itself.'[16]

But is it a sudden transformation? Hardly that, for the cat's eye marble has always had a duplicitous existence: 'The cat's eyes really are like eyes, but not the eyes of cats. They're the eyes of something that isn't known but exists anyway... like the eyes of aliens from a distant planet. My favourite one is blue' (pp. 62–3). Invested by the nine-year-old girl with supernatural powers to protect her, it becomes for her a talismanic object and the sign of her own difference: 'She doesn't know what power this cat's eye has, to protect me. Sometimes when I have it with me I can see the way it sees.... I am alive in my eyes only' (p. 141).

Cat's eyes, planets and stars swirl together in Elaine's power dream, when the cat's eye enters her body:

It's falling down out of the sky, straight towards my head, brilliant and glassy. It hits me, passes right into me, but without hurting, except that it's cold. The cold wakes me up. My blankets are on the floor.   (p. 145)

The cat's eye functions as the nexus for all those contradictory feelings of fear and longing, love, hatred and resistance that she feels towards Cordelia, Grace Smeath and Carol Campbell 'In the endless time when Cordelia had such power over me' (p. 113). Indeed, it is already functioning beyond her consciousness as her Third Eye when, deserted by her friends and lying in the snow in the dark, she has her vision of the Virgin Mary, 'Our Lady of Perpetual Help', floating over the footbridge in the Toronto ravine. Elaine's reassumption of her own independence after this agony is marked by the sign of the cat's eye: 'I am indifferent to them. There's something hard in me, crystalline, a kernel of glass. I cross the street and continue along, eating my licorice' (p. 193); much later Elaine will recognise it as the sign of the artist's powers of vision, and it will appear again and again in her paintings as her signature (the pier-glass, the globe, the cat's eye marble). She will use it to figure curved space where 'Nothing goes away'.

The cat's eyes disappear entirely from her memoir narrative of adolescence and early adulthood in a complex process of repression: 'I've forgotten things, I've forgotten that I've forgotten them' (pp. 200–1). However, in the double mode of figuration employed in this novel, the discontinuous narrative constructed by Elaine's paintings tells a different story about Elaine as subject. Though she may feel like 'nothing' but a 'seeing eye', her paintings display an excess of signification that goes beyond the discursive narrative produced by her conscious mind. They are truly 'sub-versions', uncovering that highly complex network of conflicting energies, conscious and unconscious, which make up any individual's subjectivity. The presence of the cat's eye is signalled in Elaine's fascination with the effects of glass when she is studying the history of visual styles, and a little drama of substitution is played out for the reader (though not for her) in her particular concern with the pier-glass in Van Eyck's picture *The Arnolfini Marriage*, where the 'round mirror is like an eye' (p. 327). The cat's eye is there, multiplied, in some of her early still lifes, though scarcely visible: 'far back in the dense tangle of the glossy leaves, are the eyes of cats' (p. 337). Arguably, it is through that alien lens that Elaine paints her savage exposures of Mrs Smeath: 'One picture of Mrs. Smeath leads to another. She multiplies on the walls like bacteria, standing, sitting, flying, with clothes, without clothes, following me around with her many eyes' (p. 338). This is a form of revenge that her conscious mind fails to understand, both at the time of painting and when her pictures are attacked by the ink-throwing woman at the feminist art show in Toronto: 'It's still a mystery to me, why I hate her so much' (p. 352). The answer hovers in the reader's mind as the words of Atwood's prose poem whisper, 'The third eye can be merciless, especially when wounded.'[17]

What is never explained in either the discursive or the figural narrative is Elaine's moments of revelation: her childhood vision of the Virgin Mary or that moment when, back in her parents' house after her father's death, she finds the cat's eye marble in her old red plastic purse; as she looks through that lens, she suddenly sees her 'life entire' (p. 398). Yet these are perhaps the crucial moments which have determined her life as an artist and they both figure together in her final painting, where the Virgin Mary holds 'an oversized cat's eye marble, with a blue centre' (p. 408). ('Vision...a vision: something it's assumed you've seen...something it's assumed you haven't.') Through the logic of the image, Elaine's paintings present 'a vision' as 'vision', so that as we follow the verbal descriptions of the paintings, the act of reading changes to gazing. We 'see' through Elaine's mediating eye, which dissolves the boundaries between the visionary and the visible.

The retrospective exhibition occurs in the chapter 'Unified Field Theory', which with its echoes of Stephen's lecture 'The First Picoseconds and the Quest for a Unified Field Theory: Some Minor

Speculations' (p. 331), places it in a relational context and also signals its function in this autobiographical narrative. Within the parameters of theoretical physics Elaine traces her figural interpretation of her life story, which offers a significantly different series of projections from her discursive memoir. By way of explanation for such differences, we might consider briefly Norman Bryson's emphasis on the double nature of painting in the Western tradition, which he calls 'the divided loyalty of the image': 'A sign is always divided into two areas, one which declares its loyalty to the text outside the image, and another which asserts the autonomy of the image.'[18] This seems a useful way to describe the fissure within Elaine's remembering process, between her conscious mind's discursive narrative and the figural narrative of her imagination. From physics comes the definition of a 'field':

> In physics a field can only be perceived by inference from the relationships of the particles it contains; the existence of the field is, however, entirely separate from that of the particles; though it may be detected through them, it is not defined by them.[19]

Unified field theory itself (the attempt to formulate a comprehensive theory of the laws that govern the universe) belongs to the discourse of theoretical physics; to a non-physicist like Elaine, her brother's lecture sounds as close to metaphysics as to physics.[20] At the end of it, after his speculation on picoseconds, space–time and matter–energy, Stephen does, however, give her a sentence which is crucial to her project of self-representation: 'But there is something that must have existed before. That something is the theoretical framework, the parameters within which the laws of energy must operate' (p. 332). It is this relationship between the cosmic and the humanly particular that Elaine figures in her paintings, none of which offer a totalised representation of her 'self', though maybe that self is the 'field' that might be inferred from the constructions of her pictures.

At the retrospective exhibition we are invited to 'read' the pictures in sequence as we are led by Elaine past the 'early things' and the 'middle period', all of which we have already 'seen' in the text, to her five most recent paintings, which she has never shown before. These are described in detail, and we realise that these paintings have a double significance as representations. There is a personal rationale behind the collocation of images in each picture, which Elaine interprets for us, for these are plain statements in her own private narrative of crises, revelations and memories. However, as the wickedly satirical extracts from the catalogue commentary suggest, they also have a public life as paintings in an exhibition, available to the viewer's interpretation, so that plain statements become riddles provoking other people's narrative solutions: 'I can no longer control these paintings, or tell them what to mean. Whatever energy they have came out of me. I'm what's left over' (p. 409).

The second thing we notice is that these late paintings share a common structural feature: they all introduce further dimensions of meaning into the figural image by their pier-glass motifs or their triptych designs, which initiate shifts in perspective. A host of possible meanings are generated through different spatial patterings, different time dimensions, executed in different painterly techniques. As each painting contains several styles of representation, so the referentiality of any single image is undercut. These multiplicities are quite simply illustrated in Elaine's self portrait, *Cat's Eye* ('There is never only one, of anyone', and anyway her portrait, like the one she painted of Cordelia, is only 'Half a Face'), while more complex representations of space–time and vision are developed in *Unified Field Theory*. The structural feature of the convex lens also highlights artifice, for these paintings reveal themselves as postmodern constructions where realistic images juxtaposed in different dimensions are used to map a psychic landscape in Elaine's project of painting time.

It is important in the double mode of figuration of this novel to note that the paintings effect quite significant revisions in Elaine's retrospective narrative, for they encode insights that she herself only realises later when she looks at the paintings. Now she reads the Mrs Smeath paintings differently, understanding at last not only why she had hated that woman so much but also how vengeful she had been as a younger woman, and how her earlier self lacked the compassionate recognition which she had actually painted into Mrs Smeath's eyes:

> It's the eyes I look at now. I used to think these were self-righteous eyes, piggy and smug inside their wire frames; and they are. But they are also defeated eyes....Mrs. Smeath was a transplant to the city, from somewhere a lot smaller. A displaced person; as I was.   (p. 405)

This process of moving from the blindness of consciousness to the insight of imaginative seeing occurs in Elaine's reading of all her late paintings, with her questioning of the reliability of memory in *Picoseconds*, her awareness of the kindness of strangers in *Three*

Muses, her ignorance of her brother's last moments in *One Wing*, and her recognition of what her childhood torments were and how they were crucial to the development of her artistic powers. It is the last painting, *Unified Field Theory*, which marks the most significant revision of all in its effort at synthesis. Elaine's figuration of her vision of the Virgin Mary holding the cat's eye marble and floating above the bridge of her childhood traumas combines with her brother's cosmic imagery ('Star upon star, red, blue, yellow and white, swirling nebulae, galaxy upon galaxy'). This representation of the night sky could also be read as a black hole under the ground, as the secret place of her brother's buried treasure, or as 'the land of the dead people', one of the many terrors of her childhood. Here the figural presents oppositions as co-existing on the same plane: the past and the present, 'a vision' and 'vision', the sacred and the profane, science and art, the universal and the particular. This is Elaine's attempt to present her 'life entire' in an impersonal vision of wholeness, painting the forces which govern the laws of her being. All this is carefully spelled out by Elaine, with no comment from the catalogue this time, and as readers we probably believe her interpretation because it gathers up so many anecdotes from her memoir text, offering a possible site for accommodating the Virgin Mary vision. The meanings work forwards as well as backwards to enhance Elaine's discursive narrative when she will record her last 'vision' of Cordelia, in language which sets up parallels and echoes with the account of the first vision. However, the painting might also work another way, to problematise further her memoir narrative by highlighting its gaps and omissions. In a universe where 'Nothing goes away' (p. 3), 'what have I forgotten?' (p. 334) always remains an open question.

Of course, the last painting, like the retrospective or the memoir, offers only a theoretical framework for the definition of Elaine's self, providing an illusion of completeness which is dispelled by the final chapter, entitled 'Bridge', where the narrative takes up once again the quest for Cordelia and Elaine's registration of lack and loss. Our view of Elaine herself remains partial and provisional; though we have learned to see through her eyes, we have only ever seen half her face or her face 'defaced'. Apparently the human subject is as mysterious as the universe: 'The universe is hard to pin down; it changes when you look at it, as if it resists being known' (p. 388).

In this version of life-writing in the feminine, with its double project for constructing female subjectivity through the discursive and the figural modes, the emphasis on displacements, doublings and 'defacements' underlines the inherent instability of the narrating subject at the same time as it 'undoes the model [of autobiography as a genre] as soon as it is established'.[21] Though we may be persuaded that Elaine succeeds in locating her own distinctive position in her figural constructions of space–time, the discursive narrative as a 'textual system made up of tropological substitutions'[22] will always register some incompleteness in the construction of subjecthood, a lack that is confirmed at the thematic level by Elaine's failure to find Cordelia and her recognition that she is alone in Toronto. A manuscript note clarifies this point while amplifying it in interesting ways: 'Cordelia is gone, this is empty landscape. Or not empty. Full of whatever is there without our hatreds and desires.'[23] Elaine is left stranded in the present, surrounded by the wash of time:

> This is what I miss, Cordelia: not something that's gone, but something that will never happen. Two old women giggling over their tea.   (p. 421)

Through the multiple modes of narrative representation, Elaine, like Offred or Cordelia, 'slips from our grasp and flees'. By telling the reader so much, Atwood has paradoxically exposed the limits of autobiography and its artifice of reconstruction. The best Elaine Risley or Margaret Atwood can offer is a Unified Field Theory from which inferences about the subject may be made, but the subject herself is always outside, or somewhere beyond the figurations of language; the 'I' remains behind the 'eye'. At the end, Elaine recedes back into her seeing eye, voided of personality, as her narrative dissolves into light:

> Now it's full night, clear, moonless and filled with stars, which are not eternal as was once thought, which are not where we think they are. If they were sounds, they would be echoes... Echoes of light, shining out of the midst of nothing.
>   It's old light, and there's not much of it. But it's enough to see by.   (p. 421)[24]

SUGGESTIONS FOR FURTHER READING

Bouson, J. Brooks, *Brutal Choreographies: Oppositional Strategies and Narrative Design in the Novels of Margaret Atwood* (Amherst: University of Massachusetts Press, 1993), pp. 159–84.

Davidson, A. E., *Seeing in the Dark: Cat's Eye*, Canadian Fiction Studies, 35 (Toronto: ECW Press, 1997).

Kirtz, Mary K., '(Dis)unified Field Theories: the Clarendon Lectures seen through (a) *Cat's Eye*', in Sharon R. Wilson (ed.), *Margaret Atwood's Textual Assassinations* (Columbus: Ohio State University Press, 2003), pp. 54–73.

MacMurraugh-Kavanagh, Madeleine, *Cat's Eye*, York Notes Advanced (London: York Press, 2000).

Man, Paul de, 'Autobiography as De-facement', *Modern Language Notes*, 94 (1979): 931–55.

9

The Robber Bride

'The Other Woman will soon be with us,' the feminists used to say. But how long will it take, thinks Roz, and why hasn't it happened yet?

(Margaret Atwood, *The Robber Bride*, p. 392)[1]

With *The Robber Bride*, Atwood returns to her favourite genre of female Gothic romance, but in the 1990s she turns Gothic romance upside-down by using and revising its conventions to produce a worldly text which engages not only with questions of sexual politics and fantasies of femininity but also with questions of national identity in an urban postcolonial context. *The Robber Bride* is a mutant form of Gothic romance, with the return of a demonic woman from the dead in a story about transgressions, magic mirrors, shape changers and dark doubles, betrayals and omens of disaster, until the final defeat of the villainess by three women friends when her body is burned up and its ashes scattered over the deepest part of Lake Ontario. There is also a multiple homecoming and the restoration of social and family order at the end. Here we find the key Gothic elements of the unspeakable and the buried life, together with a whole range of traditional motifs like vampires and monsters, spells, soul stealing and body snatching, while the plot conforms to the traditional Gothic pattern as a 'narrative of disclosure and reparation' where 'the weight of the past...may be escaped only when its secrets are brought to light through the process of discovering connections between past and present'.[2] It could be argued here that the traditional Gothic plot is turned 'upside-down somehow', for though there are female victims there are no rescuing heroes and the novel is structured around the adventures not of a villain but of a villainess, who seems to be a figure out of nightmare and whose existence blurs the borderlines between realism and fantasy. This is the demonic woman of the title, Zenia the Robber Bride herself, that 'Other Woman' who has come all the way from central Europe as an immigrant to torment three innocent women who live in modern

Toronto. If it were possible, Zenia could be Dracula's daughter, for this is a story about the Un-Dead. Yet there are no tombs, mazes or haunted castles here; in this story all the blood belongs to history and to metaphor.

So, what is happening here? Margaret Atwood has produced a postmodernist fiction which exploits the shock effects that occur when Gothic fairy tale migrates into totally different genres like the failed family romance, the detective thriller and documentary history. Tony, the professional historian among the three friends, knows this technique and how it might be used to engage the interest of listener and readers: 'She likes the faint shock on the faces of her listeners. It's the mix of domestic image and mass bloodshed that does it to them' (p. 3). The novel is both like a fairy tale as its title indicates, and like history, which – as Tony the female military historian explains – is always 'a construct' (p. 6), being the combination of different kinds of textual evidence: social documentary, private memory narrative and imaginative reconstruction. History is a discontinuous text with crucial gaps, so that different interpretations of the facts are always possible, for 'every sober-sided history is at least half sleight-of-hand' (p. 461). Tony's words recall those of the American historiographer Hayden White, who has suggested that the narratives of history always reconstruct the available facts of the past for readers in the present according to congenial ideological perspectives and identifiable literary patterns, like the quest of the hero or fables of decline and fall.[3] In this chapter I am concerned primarily with Zenia's role as the Other Woman and with teasing out the different dimensions of her otherness, though I shall also pay attention to history, for the personal histories of Zenia and her three friends are situated in a wider context of Canadian and international history as well.

The Robber Bride is the story of Zenia as told through the multiple narratives of her three friends, Antonia Fremont (Tony), Roz Andrews, and Charis. As each of the three tells her own life story, different overlapping frames of reference are set up through which Zenia's character and significance are given meaning, though Zenia never exists independently of the stories of others. It is through her relationships that Zenia's identity is constructed, but it is also transformed as it is refigured through the perspectives of a military historian (Tony), a successful businesswoman (Roz) and a New Age mystic and shop assistant (Charis). These women are all living in Toronto on 23 October 1990, a crucial date for the narrative as on that day they are having lunch together at a fashionable Toronto restaurant called the Toxique, and 'Zenia returns from the dead' (p. 4). Through the swirl of contemporary history, which Atwood sketches as a globalised scene of disasters, the novel focuses on this one particular event, the kind of 'definitive moment' so useful to historians – and to novelists – after which 'things were never the same again. They provide beginnings for us, and endings too' (p. 4). The postmodern self-reflexivity of the narrative is signalled in the first and last sections, entitled 'Onset' and 'Outcome', told by Tony, who has a 'historian's belief in the salutary power of explanations' while realising the 'impossibility of accurate reconstruction'. Yet for all its enigmas and secrets and dark doubles – traditional Gothic elements which, we are reminded, are also the features of historical and psychological narratives – the novel is structured quite schematically, moving out from the crisis of Zenia's Gothic reappearance in the restaurant five years after her memorial service, then scrolling back through the life stories of all three in an attempt to track Zenia down, only to return to the Toxique again about a week later, where the final crisis occurs. Though the three friends have met to exchange stories of their confrontation with Zenia, whom they have all encountered on the same day, and to celebrate their resistance and her defeat, they discover something even more startling has happened: Zenia is dead, really dead this time. As Tony's husband West says, 'Again? I'm really sorry' (p. 449); and there is a second memorial service for Zenia a year later which is a replay of the earlier one, when the friends scatter her ashes and return to Charis's house to tell stories about Zenia all over again.

Within that contemporary frame the memory narratives of Tony, Charis and Roz all occur in chronological sequence, charting the history of changing cultural fashions in Toronto over the previous 30 years. Tony's section ('Black Enamel') recounts her memories of meeting Zenia as a student in the 1960s as it tracks back through Tony's unhappy childhood, and recounts Zenia's many attempts to rob Tony of her money, her professional reputation, and her beloved West. Charis's section ('Weasel Nights') focuses on her memories of Zenia in the 1970s, the era of hippies and draft dodgers, her American lover Billy and their daughter August, with flashbacks to her childhood as a victim of sexual abuse; it ends with Zenia's seduction of Billy and his disappearance. Roz's section ('The Robber Bride') recounts her meetings with Zenia in the 1980s and follows a similar pattern of recall: childhood memories, marriage, motherhood and a successful business career, up to Zenia's seduction of Roz's husband Mitch and his eventual suicide. Only Tony survives with her man, and it is left to her to give a narrative shape to the fragments of Zenia that exist in the multiple anecdotes of these women: 'She will only be history if Tony chooses to shape her into history' (p. 461). For all three, Zenia is the 'Other Woman' in the romance triangle, and her existence challenges the optimistic assertion of the early 1970s feminists, which Roz recalls with some scepticism in 1990. I have chosen Roz's ironical remark as the head quote for this chapter because it highlights Zenia's significance in feminist readings of the novel, though in typically Gothic style it veils the more uncanny dimensions of her otherness. Zenia represents a powerfully transgressive element, which continues to threaten feminist attempts to transform gender relations and concepts of sexual power politics. It is the otherness of Zenia which is figured in her three avatars in this novel, identified in the different life stories told by the three friends. One avatar is from fairy tale: *The Robber Bridegroom* by the Brothers Grimm, which is here feminised by Roz's twin daughters and savagely glossed by her through the parodic mode of double coding:

> *The Robber Bride*, thinks Roz. Well, why not? Let the grooms take it in the neck for once. The Robber Bride, lurking in her mansion in the dark forest.... The Rubber Broad is more like it – her and those pneumatic tits. (p. 295)

A second avatar is from the Bible, the figure of Jezebel in the Old Testament (1 Judges: 21). This is prefigured as far back as Charis's childhood when with her grandmother she used to choose revelatory passages from the Bible at random, and once lit on the death of Jezebel; that 'message' is confirmed on the very day of her last confrontation with Zenia, by her morning Bible reading:

> She realized it as soon as she got up, as soon as she stuck her daily pin into the Bible. It picked out Revelations Seventeen, the chapter about the Great Whore. (p. 420)

There is a third avatar advanced by Tony near the end, that of the medieval French Cathar woman warrior Dame Giraude, who in the thirteenth century defended her castle against the Catholic forces of Simon de Montfort. She was finally defeated and thrown down a well. This is the most unsettling of Zenia's avatars because it introduces a new perspective on her otherness which extends beyond gendered antagonisms and the demonic. Just as Tony very much admires the reckless courage of Dame Giraude, fighting for a lost cause, so too she has a sneaking admiration for Zenia as a guerrilla fighter, despite her own humiliations at her hands:

> Zenia is dead, and although she was many other things, she was also courageous. What side she was on doesn't matter; not to Tony, not any more. There may not even have been a side. She may have been alone.   (pp. 469–70)

This heterogeneous collection of women out of history and legend is a recognition of the 'otherness' of Zenia, which cannot be accommodated within the parameters of the friends' stories. Tony has always associated Zenia with war – or 'Raw' in terms of her own subjective life. As a result of having known Zenia, Tony contemplates writing a book about female military commanders: '*Iron Hands, Velvet Gloves*, she could call it. But there isn't much material' (p. 464). It is also Tony who wishes to give Zenia's ashes a sort of military burial on Armistice Day: 'An ending, then. November 11, 1991, at eleven o'clock in the morning, the eleventh hour of the eleventh day of the eleventh month' (p. 465).

Whichever way we look at it, the most interesting figure in the novel is Zenia; she is there in the title and it is her story which defines and focuses the narrative. How is it that this traditionally Gothic figure survives as such a powerful force in Atwood's novel about contemporary social reality in 1990s Toronto? I wish to suggest that Atwood herself has done a Dr Frankenstein performance here, reassembling parts of old legends and fairy tales in order to create her female monster, who strides through three Canadian women's stories from the 1960s to the 1990s haunting their lives and wreaking havoc. However, Atwood revises the *Frankenstein* ending for it is the monster who destroys herself and it is the three friends who survive, though their memories of Zenia will live on. This is perhaps putting it rather melodramatically, but what Zenia represents will always exceed the bounds of decorum. Her power is the power of female sexuality, and the figure of Zenia relates directly to contemporary social myths about femininity; it also relates to male (and female) fantasies about the feminine; and in addition it challenges feminist thinking about gender relations. Female sexuality has always been a problem for real women and real men, just as it is a problem for feminism: 'Male fantasies, male fantasies, is everything run by male fantasies?' (p. 392). Have women internalised these fantasies to such an extent that, as Roz fears, 'You are a woman with a man inside watching a woman'? Atwood answers Roz's rhetorical questions by investigating the effects of fantasies of desirable femininity on women themselves. Zenia inhabits that fantasy territory:

> The Zenias of this world...have slipped sideways into dreams; the dreams of women too, because women are fantasies for other women, just as they are for men. But fantasies of a different kind. (p. 392)

Atwood is using her Gothic villainess to highlight the way fantasy works, with its distorting images of desire and lack, as in the photograph of Zenia which Roz shows to her assistant and to the reader in the course of a business deal about the take-over of a cosmetics firm:

> What she hands him is an eight-by-ten colour glossy of Zenia, a studio portrait, the same one they'd used for *WiseWomanWorld* when Zenia was the editor....A dark dress with texture, plushy, V-necked of course – if you've got it, flaunt it, even if it's styrofoam; the long white throat, the dark electrical hair, the left eyebrow quirked, the mulberry-coloured mouth curved up at the edges in that maddening, secretive smile.
> My own monster, thinks Roz. I thought I could control her. Then she broke loose. (p. 95)

This photograph of Zenia that Roz displays is an image of the Femme Fatale, the exciting and dangerously sexy lady, that illustrates contemporary cultural constructions of desirable femininity. But she is also likened to Frankenstein's monster, where Roz is in the role of Dr Frankenstein. So we need to ask what kind of a fantasy she is for Roz when there is such an obvious tension in Roz's mind between the glamorous image and her ironic exposure of its falsity. Through the photo and Roz's gazing at it, Atwood exposes the power politics within feminism in the 1980s as different kinds of female power come into conflict: Zenia has a sexual power, whereas Roz has the financial power to make or break another woman's career. However, Zenia has run off with Roz's husband, showing Roz that her power has limits, and it is the projection of Roz's personal chagrin which is being described here in all its complexity. Interestingly, this is not a male fantasy but Roz's, for Atwood is drawing attention to the ways in which popular fantasies of femininity continue to affect women's images of their own identities. Roz's Frankenstein reference recalls Atwood's early poem 'Speeches for Dr Frankenstein', when he addresses his 'sparkling monster', telling it that it has absorbed everything he once valued, but the monster responds only with defiance: 'I will not come when you call.'[4] Bereft of even the illusion of mastery, Frankenstein like Roz is left with nothing but longing: he becomes the monster's shadow. It is no wonder that sometimes Roz would like to be somebody else: 'But not just anyone. Sometimes… she would like to be Zenia' (p. 393).

Zenia seems to be real but, as Roz's photograph suggests, she has a double existence for she belongs to two different fictional discourses, those of realism and of fantasy. She is a very transgressive figure who exists both as a character in a realistic fiction and also as the projection of three women's imaginations. As the Other Woman, her identity is fabricated through their stories about her, which are all stories of seduction, betrayal and humiliation. She herself is an enigma. Indeed she derives meaning only within the signifying structures of other people's stories and then always retrospectively. Zenia is a liar, a floating signifier, possibly a void and certainly a fraud. There is no indication that she has any independent subjective life, unless it is her 'aura', which is savagely at variance with her glamorous appearance; it is, according to Charis, 'a turbulent muddy green… a deadly aureole, a visible infection' (p. 66). At least this is how Zenia appears to one of her victims, always on the loose and ready to rob them of whatever is most precious to them. Zenia is everything they want most and everything they fear, for she represents their unfulfilled desires just as she represents their repressed pain-filled childhood selves come back to haunt them in adult life. This is where Zenia's otherness assumes its uncanny dimensions, for her reappearances remind them of something that is 'deeply familiar but which has become alienated through repression', as Freud would remind us. She is the dark double of them all, having multiple identities but no fixed identity as she migrates from one woman's life story to another's. As Tony discovers after systematic research:

> Even the name Zenia may not exist…. As for the truth about her, it lies out of reach, because – according to the records, at any rate – she was never even born.   (p. 461)

There are three totally different versions of Zenia's life story, which have been tailored to fit the lives of Tony, Charis and Roz.

She is what they most desire and dread to be. Like Roz, both Tony and Charis think occasionally that they would like to be someone other than the persons they are; most of the time they would like to be Zenia. It is no wonder that Tony reaches this conclusion:

> As with any magician, you saw what she wanted you to see; or else you saw what you yourself wanted to see. She did it with mirrors. The mirror was whoever was watching, but there was nothing behind the two-dimensional image but a thin layer of mercury. (p. 461)

Zenia's name (pronounced 'with a long *e*, as in *seen*', Atwood advises us in her Acknowledgements) emphasises surfaces and appearances, and we may recall that her return from the dead is signalled by her appearance in the mirror of the Toxique restaurant. The novel is full of mirror images, with Zenia on one side of the mirror and the three friends on the other, as all of them see themselves reflected in her. As the critic Shannon Hengen has argued in her essay on 'Zenia's Foreignness'[5] it is her otherness which forces these women to confront dimensions of otherness within themselves, a fact obscurely recognised by Tony at the beginning of her relationship with Zenia when, looking into her eyes, Tony sees herself as more heroic and assertive than she has ever been in real life, for she 'sees her own reflection: herself, as she would like to be. *Tnomerf Ynot.* Herself turned inside out' (p. 167). Even Charis, for all her unworldliness and New Age mysticism, dreams of being a different, stronger self when she sees her own image and Zenia's merging together in her first power dream:

> Zenia's edges dissolve like a watercolour in the rain and Charis merges into her.... She looks out through her eyes. What she sees is herself, herself in the mirror, herself with power. (p. 398)

Only for Roz does the mirror reflect her limits of power; much as she wishes to be Zenia, her magic mirror out of the Snow White fairy tale refuses to co-operate, only giving her truthful practical answers:

> *Mirror, mirror on the wall,*
> *Who is the evilest of us all?*
>
> *Take off a few pounds, cookie, and maybe I can do something for you.*
> (p. 393)

These mirror images, always closely associated with Zenia, make the friends see unacknowledged dimensions of desire and lack within themselves, just as Zenia forces them to remember and to tell all the unspeakable secrets of their past lives. Her otherness acts as a catalyst in their redefinitions of personal identity.[6]

We begin to see why the three women cannot let Zenia go, when they believe she is dead and when they have been to her memorial service five years earlier. Having been tricked and robbed by Zenia of men, money and self-confidence, they keep on meeting once a month for lunch because of her. The positive outcome is that they become fast friends, and it is worth noting that this is the first time such a group of loyal female friends has appeared in Atwood's fiction. However, the fact remains that they meet to tell stories about Zenia, and in fact it is their collective need of her which brings her back from the dead – or would do so, if she were really dead. When she commits suicide the three friends stand looking at her, still needing to believe that she is looking at them:

> Zenia revolves slowly, and looks straight at them with her white mermaid eyes.
> She isn't really looking at them though, because she can't. Her eyes are rolled back into her head.   (pp. 446–7)

The switch in narrative perspective reminds readers of whose is the active needy gaze, and it is not Zenia's. Even when they have scattered her ashes in Lake Ontario at the end, their stories will still be about Zenia. They need her, or their stories about her, in order to define themselves, for the 'good' women are shown to be as dependent on the 'Other Woman' as she is on them. Zenia is inside each one, for she represents their unfulfilled shadow selves: 'Was she in any way like us? thinks Tony. Or, to put it the other way around: Are we in any way like her?' (p. 470). The dark reflection in the magic mirror is still there, in that 'infinitely receding headspace where Zenia continues to exist' (p. 464). Atwood has given some clues to Zenia's role in her speech on 'Spotty-Handed Villainesses':

> But female bad characters can also act as keys to doors we need to open, and as mirrors in which we can see more than just a pretty face. They can be explorations of moral freedom – because everyone's choices are limited, and women's choices have been more limited than men's, but that doesn't mean that women can't make

choices. Such characters can pose the question of responsibility, because if you want power you have to accept responsibility, and actions produce consequences. I'm not suggesting an agenda here, just some possibilities…[7]

In her discussion of Daphne du Maurier's *Rebecca*, that story of another demonic woman, Alison Light took a somewhat similar line of argument:

> It demarcates a feminine subjectivity which is hopelessly split within bourgeois gendered relations…[it] makes visible the tensions within the social construction of femininity whose definitions are never sufficient and are always reminders of what is missing, what could be.[8]

Light's remark about a woman's novel of the late 1930s needs very little updating in relation to *The Robber Bride*, written nearly 60 years later, where the concept of split feminine subjectivity is shared by all three of Atwood's protagonists. Signalled in their doubled or tripled names (Tony/Antonia Fremont/Tnomerf Ynot; Roz Andrews/ Rosalind Greenwood/Roz Grunwald; and Charis, formerly known as Karen), it is commented on explicitly in the accounts of all three. Since childhood Tony has always been able to write and spell backwards: 'It's her seam, it's where she's sewn together; it's where she could split apart' (p. 19). Similar comments are offered about Charis, who was 'split in two' as a sexually abused child (p. 263), and about Roz, whose life was 'cut in two' when her Jewish father returned to Toronto after the Second World War (p. 332). All three have a seam, a split, which is the space of repression occupied by their 'dark twins', and Zenia operates on this edge of desire and lack, which is the borderline territory of the Gothic Other.

Zenia is a threat because of her flaunting sexuality, her deceptions and betrayals, her ruthless contempt for others and her random destructiveness. With her siren song she seduces men, pulls them inside out and then abandons them, though as Tony realises, there is nothing gender specific about this with Zenia:

> How well she did it, thinks Tony. How completely she took us in. In the war of the sexes, which is nothing like a real war but is instead a kind of confused scrimmage in which people change allegiances at a moment's notice, Zenia was a double agent. (p. 185)

Zenia is likened to a marauder, a guerrilla fighter, a vampire, and a rattlesnake. The otherness which she represents has to be construed as deviant, dangerous, and threatening, and she has to be destroyed again and again. Her punishment is very like Rebecca's in the earlier novel when Rebecca suffered murder, vilification and cancer of the womb; Zenia commits suicide – or was she murdered? She is discredited through the revelation that she was a drug dealer and possibly an arms smuggler, and she is reputed to be suffering from ovarian cancer. As Tony repeats, 'Zenia is history,' which does not mean that she is dead and out of the way but that her story will continue to be retold in different versions and endlessly speculated upon. It is symptomatic that even her funeral urn splits in two and her ashes blow about all over the three mourners. In this Gothic fairy tale told from a feminist perspective, Zenia is a very disruptive figure for she is the spectacle of desirable (and possibly fatal) femininity, a beautiful façade which hides whatever is behind it. (Is it neurotic insecurity? Or frigidity? Or nothingness? Or is it ruthless egoism?) The final image of Zenia is given by Tony in her ambiguous elegy:

> She's like an ancient statuette dug up from a Minoan palace: there are the large breasts, the tiny waist, the dark eyes, the snaky hair. Tony picks her up and turns her over, probes and questions, but the woman with her glazed pottery face does nothing but smile. (p. 470)[9]

Yet there is another way of looking at Zenia as the Other Woman, which Tony is willing to contemplate right from the beginning:

> *Pick any strand and snip, and history comes unravelled . . .*
> But Zenia is also a puzzle, a knot: if Tony could just find a loose end and pull, a great deal would come free, for everyone involved, and for herself as well. Or this is her hope. She has a historian's belief in the salutary power of explanations.   (p. 3)

As these women's personal histories are revealed through their relationships with Zenia, Atwood pulls apart comfortable assumptions about authentic white English-Canadian identities, showing up the fault lines in any identity construction. It is an interesting symptom of the same processes of historical and cultural change that Atwood records in her novel that since the late 1990s there has been a shift in the critical reading of Zenia's otherness which extends beyond a specifically feminist framework into wider dimensions of social history focused on multiculturalism and immigrant identities in the Canadian context.[10] In such readings Zenia is still the focus, but the Gothic Other has now become the figure of the immigrant, the *étrangère*, whose dislocated identity mirrors dimensions of alienation within those who have stayed at home. As we have previously seen, Roz, Tony and Charis are all split subjects, though gender is only one of the factors that have contributed to the dislocation and self-division which is evident in all their life stories. All of them have repressed traumatic memories of unhappy childhoods and have reinvented their social identities as adults, though hidden histories of unbelonging, immigrant parents, sexual abuse, and isolation characterise all three, so that they feel like outsiders in the country of their birth. As Rao comments on their shared sense of foreignness: 'A preoccupation with questions of home and estrangement, national identity and belonging runs throughout a text populated by characters who experience a literal or metaphorical exile,' and Zenia's foreignness reflects back to all these women in exaggerated form their own instabilities of identity.[11]

Zenia may be a European postwar immigrant to Canada (a White Russian aristocrat on her mother's side and with any one of three possible fathers, in the version of her life story which she tells Tony; of mixed Jewish and Roman Catholic parentage in Berlin, as she tells Roz; or the daughter of a Romanian gipsy and a Finnish communist, in her story to Charis), whereas the three friends are all Canadian born. However, they have one point in common: they were all born during the Second World War and they are all, in a sense, war casualties. Tony is the product of an unhappy marriage between a Canadian solder and an English war bride, Roz's father was a Jewish immigrant from Winnipeg who made his money as a black marketeer in Europe during the war and who returned to Canada as a Displaced Person, only to make his fortune in Toronto as a property developer, and Charis is illegitimate, though she grew up believing that her father was a soldier who was killed in the war. 'I guess a lot of people were,' says Zenia dismissively. 'But that's history' (p. 272). Yet the past survives into the present, and ironically it is Zenia who makes them see the 'raw war' of their personal histories set in a wider international context of European wars, dislocated identities and struggles for survival. Of the three friends, it is Roz who feels closest to Zenia's position as a displaced stateless immigrant in Canada, for Zenia reflects back to Roz her own sense of not belonging: 'She's not what she appears, a beautiful and successful career woman. She's a waif, a homeless wandering waif' (p. 365). Despite the fact that Roz is a wealthy company director and publicly recognised as one of 'Toronto's Fifty Most Influential' citizens (p. 88), she always feels like a refugee, 'just off the boat, head wrapped in a shawl, wiping her nose on her sleeve and lucky to have a sleeve at that. Which boat? There are many boats in her ancestral past.... Everyone she's descended from got kicked out of somewhere else' (p. 305).

Roz's life story reflects an important element in Canada's postwar social history with its high proportion of ethnic immigrants and culturally hybridised identities, where questions of nationality have to be renegotiated. For her, there is a strong feeling of anxiety over these issues which is directly related to her own memories of Canadian anti-Semitism during the war:

> But things are getting more confusing: for instance, how many immigrants can you fit in? How many of them can you handle, realistically, and who is *them*, and where do you draw the line? The mere fact that Roz is thinking this way shows the extent of the problem, because Roz knows very well what it's like to be *them*. By now, however, she is *us*. It makes a difference.   (p. 100)

But being *us* is for Roz always undermined by her own awareness of her father's Jewish origins and her mother's Irish Catholic working-class background, together with the painful memories of her own series of reinvented identities and changes of name, which marked her family's upward mobility. In her life Roz has shifted names and identities three times, from Rosalind Greenwood as the daughter of an Irishwoman who kept a lodging house in Toronto during the war, to Roz Grunwald, the rich half-Jewish princess, when her father returns from Europe after the war, to Ms Roz Andrews through her marriage into old Toronto WASP society. Roz is beset by insecurities and a sense of inadequacy because of her dual cultural inheritance. She feels like a misfit in any social context: 'But whereas once Roz wasn't Catholic enough, now she isn't Jewish enough. She's an oddity, a hybrid, a strange half-person' (p. 314). Though she has lived in Toronto all her life, after the war she felt like a Displaced

Person herself, and managed to survive by adopting the immigrant's strategies of wariness and mimicry, at Jewish summer camp imitating the gestures and language of the others, adding 'layers of language to herself, sticking them on like posters on a fence' (p. 345) in her performance of her new role. Even her marriage and her financial success as the inheritor of her father's business do nothing to eradicate Roz's sense of outsiderliness, for she is keenly aware that social identities are only masks, hiding a 'homeless waif' inside her skin.

Zenia's tale of her own Jewish–Catholic parentage and her arrival in Canada after the war as a child refugee give Roz back her own reflection, though Zenia adds a dimension that Roz cannot resist, in her story of Roz's beloved father's heroism in rescuing her from the Holocaust and providing her with a forged passport to Canada. But we need to remember (as Roz did not, though she was warned by Tony) that Zenia is a double agent, who not only magnifies Roz's insecurities but also exploits her vulnerability and, like the magic mirror, shows her the limits of her power as wife, mother and businesswoman. Zenia's attacks push Roz to the point of suicide, though paradoxically it is only through Zenia that Roz finally learns to accept her multiple changing identities and to realise that the choice of identities is a mark of freedom and not of dispossession: 'Roz will finally be a widow. No, she'll be something beyond that. What? She will wait and see' (p. 467).

All these women finally defeat Zenia in their own private battles with her, and their triumph at the end is a measure of their new self-confidence as they begin at last to feel at home in Toronto, having survived their encounters with Zenia and learned some painful lessons. After all, as the first epigraph to the novel reminds us, 'A rattlesnake that doesn't bite teaches you nothing'.

It would seem that after her second memorial service Zenia has finally gone, and that she can now be turned into history, 'because she is dead, and all of the dead are in the hands of the living' (p. 246). Zenia's identity remains unfixed, though ironically for a European immigrant with at least three passports, she is the only one who is ever officially classified as Canadian, in a newspaper report of her death in the Lebanon: 'Canadian Killed in Terrorist Blast' (p. 13). Always an enigma, Zenia makes her transgressive way through the novel under the camouflage of her shifting figurations. During the narrative she has taken on all the pains of the twentieth century – as the Jewish victim of Nazi persecution, as a displaced person after the Second World War, as victim of violence and sexual abuse, as suffering from cancer, AIDS, and drug addiction – just as she has been the icon of femininity, Robber Bride, Whore of Babylon and woman warrior. Zenia represents the phobic underside of consciousness for the three friends, but she also represents the social neuroses and traumatic memories that are buried in the foundations of late twentieth-century Western culture. She remains un-dead, a vampiric figure desiring 'a bowl of blood, a bowl of pain, some death' (p. 13), for she derives her life from the insecurities and desires of the living.

The ending of *The Robber Bride* is not an ending but merely 'a lie in which we all agree to conspire' (p. 465). We are reminded of Atwood's voice in *Murder in the Dark*, whispering 'I have designs on you...by the rules of the game, I must always lie.' Atwood takes Gothic conventions and turns them inside out, weaving her illusions 'like any magician making us see what she wants us to see', as she transgresses the boundaries between realism and fantasy, between what is acceptable and what is forbidden. Of course, *The Robber Bride* is a fiction created by Atwood's narrative art, but it speaks to readers in the present as it tricks us into confronting our own desires and fears. Atwood, like the old Gothic novelists, like Joan Foster in *Lady Oracle* and like Zenia, is a magician who uses the same illusionist techniques: 'she does it with mirrors'.

SUGGESTIONS FOR FURTHER READING

Atwood, Margaret, 'Spotty-Handed Villainesses: Problems of Female Bad Behaviour in the Creation of Literature' (1994). www.web.net/owtoad/vlness.htm

Hengen, Shannon, 'Zenia's Foreignness', in Lorraine M. York (ed.), *Various Atwoods: Essays on the Later Poems, Short Fiction, and Novels* (Toronto: Anansi, 1995), pp. 271–86.

Howells, Coral Ann, '*The Robber Bride*: or, Who is a True Canadian?' in Sharon Wilson (ed.), *Margaret Atwood's Textual Assassinations: Recent Poetry and Fiction* (Columbus: Ohio State University Press, 2003), pp. 88–101.

Mycak, Sonia, *In Search of the Split Subject: Psychoanalysis, Phenomenology and the Novels of Margaret Atwood* (Toronto: ECW Press, 1996), pp. 212–42.

Rao, Eleanora, *Heart of a Stranger: Contemporary Women Writers and the Metaphor of Exile* (Naples: Liguori Editore, 2002), pp. 107–19.

Wilson, Sharon R., 'Mythological Intertexts in Margaret Atwood's Work', in R. Nischik (ed.), *Margaret Atwood: Works and Impact* (New York: Camden House, 2000), pp. 215–28.

10

Alias Grace

The lure of the Canadian past, for the writers of my generation, has been partly the lure of the unmentionable – the mysterious, the buried, the forgotten, the discarded, the taboo.

(Margaret Atwood, *In Search of Alias Grace*)[1]

Atwood's retrospective impulse becomes an explicitly historicising one with her novel *Alias Grace* (1996), which is set in the context of nineteenth-century English-Canadian colonial history, a return to the same period as her early poetic sequence *The Journals of Susanna Moodie*. In this chapter I am concerned with Atwood's revisions of Canadian history in a postmodern context, looking at her narrators and narrative techniques, and investigating the connections between history, fictive autobiography, Gothic tale and domestic drama. Like *The Handmaid's Tale*, *Alias Grace* tells history from a feminine perspective, challenging and resisting the discourses of masculine authority which constitute official historical accounts, as a woman's voice declares in the opening epigraph, taken from a late nineteenth-century poem by William Morris:

> Whatever may have happened through these years,
> God knows I speak truth, saying that you lie.[2]

This is the voice of Arthur's queen, Guenevere, who refutes her accusers by reminding them that they can never know the truth about the past and therefore cannot pass judgement on her. A pattern of correspondences is suggested here between a legendary queen, a nineteenth-century Irish servant girl in Canada, and a woman novelist at the end of the twentieth century, all of whom are sceptical about the truth status of historical reconstruction. *Alias Grace* is a story about one of the almost-forgotten scandals in Canadian history where 'few facts emerge as unequivocally "known"' (Author's Afterword, *Alias Grace*, p. 541). For Atwood, 'memory, history and story all intersect' and though she does not erase the distinction between history and fiction, she is careful to point out the gaps and contradictory frames of explanation in the records, which open up a space for historical novels. Atwood's interest is in the process of historical reconstruction, focused through the testimony of one individual:

> History may intend to provide us with grand patterns and overall schemes, but without its brick-by-brick, life-by-life, day-by-day foundations it would collapse. Whoever tells you that history is not about individuals, only about large trends and movements, is lying. (*In Search*, pp. 6–7)

The story she chooses to tell is the unsolved case of a double murder committed on a farm outside Toronto back in the 1840s in pre-Confederation times. Following Atwood's lead, my discussion in this chapter will begin with Grace Marks, the enigmatic figure at the centre of the novel, who tells her story while in prison. Who was Grace Marks, and was she innocent or guilty?

This is a woman's narrative, and it eludes the attempts of male authority figures – from the church, and the legal and medical professions – to get at the truth of what happened, for Grace always claimed not to remember what happened on the day in 1843 when her employer Thomas Kinnear and his housekeeper-mistress Nancy Montgomery were murdered, the crime for which Grace and her fellow servant James McDermott were blamed. McDermott was hanged, but Grace was imprisoned in Kingston Penitentiary where she remained for thirty years until she was pardoned under a general amnesty by Canada's first Prime Minister. As Atwood has remarked, there is never any popular doubt about the man's guilt in such cases, though opinions over the woman are always sharply divided. Grace went to live in New York State where possibly she married and changed her name, but at all events she disappeared from official records. I shall set Grace's possibly duplicitous storytelling in the context of Atwood's critical deployment of mid-nineteenth-century psychological theories of split personality disorder, hysteria and insanity, combined with her sceptical exploration of the Victorian fashions for hypnosis and spiritualism. As Atwood commented, 'We cannot help but be contemporary, and *Alias Grace*, although set in the mid-nineteenth century, is, of course, a very contemporary book' (*In Search*, p. 36). Part of the reader's interest is in how those Victorian fashions of thought can be translated to provide a postmodern perspective on the problematic construction of female subjectivity and narrative reconstructions of the past. The strategies employed by Grace Marks and by Atwood in her structuring of this autobiographical fiction where the past is pieced together as 'herstory' will be discussed in relation to the motif of quilt making. Designs for quilt pattern blocks occur at the beginning of all fifteen sections of the novel; Grace is an excellent quilter herself, and the narrative ends with Grace's own marriage-bed quilt, where the Tree of Paradise pattern that she is sewing may be her silent confession – though it continues to elude definitive interpretation: 'I have to conclude that, although there undoubtedly was a truth – somebody did kill Nancy Montgomery – truth is sometimes unknowable, at least by us' (*In Search*, p. 37).

In reconstructing this historical event Atwood's research uncovered a tangle of contradictory evidence, a heroine who suffered from fits of amnesia and who may have been criminally insane, together with a welter of sex and violence, anti-Irish and anti-Semitic prejudice, shocking poverty among immigrant workers, and widespread Victorian social and sexual hypocrisy. These are some of the 'unmentionable' facts which have lured Atwood back into Canadian history, and the tale she tells is pure southern Ontario Gothic with its unspeakable secrets, murder, criminality, madness, ghostly voices and demonic possession. The fascination of a character like Grace Marks is bound up with nineteenth-century anxieties about women and their true nature: are they pure and innocent or are they lying devils, and which is Grace? Grace's is the dominant voice in the novel (though not the only one) as she tells her story to the young American psychiatric doctor Simon Jordan, who is trying to persuade her to relive the traumatic events of the day of the murders. His dual purpose is to solve the riddle of her guilt or innocence, while making his professional name in the new medical field of mental pathology. Needless to say he is unsuccessful, for though Grace tells him a great deal about the details of her daily life and her family's emigration to Canada, she always avoids any discussion about her role in the murders, claiming to suffer from traumatic memory loss. Finally Dr Jordan abandons her case without ever solving the mystery so that the fictional Grace, like the historical Grace, 'remains an enigma' (*Alias Grace*, Afterword, p. 539).[3]

Atwood's Grace is of course a fictive construction, made up out of what historical evidence there is plus Atwood's late twentieth-century reinterpretation. Her story is presented to us already framed by previous discourses, as Atwood indicates in the three opening sections, where Susanna Moodie's account from *Life in the Clearings* introduces Grace Marks as 'the celebrated murderess', followed by a collage of fragmentary evidence taken from newspaper reports of the trial, an extract from the Punishment Book of Kingston Penitentiary, portraits of Grace Marks and James McDermott published by the *Toronto Star and Transcript*, and a popular ballad. Also embedded at the beginning is Grace's prison nightmare of Nancy Montgomery's murder:

> Then up ahead I see Nancy, on her knees, with her hair fallen over and the blood running down into her eyes. Around her neck is a white cotton kerchief printed with blue flowers, love-in-a-mist, it's mine. She's lifting up her face, she's holding out her hands to me for mercy ... and then Nancy smiles, only the mouth, her eyes are hidden by the blood and hair, and then she scatters into patches of colour, a drift of red cloth petals across the stones. (*Alias Grace*, p. 6)

Does this sensationally Gothic dream of Nancy's bruised and bleeding body figure the terrible secret at the centre of Grace's traumatic history, where what is repressed 'proliferates in the dark' like the red satin peonies?[4] Is this the 'Jagged Edge' which must somehow be fitted into the narrative, as the first quilt pattern block suggests? Or is Grace embroidering her tale to interest her listener? 'This is what I told Dr. Jordan, when we came to that part of the story,' as she comments immediately after the dream account. It is impossible to know whether this 'dream' is a revelation from the unconscious or a storyteller's conscious duplicity, as Grace celebrates her power to rivet her audience's attention. In the heteroglossia of voices at the opening of the novel Atwood represents the bewildering variety of fragments out of which historical narrative is fabricated. As the American critic Earl G. Ingersoll has suggested, there are many jagged edges at the beginning, rather like a 'collection of quilting blocks, ready perhaps to be assembled' by the reader into a meaningful pattern.[5] Grace's identity would seem to be fixed: she is one of society's 'others', marginalised by her working-class immigrant background and her gender, demonised as a murderess who has been in Kingston Penitentiary and Toronto Lunatic Asylum for sixteen years. Yet the first time the reader sees her she is sitting like a visitor on the purple velvet settee in the Governor's wife's parlour, where she works as a daily domestic and seamstress, as we hear her rehearsing to herself 'all the things that have been written about me'. Is she a female demon or an innocent victim? Is she handsome, and are her eyes blue or green? Is she brisk and smart or is she sullen and stupid? Is she a good girl or is she cunning and devious? As Grace comments ironically, 'And I wonder, how can I be all of these different things at once?' (*Alias Grace*, p. 25). Those contradictory representations in the popular press open up her identity to specu-lation, and that instability is enhanced on Grace's first meeting with Dr Simon Jordan, where she is represented as a shape-shifting figure. On his first glimpse of her in the prison cell he imagined that he saw a frail hysteric, a sort of Pre-Raphaelite virgin, but when Grace stepped forward 'the woman he'd seen the instant before was suddenly no longer there. Instead there was a different woman – straighter, taller, more self-possessed' (p. 68). Under his medical gaze Grace stares back at him, 'as if it were he, and not she, who was under scrutiny', thereby managing to destabilise not only Simon's perception of her but also the conventional balance between doctor and patient, scientific observation and imaginative interpretation.

That initial encounter prefigures the dynamics of their relationship, which develops not so much as an early version of the 'talking cure' but as an elaborate guessing game where the patient keeps outwitting the doctor. Grace's suspicion of doctors and her familiarity with Simon's associationist therapy is clear, and she resists the new doctor by assuming a disguise of incomprehension: 'I have a good stupid look which I have practised' (p. 43). Yet she does oblige by talking a great deal, not following the association patterns suggested by the root vegetables the doctor brings, but following associations of her own, which are frequently prompted by the quilt patterns she is continually sewing during their interviews. I shall return to those quilt patterns, but it is worth remarking that sewing allows Grace to keep her head down both literally and metaphorically, so that Simon cannot see the expression on her face unless she chooses to look up at him. Their relationship could be crudely interpreted as a game of sexual power politics, where the doctor has the authority to affirm this female prisoner's guilt or innocence in exchange for her true confession.

However, this is power politics with a difference. It is precisely because Simon does not know Grace's secret, that she has the power to resist his authority by lying or by selecting which pieces of her story she will tell him, and so to impose her own pattern on her narrative. She also knows that she has the power to allure him by representing herself as an enigma, exploiting the myth of mysterious femininity which so seduced Victorian males: her defence lawyer was right when he called her a Scheherazade figure, telling stories which blur the boundaries between truth and falsehood: 'Perhaps Grace Marks has merely been telling you what she needs to tell, in order to accomplish the desired end' (p. 438). Grace's project of self-figuring represents a complex negotiation between teller and listener as she tries to make her story 'rich in incident, as a sort of return gift' to Simon (p. 286), while all the time resisting his attempts to define her identity: 'While he writes, I feel as if he is drawing me; or not drawing me, drawing on me – drawing on my skin' (p. 79). Indeed, her continual shifts in position make it difficult to know who or where Grace is. Though she sits quietly enough when she is with Simon Jordan, he knows that every day Grace walks between the prison and the Governor's house, where her roles switch between silenced prisoner and speaking subject. As Grace seems to have no stable location physically, so her narrative switches between present and past, between voluble detailed recollection and traumatic memory lapses, so that Simon becomes increasingly intrigued and suspicious: 'It's as if she's drawing his energy out of him – using his own mental forces to materialize the figures in her story, as the mediums are said to do during their trances. This is nonsense, of course' (p. 338).[6]

Grace is a very slippery subject. Is she suffering from a split personality disorder? Is she a hysteric? Is she mad? Or is she innocent? All these possibilities are canvassed within the novel as Atwood draws on nineteenth-century discourses of psychology for her constructions of Grace's identity. As Jenny Bourne Taylor and Sally Shuttleworth have demonstrated, Victorian medical science was fascinated with the mysteries of the human mind: 'These concerns included the complex relationship between the mind and the body; the working of individual consciousness, the power of unconscious processes and the limits of self control; the problematic boundary between normal and aberrant states of mind' in a period which saw the increasing professionalisation of psychiatric medicine.[7] In her Afterword Atwood acknowledges her indebtedness to these medical sources by citing a list of textbooks on the unconscious and dreams, on hypnotism, spiritualism and the occult which constitute her frame of historical inquiry. In addition, Dr Jordan, Dr DuPont and Reverend Verringer discuss psychological theories in their numerous conversations.

Atwood's post-Freudian representation of her female subject's condition offers a late twentieth-century critique of those theories through which any diagnoses of Grace's fainting fits, her amnesia and her hallucinations were investigated. The Gothic representation of Grace's split self corresponds to Victorian theories of 'double consciousness', which offers a different model of mind from the Freudian archaeological or 'depth' model focused on mechanisms of repression. Instead, 'double consciousness' proposes an alternate spatial model where in mentally disturbed patients the two halves of the brain operate like 'two distinct and often competing selves'.[8] This theory, ascribed to Queen Victoria's physician Henry Holland in 1839, opens the way to the divergent treatments proposed by Grace's two doctors. Whereas Dr Jordan works gently via associationism designed to lead Grace back to the centre of her trauma and so release her from its power, Dr DuPont works by the more spectacular treatment of 'artificial somnambulism' or 'neurohypnotism' developed in the 1850s by the Manchester physician James Braid, who later advised Jean-Martin Charcot about the treatment of female hysterics at the famous Salpêtrière Hospital in Paris in the 1960s. There is quite a small gap between the hypnotic trance and the spiritualist séance, a connection which Atwood exploits in the bizarre episode of the neurohypnotism scene in Chapter 48. Grace manages to elude both kinds of inquiry, leaving the reader and Simon Jordan alike fascinated by the way the narrative manages to negotiate the traumatic event of the murders without ever revealing the secret of how much Grace was implicated.

Again questions arise in Simon's mind as well as the reader's: Was Grace an 'accomplished actress and a most practised liar'? Was she innocent, or was she mad? The historical records attest that Grace spent fifteen months in Toronto Lunatic Asylum, and her private comments on madness sound very like a first-hand experience of schizophrenia:

> *Gone mad* is what they say, and sometimes *Run mad*, as if mad is a direction, like west; as if mad is a different house you could step into, or a separate country entirely. But when you go mad you don't go any other place, you stay where you are. And somebody else comes in.   (p. 37)

Yet is Grace to be trusted? She is so conscious of her own image in the popular imagination that she is quite capable of exploiting the role of criminal and mad woman:

> My hair is coming out from under my cap. Red hair of an ogre. A wild beast, the newspaper said. A monster. When they come

with my dinner I will put the slop bucket over my head and hide behind the door, and that will give them a fright. If they want a monster so badly, they ought to be provided with one.

I never do such things, however. I only consider them.   (pp. 36–7)

Grace knows what the Victorian mad woman should look like, from the stories she used to read with her fellow servant girls Mary Whitney and Nancy Montgomery as well as from newspaper accounts of her own story. Atwood appeals to the reader's textual knowledge as well, for who can read Grace's description without remembering Bertha in Charlotte Brontë's *Jane Eyre* or the melodramatic accounts in Susanna Moodie's *Life in the Clearings* where she describes seeing Grace Marks in the asylum? 'Among these raving maniacs I recognised the singular face of Grace Marks – no longer sad and despairing, but lighted up with the fire of insanity, and glowing with a hideous and fiend-like merriment' (p. 51). Mrs Moodie goes on to speculate about the possible connection between female insanity and criminality in a typically mid-Victorian way: 'Let us hope that all her previous guilt may be attributed to the incipient workings of this frightful malady.'[9] As Grace ironically interrogates contemporary cultural constructions of female monstrosity she sounds far from mad, though this imagined performance arouses a certain unease. To what extent was her madness, like her amnesia, really a performance, and was she possibly guilty after all? While Grace laughs at the popular image of her as a monster, she never says that she is innocent; she merely dismantles all the classifications imposed on her. In the end, when she is released, her only comment is: 'It was very strange to realize that I would not be a celebrated murderess any more, but seen perhaps as an innocent woman wrongly accused.... It calls for a different arrangement of the face' (p. 513). Atwood may be giving the madwoman a voice so that she no longer seems like a monster, though Grace's story leaves everything to the reader's interpretation. It serves less as a confession and more as way of keeping her secrets.

However, Grace continues to insist that she has no recollection of what happened on the day of the murders, for she had repeatedly fallen into fainting fits and can recall nothing of what she did or did not do: 'All that time is dark to me, Sir' (p. 369). She manages to frustrate his quest for the 'truth' and to challenge his certainty that nothing is lost from the unconscious: 'She knows; she knows. She may not know that she knows, but buried deep within her, the knowledge is there' (p. 338). The paradoxical possibility is that both

Grace and Simon may be speaking the truth here and that the secret is hidden from Grace herself. After all, Grace has a history of lapses of consciousness under situations of extreme stress: after her mother's death on board ship on the way to Canada, she says, she 'sat as if paralyzed' (p. 139), and after Mary Whitney's funeral as she reports to Simon, 'I did not seem to know where I was, or what had happened; and I kept asking where Grace had gone' (p. 208). And she still has the scar on her breast from when she had fainted at the trial as the death sentence was announced and she fell on the railing (p. 420). We also need to remember the time lapse between the events and Grace's reconstruction for Simon. Grace is telling her story to him sixteen years later, following her earlier reconstruction at the trial when she was instructed by her defence lawyer 'to tell a story that would hang together, and that had some chance of being believed' (p. 415).

There is still another layer which complicates Grace's story, and that is her own almost continuous interior monologue, which accompanies her oral narrative. Sometimes those private thoughts indicate her deliberate selection of what to include in her storytelling or her ironic comments on a variety of topics, but not always. Her remarkable interior monologue when she is lying in prison one night considering what she should tell Dr Jordan about the day of the murders causes the reader to wonder whether her memories are so painful that they are really unavailable to Grace herself except in disconnected fragments. Chapter 33 presents a psychodrama on the borders of consciousness between waking and sleeping which vividly figures a mechanics of repression, where Grace is haunted by echoes and images from the past as they surface in a series of questions: 'Did he say...?', 'Did she say...?', 'Did he take me in his arms?...Did I push him away?...It might have happened' (p. 343). That narrative reveals something she had not mentioned to Dr Jordan, which is the possibility that she had sexual relations with both her employer and McDermott, though the unspecific use of the pronoun 'he' makes it impossible to determine precisely who is being referred to. This slippage between pronouns and their referents is a stylistic phenomenon which Shuli Barzilai has analysed in relation to memory disturbance and repression in *Surfacing*, and which is here magnified, possibly for similar reasons.[10] Grace consistently employs strategies of displacement and doubling, mixing echoes of conversations with memories of doom-laden dreams at Mr Kinnear's house. All of these confused memory episodes are followed by the repeated phrase, 'I think I sleep.'

Grace's conscious mind veers away from her traumatic memories by reducing these fragments from the unconscious to an incoherent babble, which can only be formulated through a striking image of shattering and turbulence. This mirrors back to Grace her own disturbed state of consciousness while providing an analogy for her narrative reconstruction to Simon Jordan:

> When you are in the middle of a story it isn't a story at all, but only a confusion; a dark roaring, a blindness, a wreckage of shattered glass and splintered wood.... It's only afterwards that it becomes anything like a story at all. When you are telling it, to yourself or to someone else. (pp. 345–6)

Grace's nightmare is not entirely dispelled on waking, for though she declares 'I know where I am', her mind proceeds to move rapidly through a whole series of shifting locations – from the parlour to the scullery to the cellar of Mr Kinnear's house and finally back to her prison cell. She knows that she is trapped inside her story, 'although I hurl myself against the walls of it and scream and cry, and beg to God himself to let me out' (p. 345).

Simon Jordan's project is frustrated not only by Grace herself but by the arrival of another American, the 'noted medical practitioner' Dr Jerome DuPont. It is he who puts Grace into a trance in a highly theatrical episode in Chapter 48, where Grace is hypnotised in front of a private audience of interested parties, including of course Simon. In this curious scene Grace at last speaks out about the murders, but in a new thin voice which is not her own. Simon is bewildered: 'This voice cannot be Grace's; yet in that case, whose voice is it?' (p. 465). Her revelations under hypnosis are shockingly irreverent and erotic, though the ultimate surprise comes when the voice declares that she did the murders and then challenges her audience by declaring 'I am not Grace! Grace knew nothing about it!' (p. 467). When invited to guess whose voice it is, Simon is the person who guesses right:

> 'Not Mary,' says Simon. 'Not Mary Whitney.'
>   There is a sharp clap, which appears to come from the ceiling.
> 'I told James to do it. I urged him to. I was there all along!' (p. 468)

Evidently what began as a hypnotic trance has changed unexpectedly into a spiritualist séance where Mary's ghost has taken over Grace's 'fleshly garment' and answers in her stead. When Grace comes out of her trance as if out of a deep sleep, she speaks in her usual voice again and has no memory of what happened. In consequence of this scandalous confessional, Grace is exonerated in the opinion of all those present, on the grounds of diminished responsibility. This striking example of double voicing invites multiple interpretations, which are immediately offered by the men of science and religion. Reverend Verringer is inclined to see it as a clear case of demonic possession, while a nineteenth-century medical reading would see it as symptomatic of the condition of double consciousness. However, there is also a third possibility, which Simon wonders about: 'he may have been shown an illusion, which he cannot prove to have been one' (p. 472). This interpretation would fit with Atwood's ironic redeployment of the conventions of nineteenth-century melodrama, and when we remember that the mysterious Dr DuPont is none other than Grace's old friend Jeremiah the peddler in one of his multiple disguises, we may agree with Simon that this has been a theatrical performance and not a revelation from the unconscious. Jeremiah is a charlatan and a trickster who had once invited Grace to go away with him on a touring show as a medical clairvoyant: 'with your hair down you would have the right look' (p. 311). Whether Grace was under a hypnotic trance or not, and whether her lips were moving behind the veil it is impossible to tell, for the whole scene is refracted through Simon's viewpoint. The reader finds out later (though Simon does not) that Jeremiah is also a ventriloquist, when Grace writes him a letter where she also acknowledges that there was a trick: 'if they found you out, they would think you had tricked them, as what is done on a stage is not as acceptable, as the very same thing done in a library' (p. 492). Whatever may have happened, Jeremiah has saved Grace by allowing her to keep her secret about the murders; he has also defeated Simon, who cannot write a medical report based on such unscientific evidence and who leaves Kingston shortly afterwards, never to return.

We would be underestimating Atwood's narrative art, however, if the scene in the library were to be reduced to a tawdry 'small-town lecture hall' performance purely for entertainment, for this piece of theatre offers the spectacle of the split self invaded by its dark double, a traditional Gothic device ironically adapted and psychologised by Atwood in her postmodern historical fiction. Here it becomes a figure for the construction of female subjectivity where the conscious self is displaced by its shadowy twin, whose voice comes closest to saying what is socially unspeakable. The ghost of Mary Whitney, always a girl with 'democratic ideas', speaks out about Victorian sexual hypocrisy and especially about the appalling conditions for female domestic servants who worked in the big houses of respectable Toronto citizens and who were frequently the sexual victims of their masters. Mary died of a botched abortion, having been made pregnant by the son of the household, and Nancy Montgomery was pregnant with Mr Kinnear's child: 'The wages of sin is death. And this time the gentleman died as well, for once. Share and share alike!' (p. 466).[11] The voices of these marginalised women are heard in the neuro-hypnotism scene through a transgressive speech act, though ironically the ghostly voice is, I believe, that of a man. Once again Grace is not allowed to speak for herself any more than at her trial, when she had felt like a ventriloquist's doll and 'my true voice could not get out' (p. 342).

If, on the other hand, Mary Whitney is Grace's ghostly double and borrows her bodily form, this could surely be read as a friendship exchange, for Grace had borrowed Mary's name as her alias just as she had 'borrowed' the murdered Nancy's clothes after the murders. That principle of doubled identities extends beyond the three servant girls, however, for even Simon Jordan is forced unwittingly into the role of one of Grace's doubles as Atwood's narrative transgresses borderlines between genders as well as nationalities. Her tale has implicated him, for his obsessional pursuit of her secret has released not her memories but his own, and it is his secret life of erotic fantasy which is exposed in his shabby affair with his landlady, whom he dreams is Grace Marks. When he finally flees back to America, he suffers from partial amnesia as a result of a head wound in the Civil War, and he also insists on calling his fiancée, whose name is Faith Cartwright, by the name of Grace. In this novel where so much is doubled or susceptible to more than one interpretation, the quilt pattern 'Attic Windows' might be taken as a kind of *mise-en-abîme* for the whole narrative structure. Are the windows open or closed? As Grace advised Simon Jordan, 'you can see them two different ways, by looking at the dark pieces, or else the light' (p. 187). And what difference does it make to the meaning if Attic Windows is misheard as Attic Widows? Interpretation is evidently a matter of perception, and meaning is not fixed but changes according to the circumstances of its reception.

The patchwork quilt motif has been the main theme of critical commentary on this novel. It has been analysed from a number of angles – as graphic feature and material object, as representation of women's domestic craft skills, as topic of conversation, as metaphor for a distinctively feminine mode of storytelling, and as metafictional commentary on the reconstruction of history through narrative. Margaret Rogerson focuses on quilt making as a traditionally feminine cultural practice which refashions new artefacts from old materials, likening Grace's skill in quilting to her skills in selective storytelling, and suggesting that the reader also becomes a quilt maker by creating meaningful patterns out of disparate narrative blocks.[12] Coomi Vevaina reads that same process of assembling fragments as a metaphor for Grace's autobiographical method as she 'weaves her disparate selves into aesthetic patterns',[13] while Jennifer Murray emphasises the relation between quilting and postmodern reconstructions of history, where 'the desire to return to the past...is confronted by the awareness that there is no "real" access to the past, no key to unlock it, no guarantee of its authenticity'.[14] Earl G. Ingersoll develops a similar perception when he comments on the patches of 'found texts' stitched together in this novel, arguing for the patchwork trope as Atwood's metafictional comment on the narratives of history: 'This notion of a discoverable "truth" implicit in both traditional and modernist fiction, is clearly being problematised by Atwood's narrative, providing yet another dimension of its postmodernity'.[15] Sharon R. Wilson's detailed analysis of the quilt designs and some of the epigraphs argues that the names of the quilt patterns themselves make a metafictional comment on the narrative of which they are a part, again focusing on questions of interpretation, which are left to the reader's choice in a narrative where the reader is left 'free to invent'.[16] As Grace sits sewing her quilt blocks while talking to Dr Jordan, she quite self-consciously draws a parallel between her storytelling and quilt making:

> Some of it is all jumbled in my mind, but I could pick out this or that for him, some bits of whole cloth you might say, as when you go through the rag bag looking for something that will do, to supply a touch of colour.
> I could say this... (p. 410)

Grace would seem to have authority over her narrative, but hers is not the whole story by any means, for there are many other stories in this multivoiced novel, which offer conflicting frames of explanation for Grace's story. Nor should we forget the mass of prefatory materials at the head of every section, which introduce historical perspectives on Grace's situation as well as on Victorian literary and social history. Should these textual materials be seen as quilt borders, or are they actually part of the whole quilt design, which is of course Atwood's, and which is in its way as duplicitous as Grace's? Atwood's appropriation of traditional patchwork art highlights her postmodern reconstruction of history, which is presented here as a 'patchwork' of conflicting evidence from which the reader has to arrange a meaningful design. Attic Windows or Attic Widows?

When Grace comes to make her own quilt, she is a free woman and a respectable wife sitting in her own farmhouse in Upper New York State in the rather shadowed Victorian domestic happy ending to the novel. (Is Grace pregnant, or is she suffering from a tumour which will kill her as it did her mother? The answer would mean all the difference between life and death.) Her Tree of Paradise design has some significant variations from the conventional pattern, for it contains 'a border of snakes entwined', and she introduces three significant triangles of cloth into her pattern in order to make it into an album quilt in memory of her two dead friends, Nancy Montgomery and Mary Whitney. Grace pieces together three patches of fabric from their garments and her own: one white scrap from Mary Whitney's petticoat and one pale cotton piece, 'a pink and white floral' cut from Nancy's dress, as well as a scrap from her prison nightgown: 'And so we will all be together' (p. 534). Is this Grace's silent confession, or just her private reconstruction of her life story? It is a very different memorial from the Keepsake Album she had imagined years before in prison. Then she would have used rather more shocking materials: 'A square of bloodstained petticoat. A strip of kerchief, white with blue flowers. Love-in-a-mist' (p. 445). We are left wondering which version is more truthful to Grace's own life. Once again the focus is on questions of interpretation in what remains an ambiguous narrative with no definitive conclusions. Attic Windows or Attic Widows? We shall never know.

Certainly for someone who claimed to be suffering from traumatic memory loss, Grace's pattern is rather curious in its emphasis on memory rather than forgetting. As I have suggested elsewhere,[17] Grace's amnesia opens up a wider political interpretation of this novel as an oblique comment on Canadian history, where 'the forgotten, the discarded, the taboo' are all constitutive elements in any story of nationhood and national identity. Returning to the domestic drama however, Grace is not allowed to forget her past entirely: now married to Jamie Walsh, the boy from Mr Kinnear's whose evidence condemned her at her trial so many years ago, she is obliged within the privacy of the marriage bed to tell her husband stories of her life in prison in order to arouse him sexually and she also has to forgive him again and again for betraying her, which she regards as 'a small price to pay for peace and quiet'. Whatever disguises and aliases she assumes, Grace remains imprisoned in her story; as she foresaw in that first dream in the novel: 'the cellar walls are all around me, and I know I will never get out' (p. 7)

The mystery of Grace Marks remains, for despite her name she has 'left no marks' (p. 398), or at least none that can be reliably interpreted. The past does not yield up all its secrets, and Grace is like Offred when her story is disinterred long after Gilead has fallen, while Offred in turn is like Eurydice, that female figure out of classical myth who 'slips from our grasp and flees' (*The Handmaid's Tale*, p. 324).

SUGGESTIONS FOR FURTHER READING

Atwood, Margaret, *In Search of Alias Grace* (Ottawa: University of Ottawa Press, 1997).

Howells, Coral Ann, *Contemporary Canadian Women's Fiction: Refiguring Identities* (New York and Basingstoke: Palgrave Macmillan, 2003).

Ingersoll, Earl G., 'Engendering Metafiction: Textuality and Closure in Margaret Atwood's *Alias Grace*', *American Review of Canadian Studies* (Autumn 2001): 385–401.

Murray, Jennifer, 'Historical Figures and Paradoxical Patterns: the Quilting Metaphor in Margaret Atwood's *Alias Grace*', *Studies in Canadian Literature*, 26, 1 (2001): 65–83.

Rimstead, Roxanne, 'Working-Class Intruders: Female Domestics in *Kamouraska* and *Alias Grace*', *Canadian Literature*, 175 (Winter 2002): 44–65.

Rogerson, Margaret, 'Reading the Patchworks in *Alias Grace*', *Journal of Commonwealth Literature*, 33, 1 (1998): 5–22.

Taylor, Jenny Bourne, 'Obscure Recesses: Locating the Victorian Unconscious', in J. B. Bullen (ed.), *Writing and Victorianism* (London and New York: Longman, 1997), pp. 137–79.

Vevaina, Coomi, 'Quilting Selves: Interpreting Atwood's *Alias Grace*', in C. Vevaina and C. A. Howells (eds), *Margaret Atwood: The Shape-Shifter* (New Delhi: Creative Books, 1998), pp. 67–74.

Wilson, Sharon R., 'Quilting as Narrative Art: Metafictional Construction in *Alias Grace*', in Sharon R. Wilson (ed.), *Margaret Atwood's Textual Assassinations: Recent Poetry and Fiction* (Columbus: Ohio State University Press, 2003), pp. 121–34.

11

The Blind Assassin

Nothing is more difficult than to understand the dead, I've found;
but nothing is more dangerous than to ignore them.
(Margaret Atwood, *The Blind Assassin*, p. 621)[1]

The Blind Assassin is Atwood's Gothic version of Canadian history
in the twentieth century, told by an eighty-two-year old woman,
Mrs Iris Chase Griffen, who dies of a heart attack in 1999 just as she
finishes writing her memoir, which she leaves in a locked steamer
trunk in her kitchen as a legacy for her granddaughter who is away
travelling in India. With its shifting boundaries between subjective
and objective representations of reality and its duplicitous mixture
of fact and fiction, Iris's autobiographical narrative is a memorial to
the end of an era as it offers a retrospective view of some of the key
national and international events of the past century and of Canada's
changing social and political ideologies, though it is also the memoir
of a survivor, an old woman haunted by ghosts for whom life writing
becomes a kind of ghost writing in her prolonged negotiations with
the dead. In this novel Atwood leads her female protagonist further
into the Gothic maze than ever before as like a spider Iris spins out
the black thread of her handwriting, weaving her devious way
between the present and the past where 'dead people persist in the
minds of the living'.[2]

This is a novel about secrets and lies as Iris 'unpacks her steamer
trunk, which she's kept locked for quite a long time', as Atwood
remarked in a lecture on *The Blind Assassin*.[3] It is also a grandmother's
gift, designed to reveal to her granddaughter what is in the 'mysterious
sealed box' of her family inheritance, though from a wider perspective
it could be considered as a general inquiry into the way that history
is remembered and recorded.[4] Unlike *Alias Grace* this is a novel not
about things which have been forgotten but about things that have
been deliberately hidden, and it is this unearthing of connections
between present and past which gives this book much of its uncanny
appeal. The tangled web of family and national history is represented

in the complex structure of this novel, the implications of which will be explored in this chapter. However, my main focus will be on Iris as storyteller and her activity of remembering and rewriting the past, for this is history in the feminine gender, which offers an alternative perspective on the master narratives of official history. Who, we are tempted to ask, is the Blind Assassin of the title, and is this storytelling as memoir, as public memorial, as revenge, or as exorcism?

The most intriguing feature of *The Blind Assassin* is its multidimensional plot structure, which is as complicated as any Gothic romance or Victorian sensation novel. It contains three interlocking but apparently unrelated stories, all written in different styles and with different narrators. Iris's memoir is the frame narrative in which the other two stories are contained, and all three stories are finally locked up together in her steamer trunk, just as they are locked between the covers of the book as we read it. Enclosed within Iris's narrative is a modernist love story entitled *The Blind Assassin* written by Iris's younger sister Laura, which was published posthumously after Laura's death in a car crash in 1945, and within that is embedded a pulp science fiction fantasy about a blind assassin told by the male lover of the unnamed woman in Laura's novel. Only near the end, as in a detective story, are readers given the key to the hidden connections between them, as we come to realise that every story happens in 'another dimension of space' and that they are all versions of Iris's own autobiographical project. The initial challenge for readers is this switching between different genres, for these appear to be competing narratives, where Iris's Gothic emplotment of her life alternates with fragments of the science fiction story and the tragic romance plot of Laura's novel. The reader's attention is insistently drawn to the different conventions through which stories may be told, so that the interaction between them is a constant reminder of the artifice of storytelling. On the one hand, it stimulates that metafictional awareness that we have come to associate with postmodern narratives, while on the other hand it casts doubt on the absolute truthfulness of any of these accounts. With so many competing narratives, what is fact and what is fiction? We have to negotiate between different perspectives and different genres, but in all of them there is evidence of loss and devastation for these are the scenarios of a world in ruins, projected through different representations of geographical and psychological space.

The novel opens with Iris's memoir and her account of Laura's death over fifty years earlier:

Ten days after the war ended, my sister Laura drove a car off a bridge. The bridge was being repaired: she went right through the Danger sign. The car fell a hundred feet into the ravine, smashing through the treetops feathery with new leaves, then burst into flames....Nothing much was left of her but charred smithereens. (*Blind Assassin*, p. 3)

Then, within the first thirty pages three more deaths are recorded, not in Iris's voice but through newspaper obituaries on the deaths of Iris's husband Richard Griffen in 1947, of their daughter Aimee twenty-five years after that, and then in 1998 the death of Iris's sister-in-law Winifred Prior. As the Australian critic Dorothy Jones has noted, 'Death overshadows *The Blind Assassin* where so many characters first enter the text through their obituary notices and lives are shaped and mangled by two world wars.'[5] Certainly Iris's death occurs at the end and there are other deaths in the novel, but it is that multiple-death opening with its uncanny repetitions which arouses the reader's curiosity. We begin to wonder if there is any link between these deaths and why the novel is called *The Blind Assassin*. So much is left unexplained that we suspect there is more here than meets the eye and that this is another of Atwood's southern Ontario Gothic mysteries. We may be inclined to blame Iris, but after all she was not present when any of these deaths occurred. She is merely the survivor, who is telling the story years later when she is living alone in the small Ontario town where she was born. Only after the strange opening collage of newspaper fatalities interspersed with several chapters of Laura's novel and episodes from the science fiction tale do we hear Iris's voice again, speaking in the present on the day when she begins to think about writing her memoir.

Iris's narrative is grounded in the realistic circumstances of her everyday life, but there is a continual slippage away from realism as she escapes from the loneliness of the present and from her intense irritation with her bodily infirmities back into the secret spaces of private memory. As a very old person, Iris lives in a permanent condition of double vision, where the boundaries between the present and the past are frequently blurred. Taking her solitary walks around the town, Iris is continually stepping out of present time back into local history, which is also her own family's history, for Port Ticonderoga was founded by her grandfather in the 1870s as a factory town. Everywhere she goes she is surrounded by reminders of her family's past greatness, whether she walks to the cemetery to visit the Chase family monument where her parents and grandparents and Laura's ashes are buried, or whether she goes past her grandfather's Button Factory, now refurbished as a tourist centre, or past her grandparents' Gothic mansion where she and Laura were brought up, though it has now been converted into an old people's home and its name has been changed from Avilion with its Tennysonian resonances to Valhalla. ('As I recall, Valhalla was where you went after you were dead, not immediately before,' as Iris sardonically remarks, pp. 71–2.) For her, the modern town is overlaid with her memory map of 'another dimension of space' peopled by ghostly inhabitants, so that her memoir reads like a tour of the Underworld or a letter written by her and addressed to the dead.

Her memoir is part confession, part historical reconstruction, and part public memorial, like the memorials from the First World War which figure so prominently in the earlier part of the novel. However, Port Ticonderoga's monument of the Weary Soldier, donated by Iris's father, the local manufacturer and himself a war veteran, subverts the popular rhetoric of military heroism by its representation of a rumpled figure carrying a malfunctioning rifle. Iris would seem to have inherited his scepticism and ferocious irony, to judge from her own description of the moral ambiguity of memorials:

> But what is a memorial, when you come right down to it, but a commemoration of wounds endured? Endured, and resented. Without memory, there can be no revenge.
>
> *Lest we forget. Remember me. To you from failing hands we throw.* Cries of the thirsty ghosts.   (p. 621)

Her attitude to memory and memorials raises questions about why she would want to write her memoir, and these questions are similar to the ones Atwood asked about writing in her Cambridge lecture several months before the novel came out: '*Who are you writing for? Why do you do it? Where does it come from?*' (*Negotiating*, p. xix). Intriguingly Iris's initial impulse to write comes on the day when she has to present the first Laura Chase Memorial Prize at the local high school in honour of her sister, whose novel had caused such a scandal fifty years earlier and whose cult followers still cause Iris intense annoyance as she vengefully gathers up the flowers left on her sister's grave and throws them away. It is that memorial occasion in celebration of Laura which spurs Iris on to writing her own memoir, though Iris seems to regard it with a feeling of dread and likens the process of writing to a kind of bleeding to death: 'But the old wound has split open, the invisible blood pours forth. Soon I'll be emptied' (p. 51).

Iris tells her life story as a family saga stretching back through her parents' and grandparents' generations to the ruins of the family fortune as a result of the First World War and the Great Depression of the 1930s when the Button Factory was burned down in a riot and a man was killed. Clearly her autobiography is enmeshed in the wider currents of the nation's history, though the main focus is always on Iris's relationship with her sister. Iris emphasises their intense closeness growing up together as motherless girls in their shabby Gothic mansion under the care of their housekeeper Reenie and their war-damaged alcoholic father: 'This is his home, this besieged castle; he is its werewolf' (p. 102). Iris's identity is defined by her gender, her class and her role as 'good sister to Laura', and her feminine destiny is already laid out for her: as the eldest daughter of an old Anglo-Canadian family it is her duty to marry well in order to restore the family fortunes and to safeguard Laura's interests. Iris would have liked to travel, but she is always 'needed at home' to protect her younger unworldly sister, though on one significant occasion Laura manages to escape Iris's surveillance. That is the memorable event of the Chase Factory Picnic on Labor Day 1934, when Laura is discovered sitting under a tree talking to an unknown young man of indeterminate social class whose name is Alex Thomas. On that day as Iris records, a photograph of the three of them was taken by the local newspaper cameraman, the same photograph which becomes such a crucial piece of evidence in both sisters' narratives. When Alex turns out to be a Communist agitator on the run from the police, the girls enter into a conspiracy to shelter him in their father's house: 'He was our guilty secret' (p. 264).

He remains their guilty secret though it is no longer shared, for both the sisters fall in love with him. Iris later wonders if the day of the picnic was the beginning of her clandestine love affair with Alex, which runs as subtext beneath the years of her marriage; and her daughter as she later reveals is Alex's child and not her husband's. The day of the picnic also marks the beginning of Iris's relationship with the wealthy industrialist Richard Griffen and prefigures their disastrous marriage, when she sacrifices her life for the interests of her family, a pointless sacrifice as it turns out. Iris recalls her high society wedding as the erasure of her own identity: '(I say "her," because I don't recall having been present, not in any meaningful sense of the word') (p. 292). However, she does remember Laura's warnings against the marriage and her suggestion that they both run away together and get jobs as waitresses, dismissed by Iris as impractical. Laura is forced to join the Toronto household though she is always in rebellion, puncturing her sister's complacency like the voice of conscience, until the point when Laura is committed by Richard and Winifred to a clinic for the mentally ill just before the birth of Iris's daughter Aimee. Only much later does Iris hear Laura's version of that story after she escapes from the clinic, and even then Laura conceals the truth of Richard's sexual abuse. That is only revealed after Laura's suicide when Iris reads her coded confession in the notebooks. After Laura's death Iris leaves Richard, taking her daughter with her back to Port Ticonderoga; Laura's novel is published two years later, and Richard commits suicide at Avilion. In a sense, the rest of Iris's long life is an afterlife, for she has lost everyone she has ever loved and even her granddaughter Sabrina has been alienated from her.

However, this brief plot summary of Iris's memoir fails to account for the grief and anguish that infuse her memories of Laura, nor does it account for the fragmented quality of her narrative reconstruction. Iris presents Laura as a tragic heroine whose story unfolds with dramatic irony:

> In a painting she'd be gathering wildflowers, though in real life she rarely did anything of the kind. The earth-faced god crouches behind her in the forest shade. Only we can see him. Only we know he will pounce.   (p. 509)

In retrospect Iris may see the mythic overtones of Laura's story, but the narrative makes it plain that she was frequently irritated by Laura and blind to her distress. Her telling represents a tangle of emotions where guilt at having failed her sister is mixed with self-justification: 'I'm on trial here. I know it.... Should I have behaved differently? You'll no doubt believe so, but did I have any other choices? I'd have such choices now, but now is not then' (p. 522). It is surely part of Iris's retribution that she finds herself cast in the role of her sister's biographer and cursed with the historian's double vision:

> Historians attempt to represent the past as contemporaries witnessed and experienced it while simultaneously aware that

their interpretations depend on their own knowledge of how things turned out. The meaning of historical narratives may therefore be immanent from their beginnings and seem to determine events, while their credibility hangs on the tension maintained between the immanence of meaning and the open-endedness of the human actions they represent.[6]

At the centre of Iris's anguish is her memory of Laura's suicide, and its crucial importance is signalled in the flashback at the beginning together with a replay of the same memory in later chronological sequence. Such repetition both hides and reveals the secret at the heart of Iris's memoir and the main motivation for her retrospective narrative, though her mind insistently circles around the central trauma in a series of complex displacements. However, at last she is forced to confront the knowledge that she has so assiduously repressed: 'Now I'm coming to the part that still haunts me. Now I should have bitten my tongue, now I should have kept my mouth shut' (p. 595). She has to recognise that it was she who drove her beloved sister to suicide by telling her that Alex had been killed in Holland and then adding almost gratuitously that they had been lovers for a long time. Not only does Iris remember every detail of that conversation but she also recalls her sister's strange look when she learns the news, 'terrified, cold, rapturous. Gleaming like steel' (p. 596). The uncanny quality of this moment is emphasised by a strange slippage back in time to childhood memory, as if the present situation is a replay of something which is 'deeply familiar but which has become alienated through repression', as Freud would remind us.[7] Iris recalls seeing that same look on Laura's face the day she rescued her from drowning in the Louveteau River after Laura had deliberately thrown herself in, and she also sees herself acting from the same old spiteful impulse she had felt on the day of their mother's funeral when she pushed Laura off a statue in the garden. The next day Laura leaves her sister a message: 'Tell Iris I'll talk to her later' (p. 599); she then drives off the bridge in Iris's car, and immediately afterwards Iris finds Laura's hidden notebooks. So Laura initiates a dialogue across the frontiers between life and death, which becomes a major source of Iris's narrative impulse, an impulse confirmed in her later assertion that she and Laura were collaborators in authorship: 'We wrote the book together' (p. 627). I shall return to this question of writers and writing later, though it is worth mentioning that Iris always has a sense of Laura's continuing presence. Every time she sees the graffiti written in the town's public toilets she reads them as Laura's messages addressed to her.

Iris's relationship with the past is not merely a passive recording but a sustained negotiation with the dead for she is haunted by her memories of Laura, who is her own 'slippery double', both like and unlike her, where 'Each empties his or her vital substance into the other. Neither can exist alone' (*Negotiating*, p. 47). To return to that photograph of the two sisters with Alex taken at the Labour Day Picnic, it would seem to be emblematic of the doubleness and duplicity inherent in the sisters' relationship, at the same time as providing a vital link between their stories. That photograph appears and reappears in Iris's memoir, and though it is always connected with Laura's narrative and not her own, it does have a crucial bridging function.[8] Indeed, there are two versions of the photograph for Laura made two prints, one with Alex and herself and one with Alex and Iris, 'Because that's what you want to remember' (p. 261). The uncanny feature is on the margin:

> The photo has been cut; a third of it has been cut off. In the lower left corner there's a hand, scissored off at the wrist, resting on the grass. It's the hand of the other one, the one who is always in the picture whether seen or not. The hand that will set things down. (p. 632)

That severed hand, coloured yellow in one picture and blue in the other to signify the different colours of the girls' psyches, becomes a fitting emblem for the activity of writing in this curiously doubled novel. As Dorothy Jones says, 'Iris and Laura represent two different kinds of vision writers require – a keen eye for the significance of surface detail and the nuances of social interaction on one hand [Iris] and on the other, an ability to see into people's souls [Laura].'[9] At the same time, each photograph provides only half the picture, which suggests the subtle falsification and omissions in Iris's memoir. She herself acknowledges that what she has written is only half true, 'not because of what I've set down, but because of what I've omitted' (p. 484). When Iris reveals at the end of the novel that it was she and not Laura who wrote *The Blind Assassin* and that she took Laura's name as her pseudonym, it is to the photograph that she appeals for her justification:

Laura was my left hand, and I was hers. We wrote the book together. It's a left-handed book. That's why one of us is always out of sight, whichever way you look at it.   (p. 627)

Just as the photograph always conjures up its mirror image, reminding Iris of what she has lost, 'All drowned now. Drowned, but shining' (p. 8), so any version of the narrative gestures towards an absent presence. But why 'left-handed' when 'Left hands are supposed to be bad' (p. 627)? American critic Karen Stein suggests that whereas Laura thinks of Heaven as a place where 'everyone sits at everyone else's right hand' (p. 627), Iris's perspective is firmly earthbound. 'Accordingly, because her story reveals the sinister aspects of life that we usually try to overlook or hide, she names it a "left-handed book".'[10]

The sibling relationship between Iris and Laura literalises the familiar Atwoodian construction of split feminine subjectivity as well as the doubleness of the writer: 'In "good double" stories . . . both "halves" are as bound together as they are in "bad double" stories: on the fate of one depends the fate of the other' (*Negotiating*, p. 33). It is that interdependence which underlies Iris's adoption of the Laura persona for her modernist romance about the illicit love affair between a young married socialite and a Communist agitator on the run from the police in Toronto of the 1930s. He goes off to fight in the Spanish Civil War, unknowingly leaving her pregnant, and a few years later he is killed in Europe during the Second World War. Iris scrupulously maintains the anonymity of her protagonists, always referring to them as 'he' and 'she', though there are shadowy parallels between that story and her autobiographical narrative so that the reader begins to wonder which sister is writing which story. By this means Iris is able to explore the social spaces of immigrant and working-class Toronto, which would have been out of bounds in any story of her own life as a member of the Anglo-Canadian establishment. It is a strangely edgy love affair told in the 'hard-boiled' style of a Raymond Chandler or Dashiell Hammett thriller, and pervaded by mutual class antagonism. 'She' is disgusted by the seedy rooming houses and shabby eating places where they are forced to meet, and 'he' never lets her forget that she is a capitalist's daughter and a capitalist's wife. 'He' teases her about her wealth while they are making love, though he also tells her a science fiction story about a blind assassin, which runs in instalments throughout their affair and which 'she' finishes after 'he' is killed.

Iris claims that she wrote 'Laura's' novel as another form of collaborative memoir, though her reasons for taking Laura's name appear to be more ambiguous than she admits. Adopting an epigram from one of Alex's science fiction tales, she confesses: 'The real author was neither one of us: a fist is more than the sum of its fingers' (p. 626). It is that aggressive word 'fist' combined with Iris's sceptical comments about memorials and the reasons for not forgetting ('without memory, there can be no revenge') that alert the reader to another possible reason for the pseudonym. Not only did Iris wish to hide her own identity, but perhaps after all she was not unhappy for the novel to be read as Laura's autobiography – just in case Laura too had been having an affair with Alex. There is much ambiguity in Iris's mind on this question, though it is not a possibility that she dares to contemplate openly. However, there are many blank spaces in Laura's life story that remain unaccounted for and there are certainly hints of jealous triumph in Iris's confession to Laura of their love affair. But as Iris comes to realise, revenge is a double-edged sword wielded by the two blind gods of Love and Justice and it is 'a pretty good recipe for cutting yourself' (p. 608). Instead of being vilified for her scandalous novel, Laura becomes a cult heroine and Iris is forced to live the rest of her life in the shadow of her sister's name as a famous novelist, reminded of this by frequent new editions of *The Blind Assassin* (all of which she stows away in her steamer trunk) and by scattered floral tributes and graffiti, all of which invoke the name of Laura Chase. Iris cannot ignore Laura dead any more than she could when she was alive, and as I have suggested, her whole memoir provides the evidence of their ongoing dialogue.

The other ghost with whom Iris continues to negotiate is Alex Thomas, in her dreams and also through the science fiction fables about the blind assassin and the tongueless virgin in the lost city of Sakiel-Norn.[11] These tales have been criticised as pointless digressions from Iris's life story, but that is an overly simplistic judgement on this multidimensional novel for there is nothing in the science fiction sections which is irrelevant to Iris's narrative. Instead, the different generic perspectives interact to amplify the political resonances of her memoir. At the beginning the Sakiel-Norn sequence is presented as an entertainment, when the lover jokingly offers the young woman a choice of genres for his storytelling:

What will it be, then? he says. Dinner jackets and romance, or shipwrecks on a barren coast? You can have your pick: jungles, tropical islands, mountains. Or another dimension of space – that's what I'm best at.   (p. 11)

She chooses the science fiction scenario over the popular romance, though already by the second episode his narrative of an exotic ancient civilisation has begun to look rather like contemporary social satire with the appearance of the ruthless upper-class Snilfards who wear face masks of woven platinum and mercilessly exploit their women and the lower classes. By the third and fourth episodes, 'he' has introduced the blind assassin and the sacrificial tongueless virgin 'like a pampered society bride' (p. 29). When we consider that the teller is Alex the young Communist, it is not difficult to see that story as a savagely Marxist critique of class differences and the economic oppression of the capitalist system, which were so glaringly obvious in Canada during the Great Depression. Only gradually does it become a romance, when the blind assassin falls in love with the blue-blooded Snilfard princess 'against all odds' (p. 256), and they manage to escape together from Sakiel-Norn. Yet there is a clash of perspectives between the lovers over the endings they propose for the 'The Blind Assassin' story: 'she' prefers a happy-ever-after ending, but 'he' chooses a tragic ending as more true to life: 'All stories are about wolves. All worth repeating, that is. Anything else is sentimental drivel' (p. 423).

In this strangely striated novel there is a continual blurring of borders not only between fiction and Iris's real-life memoir, but also between the Sakiel-Norn fantasy and the lives of the two lovers in Toronto. This is paralleled in the increasing tendency to blur the narrative voices between the three genres: who is telling the science fiction tales or the modern romance? Likewise the news of Alex's death shimmers on the edges of fact and fiction, with the military death telegram recorded first in Laura's novel and only much later in Iris's memoir. In the novel the woman betrays her lover's memory by publicly denying all knowledge of him, only to be confronted in her dreams by his ghostly reappearance (p. 573). That dream of desolation and grief, displaced into a chapter called *The Blind Assassin: The destruction of Sakiel-Norn*, resonates against Iris's dream earlier in her memoir when she sees the same ghostly figure with the 'smile a white slash across the dark oval of his face', and realises that memory and dreams, like the dead, exist outside time. 'Time in dreams is frozen. You can never get away from where you've been' (p. 485).

Returning to Atwood's three questions about writers and writing, they may in Iris's case be answered in reverse order. The question, *Where does it come from?* is the one most easily answered, for Atwood provides a very Gothic answer herself in *Negotiating with the Dead* when she asserts that 'perhaps all writing, is motivated, deep down, by a fear and a fascination with mortality' (*Negotiating*, p. 140) as the writer ventures into the subjective spaces of memory and desire. Once she has begun her memoir, Iris writes obsessively. She writes in all weathers as she keeps reminding us, at her kitchen table or in her garden, aware that she is in a race against time ('a slow race now between me and my heart', p. 272). To the question, *Why do you do it?* the answers are more complicated. Iris herself gives a variety of answers: she writes against her fear of death and against being forgotten, for as she says, 'What we all want: to leave a message behind us that has an effect, if only a dire one; a message that cannot be cancelled out' (p. 513). Only near the end of her memoir does she confess that one of her motives in writing was revenge – possibly against Laura ('for wrongs endured, and resented'), and certainly against Richard for his treachery towards herself, her sister, and their father. 'Laura's' novel becomes a lethal weapon which drives Richard to take his own life, and twenty-five years later it causes her daughter to commit suicide, though by then the novel has a life of its own far beyond Iris's control. However, perhaps Iris's deepest narrative impulse was not revenge but something closer to that quest 'to bring something or someone back from the dead' which Atwood mentions as one of the reasons a writer would make the risky journey to the Underworld (*Negotiating*, p. 140). 'Life of a sort can be bestowed by writing' (p. 154) and Iris's elegy to Laura and Alex and to her father and mother becomes a kind of resurrection where they exist again and their voices may be heard through the medium of her handwritten script. This novel is full of references to handwriting and to writing hands – often surrealistically disembodied like the one in the Labour Day Picnic photo – and to moving fingers which endlessly trace out the lines of the past.

Iris takes a long time to answer the final question, *Who are you writing for?* When she begins her memoir, she finds herself in the position of writing for nobody:

> For whom am I writing this? For myself? I think not.... Perhaps I write for no one. Perhaps for the same person children are writing for, when they scrawl their names in the snow.   (p. 53)

Later she comes to believe that 'the only way you can write the truth is to assume that what you set down will never be read' (p. 345), but as Atwood has commented: 'Despite the hazards a reader may pose, a reader must be postulated by a writer, and always is' (*Negotiating*, p. 120). When Iris does locate her ideal reader, it turns out to be her only surviving relative, the estranged granddaughter for whom she has waited and yearned throughout the narrative:

> When I began this account of Laura's life – of my own life – I had no idea why I was writing it, or who I expected might read it once I'd done. But it's clear to me now. I was writing it for you, dearest Sabrina, because you're the one – the only one – who needs it now. (p. 627)

Iris claims to be offering Sabrina the truth about her family's history as a way to free her from false narratives of origin and identity, but after all Iris's narrative sleights of hand, maybe she is offering a duplicitous gift after all. Atwood's narrators have never been very good at telling the truth, and truth itself is a very slippery concept for Iris:

> I didn't think of what I was doing as writing – just writing down. What I remembered, and also what I imagined, which is also the truth. I thought of myself as recording. A bodiless hand, scrawling across a wall. (p. 626)

Her legacy to Sabrina locked in the steamer trunk consists of her handwritten memoir, supplemented by multiple copies of Laura's novel, Laura's notebooks, and a mutilated photograph, the tangled evidence of two sisters' life and times. Altogether, this evidence provides no definitive interpretation of either her family's or the nation's history, but rather the opposite in what looks like a deliberate destabilisation of the truth claims of historical writing in a postmodern context. If, as the historiographer Hayden White argues, the facts of the past are transformed into narrative according to the historian's choice of a particular story pattern, what happens to historical representation when multiple kinds of generic emplotment are used?

> Here, the conflict between 'competing narratives' has less to do with the facts of the matter in question than with the different story-meanings with which the facts can be endowed by emplotment....

Can it be said that sets of real events are intrinsically tragic, comic, or epic.... Or does it all have to do with the perspective from which the events are viewed?[12]

By the time Sabrina reads the contents of the steamer trunk, her grandmother will have joined the family ghosts, though she still manages a traditionally Gothic performance by speaking from beyond the grave: 'By the time you read this last page, that – if anywhere – is the only place I will be' (p. 637).

The question remains: How do private memoirs, fictional texts and public memorials function as refigurings of the past in different versions and is there any point of convergence between them? For Atwood the common ground is history itself, for we are all victims of historical process or casualties of historical accident. *'L'histoire, cette vieille dame exaltée et menteuse'* is invoked twice, both in references to cheating or catastrophe (p. 199 and p. 573). It is particularly interesting in the context of Iris's memoir writing that the image Atwood should choose to describe history is Maupassant's figure of an over-excited lying old woman, for inevitably some of those negative associations rub off on Iris as well. After all, she acknowledges in her memoir that her bones 'ache like history: things long done with, that still reverberate as pain' (p. 70) as she tells the story of English Canada in the twentieth century from her dissident feminine perspective. In her 'left-handed book' she succeeds in undermining the accounts of official history with her Gothic tale of secrets, scandals and betrayals which cross the boundaries between generations, genders and classes. Iris's memoir is her version of history written for the future, generated by her negotiations with the dead and written in 'invisible blood' (p. 51), which is the price she must pay to bring back the lost as she wanders through her private landscape of desolation at the end of her life: 'It's loss and regret and misery and yearning that drive the story forward, along its twisted road' (p. 632).

SUGGESTIONS FOR FURTHER READING

Atwood, Margaret, *Negotiating with the Dead: A Writer on Writing* (Cambridge: Cambridge University Press, 2001).
——, 'Entering the Labyrinth: Writing *The Blind Assassin*', in Gerry Turcotte (ed.), *Margaret Atwood: Entering the Labyrinth: The Blind*

Assassin (Wollongong: University of Wollongong Press and Centre for Canadian–Australian Studies, 2003), pp. 15–30.

Howells, Coral Ann, 'Sites of Desolation', in Turcotte (ed.), *Margaret Atwood: Entering the Labyrinth: The Blind Assassin*, pp. 31–46.

Jones, Dorothy, 'Narrative Enclosures', in Turcotte (ed.), *Margaret Atwood: Entering the Labyrinth: The Blind Assassin*, pp. 47–67.

Stein, Karen F., 'A Left-Handed Story: *The Blind Assassin*', in Sharon R. Wilson (ed.), *Margaret Atwood's Textual Assassinations: Recent Poetry and Fiction* (Columbus: Ohio State University Press, 2003), pp. 135–53.

White, Hayden, 'Historical Emplotment and the Problem of Truth', in *The History and Narrative Reader*, ed. Geoffrey Roberts (New York and London: Routledge, 2001), pp. 375–89.

12

Oryx and Crake

And nothing has happened, really, that hasn't happened before.
(Margaret Atwood, *Wilderness Tips*, p. 221)[1]

At zero hour when all the clocks and watches have stopped in Atwood's futuristic dystopia *Oryx and Crake*, it is perhaps time to revise historical discourse itself, for disaster has already struck and this novel looks like the end of history. In this post-apocalyptic scenario only one man has survived a mysterious worldwide plague which has destroyed human civilisation, and Snowman as he calls himself is living (and possibly starving to death) on the beach in a devastated landscape on the east coast of the United States, populated by monsters. This is a world where everything has become altered almost beyond recognition by global warming and genetic engineering, so that instead of natural species there are unnatural gene-spliced animals like wolvogs, pigoons and rakunks, and instead of human beings there is a mysterious gentle tribe of humanoid creatures called Crakers, for whom Snowman finds himself responsible. The Last Man is trapped in a nightmare which uncannily is not his own but somebody else's: 'Every moment he's lived in the past few months was dreamed first by Crake. No wonder Crake screamed so much.'[2]

Who is this mysterious Crake figure, and how did the end of the world happen? And could history be said to have stopped in a novel which is haunted by Snowman's memories of the past? He finds himself alone in a wilderness littered with the wreckage of a civilisation very much like our own, where the green-eyed Craker children pick up flotsam on the beach – plastic bottles, tins of motor oil, and a dead computer mouse 'with a long wiry tail'. This unfamiliar space does not exist outside time, however, for Snowman is still 'embedded in time'[3] and during the course of the narrative changes do take place – in the world around him, in himself, and even in the Crakers. As Atwood reminds us: 'Narration – storytelling – is the relation of events unfolding through time. You can't hold a mirror up to Nature and have it be a story unless there's a metronome ticking somewhere'

(*Negotiating*, p. 142). Even though Nature has been genetically modified and the metronome has become merely metaphorical, time is not eliminated, for 'zero hour' at the end has a different meaning from 'zero hour' at the beginning, with the narrative poised on the edge of a future where history may be about to repeat itself. This figuring of time where the past haunts the present and the future may already be scripted is emblematic of the patterns of doubling and repetition in *Oryx and Crake*, and it is with the distinctive features of Atwood's double vision that this chapter is concerned.

In characteristic fashion Atwood splices together a variety of generic forms: dystopia, satire, wilderness survival narrative and castaway narrative, tragic romance triangle, and the quest to the Underworld. This transgeneric construction highlights the fabricated quality of her narrative while making it impossible to label the novel simply as science fiction, for Atwood always includes 'something which isn't supposed to be there' in order to 'surprise the reader'.[4] Atwood's readers should not really be surprised, for she has always been concerned with the ethics as well as the aesthetics of fiction. Within the virtual reality of the novel Atwood is asking the same question that serious moralists have always asked: What does it mean to be human? This is a question which is becoming increasingly difficult to answer in the twenty-first century with its miracles of biotechnology and genetic engineering, which may soon produce pigoons (far more terrifying than their ancestors in *Animal Farm*) with human neocortex tissue in their 'craft wicked heads', or physically perfect beings like the Crakers, from whose brains all negative human impulses have been erased and who smell like citrus fruit. In this post-human world the monstrous and the human have changed places and *Homo sapiens* is now the anomaly, as Snowman's ironic self-naming suggests: 'The Abominable Snowman – existing and not existing, flickering at the edges of blizzards, apelike man or manlike ape' (*Oryx and Crake*, p. 8). Yet Snowman, wrapped in a bed sheet, stinking and starving, is all too recognisably human, a tragic figure like King Lear, reduced at zero hour to his primal condition as a 'bare, forked animal', but still possessed of memory and imagination and the power of words, all contained in 'the burning scrapbook in his head' (p. 11). Indeed, it is he, 'goon, buffoon, poltroon' (p. 361), who becomes the unlikely hero of the novel, bridging the gaps between past, present and future for the Crakers and for the readers.

To return to the main topic of this chapter, the most striking feature of *Oryx and Crake* is the way everything is doubled, not only the title and the epigraphs but also the narrative structure, while not surprisingly there are two dystopian visions – one a bioengineered wilderness nightmare and the other a savagely satirical version of late capitalist Western society. The strangeness of the novel is signalled in its title. Who are Oryx and Crake? We learn that they are the names taken by the heroine and the superhero (or is he the hero–villain?) from the non-human species world, for an oryx is 'a gentle water-conserving East African herbivore' (p. 365) and the red-necked crake is a rare Australian bird.[5] More disturbingly, we also learn that they are the names of dead animals, taken from the video game Extinctathon, which Snowman (formerly Jimmy) and his best friend Crake (formerly Glenn) played as schoolboys and at which Crake became a grandmaster. Ideas of the exotic and the threat of extinction hang over the novel, supplemented by the two opening epigraphs – one from Jonathan Swift's eighteenth-century satire *Gulliver's Travels* and one from Virginia Woolf's modernist novel *To the Lighthouse*. Here male and female voices are in counterpoint, where Gulliver's statement insisting on objectivity and 'plain matter of fact' in his tale is immediately challenged by Woolf's female artist figure who places her emphasis on human emotions with all their uncertainties and also their moments of vision. Reason versus imagination, science versus art, but do such binaries really exist (especially when we remember that *Gulliver's Travels* is both a fantasy and a satire)? The opening quotations unsettle those boundaries by implying that the creative imagination is a distinctively human capability shared by scientists and artists alike, and that it is not gender specific. Looking forward into the narrative, where Atwood demonstrates how a female novelist's creative imagination may be fired by scientific experiment, the most important pairing is between two men: Snowman, who is the artist figure, and Crake the brilliant genetic scientist. He is a demonic figure perhaps, like H. G. Wells's Dr Moreau, but also a failed visionary like Mary Shelley's Frankenstein, whose utopian project results in the near extinction of the human race.

The novel opens in the fictive present with Snowman waking up before dawn in a wilderness landscape which bears mysterious marks of environmental and biotechnological destruction. If one of the functions of dystopian writing is to negotiate cultural anxieties by reading signs of the future in the present as a way of warning against the possible dangers of activities taking place within the writer's own social context, then Atwood's ruined world is a shift into the future which contrives to cast a retrospective glance at the present after it has passed into history. Commenting on the genesis of her novel, Atwood said:

> As with *The Handmaid's Tale*, it invents nothing we haven't already invented or started to invent. Every novel begins with a *What if* and then sets forth its axioms. The *What if* of *Oryx and Crake* is simply, *What if we continue down the road we're already on? How slippery is the slope? What are our saving graces? Who's got the will to stop us?*[6]

For the first time Atwood has chosen a male narrator, or rather a male focaliser, for the story is told not in the first person but through third-person indirect interior monologue, which shifts restlessly between the narrative present and Jimmy/Snowman's memories of his own and other people's stories in a series of associative leaps, and the context is provided by an omniscient narrator who functions as his shadowy double. The effect of this technique is to displace Jimmy/Snowman from the centre of his own narrative, just as he is displaced from the post-catastrophe world around him. Atwood keys into widespread anxieties at the beginning of the twenty-first century, many of which are mutant forms of the fears of the 1980s now magnified on a global scale, where the news carries daily threats of apocalypse, with 'more plagues, more famines, more floods, more insect or microbe or small-mammal outbreaks, more droughts, more chicken-shit boy soldier wars in distant countries' (p. 298). That catalogue of fears and phobias has increased with the advancement of science and attendant popular anxieties about climate change and global warming, genetic engineering and bioterrorism. Atwood's nightmare scenario is a remarkable blend of fact and fiction as she imagines a world which has become 'one vast uncontrolled experiment' (p. 267).

Though Jimmy/Snowman's retrospective opens like a fairy tale with 'once upon a time', it actually has a very specific temporal location, beginning with his childhood memory of the huge bonfires of slaughtered cattle, which will remind readers of images from the foot-and-mouth epidemic in Britain in 2001. This allusion underlines the urgency of Atwood's warnings against a future possibly only decades away, and indeed harbingers of that future are already with us. Atwood insists that she is writing speculative fiction, and not science fiction, based on an accumulation of well-documented research, 'so there's nothing I can't back up.'[7] For years she had been clipping news items from papers and popular science magazines and 'noting with alarm that trends derided ten years ago as paranoid fantasies had become possibilities, then actualities'.[8] She used a similar research method with her clippings file for *The Handmaid's Tale*, though for this second dystopian novel there is also a webpage in her Acknowledgements, www.oryxandcrake.com, citing references consulted. Either by strategy or by uncanny coincidence *Oryx and Crake* was published the same year as the fiftieth anniversary of Crick and Watson's discovery of the double helix structure of DNA, spelling out the secret code of every living organism, which opened up the book of life – or was it Pandora's Box? Visions of progress in the life sciences are shadowed by their dark opposites in real life as in Atwood's fiction, which is where the question of human agency comes in, for as Atwood has frequently commented, the problem is not science itself, but the uses to which it is put by human beings, who are as always influenced by 'human emotions'.[9] As a novelist, Atwood is as much engaged with the psychological and emotional complexities of her protagonists as she is with science, and it is the interaction between these two forces which provides the dynamics of the plot.

Atwood has described this post-apocalyptic scenario as being more like John Wyndham's *The Day of the Triffids*, where a superhuman force is unleashed, though in the case of *Oryx and Crake*,' the problem is man-made'.[10] That man-made global disaster is foreshadowed by the second dystopia in the novel. As Offred remarked in her analysis of social change, 'Nothing changes instantaneously; in a gradually heating bathtub you'd be boiled to death before you knew it' (*The Handmaid's Tale*, p. 66), and it is through Jimmy/Snowman's memory narrative that Atwood constructs her savagely satirical version of the American Dream. It is a world of accelerating environmental degeneration, where devastating droughts and floods have wiped out much of the east coast of America as well as the orchards and the Everglades in Florida within one generation. Human beings have become radically separated from their natural environment, and that condition of alienation finds its parallel in patterns of social breakdown. Traditional structures of government and law have been superseded by a new system of social privilege based on the idealisation of science. High-ranking bioengineers and geneticists employed by the huge multinational corporations live and work in gated Compounds, quite literally sealed off from the rest of the population. Those others, derisively known as Pleeblanders, inhabit the old, decaying, urban centres, and their only value seems to be as subjects of the scientists' experiments and as mass-market consumers of synthetic products that range from cosmetics and antidepressants to hallucinogenic drugs. As the children of scientists, Jimmy and Crake grow up cocooned in the material privilege of life in the Compounds, but already the dark side of this utopian illusion shows itself in family life. Jimmy's mother has a nervous breakdown and then vanishes, Crake's father committed suicide or possibly was murdered, and both boys are left to cope with the legacies of their parents' failed idealism. Their emotional deprivation finds solace in the vicious computer games they play after school, and here Atwood expresses a truly Swiftian disgust at the long history of human folly and brutality in games like Barbarian Stomp or Blood and Roses, which traded atrocities ('Massacres, genocides, that sort of thing', p. 91) for human achievements in art and science: 'The Blood player usually won, but winning meant you inherited a wasteland' (p. 91). The most sinister game of all is Extinctathon, entirely dedicated to death in its searches for the names and characteristics of extinct species ('*Adam named the living animals. MaddAddam names the dead ones. Do you want to play?* p. 92). However, Atwood reserves her strongest condemnation for the internet porn sites, with names like HottTotts and hedsoff.com, brainfrizz.com or nitee-nite.com, which trade in sex and violence, featuring atrocities and crimes in real-time coverage, where human suffering is reduced to virtual reality. The difference between the two boys is marked by their responses to such shows: Crake finds such sites hilarious but they make Jimmy very uneasy, and he prefers the site where an actress named Anna K. reads from *Macbeth*, because he likes Shakespeare's language.

Though Atwood does not venture into the cyberspace territory mapped by William Gibson in his novel *Neuromancer*, she does explore the psychological effects of living in a high-tech world of artificially constructed reality. The boys often use the word 'bogus', which is a convenient way of blurring the boundaries between fiction and reality as well as a means of repressing any sense of emotional involvement and moral responsibility. This raises questions about a politics of representation where everything is mediated and rescripted so that nothing is verifiable. How, for example, can Jimmy make sense of the video of his mother's execution which the Compound guards show him when he knows how easily it could have been digitally faked? The answer comes when he hears his mother's voice speaking directly to him from the screen: '*Goodbye. Remember Killer. I love you. Don't let me down*' (p. 303). Jimmy's grief at the loss of his mother might be contrasted with Crake's even more traumatic experience as he watches his mother's agonising death from the other side of a glass observation window with the sound turned off. All Crake says is that it was 'impressive' and, at the time, Jimmy is puzzled by Crake's apparent lack of feeling (though later he finds a more sinister explanation for this).

Jimmy and Crake are living in a decadent postmodern culture described by Jean Baudrillard in 'Simulacra and Simulations', which 'threatens the difference between "true" and "false", between "real" and "imaginary" by undermining the foundations of referential reality'.[11] In Atwood's satirical vision of a world where everything is a reproduction of a vanished original, human beings are alienated not only from their environment but also from themselves. Repressed feelings, however, have the uncanny habit of returning in monstrous forms, for as Baudrillard notes, the process of simulation is always imperfect and it is impossible to keep it entirely separate from reality. Citing his example of a fake hold-up, '(a police officer will really shoot on sight; a bank customer will faint and die of a heart attack; they will really turn the phoney ransom over to you). In brief, you will unwittingly find yourself immediately in the real.'[12] And so it is with Crake's disastrous project to alter human history; he never stops playing computer games, for as he reminds Jimmy when they are both adults, 'Those were definitive times' (p. 353). Grandmaster Red-necked Crake plays out Extinctathon to its end, when virtual reality suddenly shifts into the dimensions of the real and causes a worldwide catastrophe. As sole survivor, Jimmy/Snowman is riddled with guilt at his own moral stupidity in confusing 'not real' with 'real' as he realises he has been duped as much by his own wilful ignorance as by Crake's treachery: 'He'd meant well, or at least he hadn't meant ill. He'd never wanted to hurt anyone, not seriously, not in real space-time. Fantasies didn't count' (p. 334). He carries the mark of his moral myopia with him into the post-human world, for his sunglasses are missing one lens, and what are we to make of his exchange for a pair of 'new two-eyed sunglasses', which he finds on his return to the RejoovenEsense Compound at the end of the novel?

It is to the curious partnership between these two men that I wish now to turn in my exploration of doubles. Best friends from school-days, later business partners and rivals in love, betrayers and betrayed, murderers both, and finally the dead and the living dead, their relationship bears a strong resemblance to the comic book stories of Superman alias Clark Kent or Captain Marvel alias Billy Batson, which Atwood read as a child. She has explained the appeal of such double identities: 'The superhero, large and powerful and good, was what we wished to be; the "real" alias, the one who lived *dans le vrai* and was small and weak and fallible...was what we actually were' (*Negotiating*, p. 27). The Crake–Jimmy pairing is the first time that Atwood has explored this doubles theme in relation to men, where the story is told from the perspective of the sidekick, who kills the superhero and survives, obsessed by Crake's ghost and riven by guilt. There are also hints of those *Boys' Own Adventures* that Atwood also read as a child: 'I used to read them, and they frequently involved adventures into other cultures, where things were arranged differently.'[13] Atwood is exploring fictions of masculinity, with Crake the personification of the urge toward male mastery through reason and science and Jimmy representing an alternative 'feminine' allegiance to the life of emotion and imagination. From another perspective Atwood is exploring the different identities of the artist figure, with Crake as amoral creative genius or as magician aspiring to be God, while Jimmy/Snowman is the 'word' man ('an adman who's a sad man' as one reviewer commented),[14] a storyteller with a sense of moral responsibility. From whichever perspective we choose to look at it, the Crake–Jimmy double act complicates stereotypes of gender and of the artist, for both protagonists are split within themselves, illustrating the contradictory impulses within human nature. As Atwood has often commented, the problem with human beings is that 'we have two hands'.[15]

Crake the biological scientist, who espouses a purely empirical approach which devalues imagination, morality and art, appears to be an emotional blank, a state of mind imaged in his 'dark laconic clothing'. A young man who can dismiss falling in love as 'a hormonally induced delusional state' and sexual pleasure as 'a deeply imperfect solution to the problem of intergenerational genetic transfer' (p. 227), is surely unusual if not dysfunctional. Several critics have suggested that Crake may suffer from Asperger's Syndrome and Atwood gives some playful support to this idea with the nickname of Crake's high-flying college, the Watson Crick Institute, being 'Asperger's U'.[16] However, there is plenty of evidence in Snowman's retrospective narrative that Crake does have very strong feelings; they are simply not articulated in ways that the young Jimmy or anybody else can understand. Instead they are figured through Crake's nightmares, which he declares he does not have, or in his condescending affection for Jimmy and the need for his friendship; it is always Crake who seeks Jimmy out and it is he who calls 'Let me in'. (That call may also be given a more sinister interpretation if we remember the calls of other dark doubles, like Zenia or Mary Whitney.) Atwood is fascinated by this mass of unacknowledged emotions that shape Crake's aspirations and his revenge. His major scientific projects – the BlyssPluss Pill and his life work of reinventing humanity with his own genetically modified Crakers – are an extraordinary mixture of vision and commercial opportunism, underpinned by an uncanny drive towards death. The two projects are 'two stages of a single plan, you might say' (p. 358). His attitude may be summed up in the paradoxical concept of BlyssPluss, a combination of viagra and sterilisation, a 'must-have pill' which will also be 'a huge money spinner', giving men and women the illusion of happiness while 'automatically lowering the population level' and implementing his grand project of bioterrorism. Crake is a double dealer who gets millions of dollars for his biological research because he promises to deliver modern miracles: '"My unit's called Paradice," said Crake... "What we're working on is immortality"' (p. 344). But just as the name 'Paradice' is itself a parody, with suggestions of trickery coded into its spelling, so Crake's atheistic definition of immortality is nothing but advertising hype. He too plays with words, though he would never admit it:

'Immortality' said Crake, is a concept. 'If you take "mortality" as being, not death, but the foreknowledge of it and the fear of it, then "immortality" is the absence of such fear. Babies are immortal. Edit out the fear, and you'll be ...'
'Sounds like Applied Rhetoric 101,' said Jimmy.   (p. 356)

Crake, as a genetic materialist, practises science minus any dimension of ethical responsibility as Jimmy realises. Though trapped in a sense of his own inadequacy and overawed by Crake, he succumbs to temptation when Crake invites him to do the ad campaign for BlyssPluss. So, Jimmy the 'wordserf' alias defender of the values of art and literature, compiler of lists of obsolete words like 'wheelwright, loadstone, saturnine, adamant' (p. 230), which he rescues like 'children abandoned in the woods', becomes Crake's accomplice. The reader is tempted to wonder what has happened to the idealism of the socially conscious artist figure, the boy who remembers his mother's dying words, 'Don't let me down,' and who as a young man feels a strong whiff of moral transgression around Crake's genetic experiments and his favourite game:

> Jimmy had a cold feeling, a feeling that reminded him of the time his mother had left home: the same sense of the forbidden, of a door swinging open that ought to be kept locked, of a stream of secret lives, running underground, in the darkness just beneath his feet. (p. 254)

This is Freud's definition of the uncanny, which shadows Jimmy's association with Crake's projects; but through a dangerous combination of diffidence and cowardice, hope and desire, Jimmy avoids any conscious recognition of how deeply he is compromised. Only after the disaster, when he returns to the ruined Paradice dome, does Jimmy/ Snowman finally confront the dimensions of his own complicity, recognising Crake as his own demonic double, 'Darker than dark, and some of that darkness is Snowman's. He helped with it' (p. 389). By an ironic twist, it is Crake the moral monster who reminds Jimmy of his moral responsibility, in words that echo those of Jimmy's mother. 'I'm counting on you' (p. 385) are his last words before Jimmy shoots him. In the end Crake has to rely on those very human qualities in Jimmy – like loyalty, honour and love – which in his arrogance he had edited out of the Crakers' brains, in order to ensure the survival of his creatures. Indelibly marked with 'the thumbprints of human imperfection' (p. 114) Jimmy becomes their reluctant rescuer, though whether he will turn out to be their saviour remains an open question. By a final irony Jimmy also becomes Crake's prophet and mythographer, publicly proclaiming 'Good, kind Crake' as the god-creator while secretly wishing to endow Crake with 'horns, and wings of fire, and allow him a tail for good measure' (p. 121).

That pattern of male doubles is overlaid by the triangular plot of heterosexual romance with the appearance of Oryx. Who is this mysterious woman with whom both Jimmy and Crake fall in love? Is she a *femme fatale* ('*Enter Oryx*. Fatal moment. But which fatal moment?' p. 361) or is she someone else entirely who refuses to be contained within the frames that the narrative offers her? The two teenage boys first see her image on the internet porn site HottTotts, where in the midst of an obscene fantasy scenario one of the little girls looks out from the screen directly at her unknown viewers: '*I see you*, that look said. *I see you watching. I know you. I know what you want*' (p. 104). That challenging look has a lasting impact on both boys, though arguably, in this male-focused narrative, Oryx never has a chance to emerge from the stereotype image of the sexually desirable Oriental female. Her life story as Jimmy later reconstructs it codes in a whole history of white imperialist oppression, where references to the history of European colonisation in the first chapter are amplified in the late twentieth-century globalised context of Third World poverty. Oryx is first a child prostitute and pornographic film star, and then later, as an immigrant in America, she is engaged in the sex trade both legally and illegally, until she reappears at RejoovenEsense as Crake's devoted acolyte and Jimmy's secret lover.

With Crake and Jimmy, Oryx is always performing her role as fantasy object, making love with them both in turn in what looks like a parody of those male fantasies of the eroticised female body. With her 'small rippling laugh' which 'disguised amused contempt' (p. 138), Oryx is a very slippery subject who may remind Atwood readers of previous duplicitous heroines like Grace Marks or Zenia, women whose stories of sexual exploitation and abuse are not unlike hers, though this time the issues do not revolve around class and gender and the female casualties of war but around race and gender. However, these women's stories provoke the same question as Jimmy used to ask when he watched the daily news: 'Why was everything so much like itself?' (p. 298). Interestingly, Grace was accused of being 'an accomplished actress and a most practised liar', so was Zenia, and so is Oryx, whom Jimmy describes as 'the best poker-faced liar in the world' (p. 369), though he excuses her in the comforting belief that she 'liked to keep only the bright side of herself turned towards him. She liked to shine' (p. 158). Jimmy does not understand Oryx at all, as she obliquely indicates on many occasions and as he dimly realises: 'That laugh of hers. What had it meant? *Stupid question. Why ask? You talk too much.* Or else: *What is love?* Or possibly: *In your dreams*' (p. 374).

Only once does Oryx's smiling mask slip, at the very end when Crake's one-man eugenics project turned global genocide is already taking effect. Oryx startles Jimmy with her tearful confession over the phone when she reveals to him the terrible secret of the plague: it was in the BlyssPluss Pills, which she had distributed internationally as Crake's business agent: '"Oh Jimmy," she said. "I am so sorry. I did not know"' (p. 380). The triangular romance plot is resolved as a melodrama of mutual betrayal and revenge, yet Oryx the unwitting bioterrorist remains for Jimmy/Snowman the ideal image of seductive femininity and female nurturing. Crake may have had the power of death over her but it is Snowman who resurrects Oryx when he mythologises her as Earth Mother in the creation myth he devises for the Crakers. Oryx is the most uncanny figure in the novel, as with her multiple shifting identities she shimmers on the borders between fantasy and reality: 'Was there only one Oryx, or was she legion?' (p. 362). Her features seem to blend to make one composite image as it appears on the internet or on the minicam in Crake's Paradice dome, but Oryx refuses to accept all these definitions of her identity: 'I don't think this is me' (p. 105). Perhaps the cover photo on the British hardback edition of the novel, featuring a woman's face broken up into a pixel representation in a digitised image, suggests the most appropriate lens through which Oryx may be viewed in the novel: like Grace and Zenia, her image can never be fixed and she remains a mysterious figure who exists behind the screen onto which male fantasies of the feminine are projected.

In *Negotiating with the Dead*, Atwood likened the creative writing process to a journey to the Underworld in quest of a lost love or forbidden knowledge, where the writer negotiates with the ghosts of private and collective memory as well as with literary tradition: 'because the dead control the past, they control the stories' (*Negotiating*, p. 159). Snowman's journey back to Crake's ruined Paradice dome is a version of that same quest, though he claims that he is going in search of objects necessary for his physical survival. Bidding farewell to the Crakers, he travels alone through a wasteland where he sees evidence of the recent catastrophe everywhere: wrecked cars, the husks of dead human bodies, abandoned homes and offices, while he has to encounter all the monsters of a mythic quest along the way, with giants in the shape of huge white crabs and demons in the form of a company of feral pigoons. The hero finally limps towards his goal, having damaged his foot on a broken bottle.

He enters the haunted space of the Paradice dome, there to confront quite literally his 'skeletons in the closet' for Paradice is also a tomb. The dead bodies of Oryx and Crake are still there as he knew they would be, or rather 'what's left of them' (p. 391) for their bones have been picked clean and are scattered about 'like a giant jigsaw puzzle' which is left for Jimmy/Snowman to piece together. Here in the secret place where all the stories happened, Snowman mourns his loss while he also gains a degree of self-knowledge, chastising himself for being 'thick as a brick, dunderhead, frivol, and dupe' as he stands there crying. He also gives his eye-witness account of the global tragedy, for he was there 'in a manner of speaking' as Crake would say, watching the extinction of the human race on a television screen. 'The whole thing seemed like a movie' (p. 399), as he remarks, and when we remember that Atwood wrote this section after 'Nine

Eleven' 2001, her fictional scenario has uncanny resonances of that real-life catastrophe. Nicholas Royle's comment on Nine Eleven in his book *The Uncanny* might serve to amplify this connection:

> As the twin towers collapsed 'live' on television, and the images of this collapse were repeatedly screened over the hours that followed, a sense of the uncanny seemed all-pervading: Is this real? Is this really happening? Surely it's a film? Is this 'our' apocalypse now?[17]

Snowman wanders like a ghost through the ruins of his past life, though he has to re-emerge into real space–time again as he did when he left Crake's dome the first time, leading the Crakers out of Paradice into the wilderness that he has taught them to call 'Home'. However, he goes back to the Crakers in a different frame of mind and wearing his new 'two-eyed sunglasses'. Moreover, the plot is taking a new direction, for there is evidence that Snowman is not the Last Man after all. In the deathly silence of the RejoovenEsense Compound he has heard the faint sound of a human voice over the wind-up radio and from the watchtower he has seen a single column of campfire smoke (p. 329). Crake's Final Solution seems to have failed by not being final enough: 'All it takes…is the elimination of one generation. One generation of anything…and it's game over forever' (p. 262).

The recurrent references to Paradice are a reminder that this text about the future is weighted with literary legacies from the past. Any creation story in Western literature is likely to refer to the Bible and to Milton's *Paradise Lost*, though instead of offering her contemporary readers Milton's theological model of 'Man's First Disobedience' and the Fall, with the expulsion of Adam and Eve from the Garden of Eden followed by the promise of Christ's salvation, Atwood offers a revision of that myth for a post-Christian world. Here it is not the laws of God but the laws of science which constitute the postmodern version of a transcendent metanarrative. Yet the imagery of the Christian tradition persists, now reshaped in parodic form not only in Crake's Paradice or his computer games but in the bricolage of Jimmy's mythologising to the Crakers. On his return he finds them chanting to an idol of himself and invoking his name, in a striking reversion to the old human practices of symbolic thinking which Crake had tried to edit out and that Jimmy/Snowman had wickedly encouraged through his storytelling: '*Watch out for art*, Crake used to say. *As soon as they start doing art, we're in trouble*' (p. 419).

Not only does Crake's grand design shows signs of disintegrating, but Jimmy/Snowman's perspective on the Crakers also begins to shift when they tell him about the arrival of three strangers like himself. The Crakers start to look less like a wave of the future and more like 'extras in a zombie film' or a primitive tribe, as he realises that their 'new' world is not in any sense a new Eden but a ruined place shadowed by a long history of oppression and brutality, from Genghis Khan to Dachau, from Rwanda back to the sack of Jerusalem.

Jimmy/Snowman is seeing differently, not because his physical space has changed but because his perspective has changed, with the prospect of entering again into human relationships. Faced suddenly with questions of choice and moral responsibility, his pulses are racing as he re-enters three-dimensional time, where the present is not static but dynamic and where 'zero hour' does not mean nil time but rather the moment for decisive action. Will he be able to protect the Crakers or not? That is his chosen role, but as he lurks in the forest, spying on the strangers around their camp fire, none of the inherited scripts of European colonialism or the Wild West which he replays in his head offer any guidance at all. As Atwood asked, 'What are our saving graces?' In the absence of God or of Oryx and Crake, Jimmy whispers his desperate plea for help into the empty air: 'What do you want me to do?' The air it seems is not quite empty, though the answer which comes is ambiguous: '*Don't let me down*' (p. 433). It could be his mother's voice or it could be Oryx's for they both used the same words, though asking him to promise to do opposite things (p. 303 and p. 378). His mother had pleaded with him to destroy all bioengineered products, while Oryx had pleaded with him to save the genetically engineered Crakers. Between those conflicting requests Jimmy/Snowman has to make a decision to act, but his dilemma is compounded by the question of what role he should adopt. Should his approach to the strangers be that of peacemaker, or negotiator, or killer? Are there any new narratives, or will history repeat itself? (And which version of history?) The answers to all these questions are left tantalisingly open to the reader's speculation at 'zero hour' as Jimmy/Snowman steps forward into the future and out of the novel: 'Time to go' (p. 433).

SUGGESTIONS FOR FURTHER READING

Appignanesi, Lisa, *Oryx and Crake* review, *The Independent*, 26 April 2003. www.enjoyment.independent.co.uk/books/reviews/story

184   *Margaret Atwood*

Atwood, Margaret, *Moving Targets: Writing with Intent, 1982–2004* (Toronto: Anansi, 2004). See 'Writing *Oryx and Crake*', pp. 328–30, and 'Arguing Against Ice Cream: *Enough: Staying Human in an Engineered Age*, by Bill McKibben', pp. 339–50.

——, 'An Interview with Margaret Atwood', 29 May 2003. www.mcclelland.com/features/oryxandcrake/interview_atwood.html

Baudrillard, Jean, 'Simulacra and Simulations', in *Jean Baudrillard: Selected Writings*, ed. Mark Poster (Oxford: Polity Press, 1988).

Bouson, J. Brooks, '"It's Game Over Forever": Atwood's Satiric Vision of a Bioengineered Posthuman Future in *Oryx and Crake*', *Journal of Commonwealth Literature*, 39, 3(2004): 139–56.

Potts, Robert, 'Profile: Margaret Atwood', *Guardian Review*, 26 April 2003, pp. 20–4.

Conclusion

It seems appropriate to begin the conclusion to this open-ended account of Atwood's fiction with the opening of the last chapter of *Oryx and Crake*, which is itself a reprise of the opening of the first chapter.

> Snowman wakes before dawn. He lies unmoving, listening to the tide coming in, wish-wash, wish-wash, the rhythm of heartbeat. He would so like to believe he is still asleep.
> On the eastern horizon there's a greyish haze, lit now with a rosy, deadly glow. Strange how that colour still seems tender. He gazes at it with rapture; there is no other word for it. *Rapture*. The heart seized, carried away, as if by some large bird of prey. After everything that's happened, how can the world still be so beautiful? Because it is. From the off-shore towers come the avian shrieks and cries that sound like nothing human.
>
> (Margaret Atwood, *Oryx and Crake*, p. 429)

Snowman is up again before dawn, but it is the dawn of a different day and Snowman is about to embark on a new adventure. He is not the Last Man as he had thought and history has not come to an end; instead, 'Events take place, in relation to other events. That's what time is. It's one damn thing after another, and the important word in that sentence is *after*' (*Negotiating*, p. 142). What will happen *after*? That is the inevitable question at the end of every Atwood novel, and it is the question any reader might ask of Atwood as a novelist. What will she write after this? Through her eleven novels to date, Atwood has shown extraordinary talent for surprising her readers with her ongoing narrative experiments and her radical questioning of contemporary social myths and fashionable ideologies. In fact, her novel writing career shows all the qualities of a good narrative: 'A story always contains some surprises: the conclusion of a good story...is not something that could have been or should have been foreseen.'[1] Yet we may be able to foresee the likely range of topics that Atwood will treat in her next novel(s) as a result of our glance back over the imaginative territory of her fiction, as we see strong continuities of thematic concern from one novel to the next. Any critical study of this kind functions as a retrospective of the writer's work, charting continuities and variations while evaluating the significance of shifts in the storyteller's perspective. There is Atwood the storyteller and there are also her many storytelling personas with their shifting narrative perspectives, for there is never only one 'true story':

> The true story lies
> among the other stories...
>
> The true story is vicious
> and multiple and untrue
>
> after all. Why do you
> need it? Don't ever
>
> ask for the true story.[2]

Atwood's novels have always highlighted the art and indeed the artifice of storytelling, where the real world is transformed and reinvented within the imaginative spaces of fiction. 'Not real can tell us about real,' as Snowman instructs the Crakers in the first stages of symbolic thinking. Yet within this seemingly infinite variety there is a recognisably Atwoodian voice, witty and funny, satirical and self-ironic, politically and morally engaged as her worldly texts respond to what is actually going on in her own place and time, spelling out her double vision of how things look on the surface and what else is happening at the same time or what has already happened before. There are also those distinctively Atwoodian topics that I have traced in this study, where it will be evident that Atwood's focus of concern has centred on the operations of power politics at every level, from national and international relations to the sexual politics of personal relationships. That topic accommodates all Atwood's other topics in a web of interrelated discourses, for her fiction canvasses such questions as Canadian national identity, Canada's relations with the United States and the rest of the world, human rights issues, and environmental issues, which initially focused on Canadian wilderness but which have assumed a globalised dimension in her increasingly urgent warnings against the danger of separating humanity from nature. There are explicit continuities between *Surfacing* and *Survival* and *Oryx and Crake*. Then there are the feminist issues (or perhaps more accurately gender issues, for Atwood has always been critical of loose ideological definitions of feminism), which include her scrutiny of social myths of femininity and most recently of masculinity, male and female fantasies about women; representation of women's bodies in art, fiction, popular culture and pornography; women's social and economic exploitation; as well as women's relations with each other, not to mention their relations with men. This list of Atwood's 'topical topics' seems to balloon out into cultural history, though there are 'definitive moments' in history so that 'We can look at these events and we can say that after them things were never the same again' (*The Robber Bride*, p. 4) – just as for us there are Atwood's eleven novels, which are our fixed points of reference.

I would like to return to the passage I quoted at the beginning of this chapter, for it seems emblematic of some of the most important features in Atwood's fiction. As a wilderness survival narrative *Oryx and Crake* might be seen as a reprise of *Surfacing*, acknowledging the Canadian literary tradition out of which Atwood writes. However, whereas in the 1970s the wilderness represented a distinctive Canadian national space in Atwood's fiction, in her post-apocalyptic scenario, 'home ground' has definitely become 'foreign territory'. Not only has the wilderness landscape been transformed through a series of man-made and environmental catastrophes but it has also been relocated in the United States; the disease 'spreading up from the south' in *Surfacing* has now spread worldwide. Does this virtual-reality scenario represent the end of our world as we know it? Yet the world remains beautiful and Snowman is still alive, at least for the present. Circumstances do change over time and revisionary readings are always possible.

Indeed, over the period of thirty-five years since her first novel was published, Atwood's own perspectives have changed in response to her widening international audience and changes in cultural politics on the international globalised scene as well as to shifts in Canadian social and political agendas. The key term for Atwood is always 'survival' in a context of environmental change which is both ecological and ideological. As I have tried to show, Atwood's view of the prospects of survival for the human race has grown bleaker even as her position has changed from her early Canadian nationalist stance to her engagement with issues of environmental degradation from man-made and natural causes. The wilderness myth almost disappeared from her fiction in the late twentieth century, only to make its uncanny comeback in *Oryx and Crake*. Atwood pushes her narratives to the verge of collapse and disaster or even over the edge, and then she shifts the perspective to a wider historical context which holds out an ambiguous hope for the future. Her narratives open up space for the transformation of attitudes and policies before it is too late. Her two futuristic dystopias sweep back to the past, only to land readers squarely in the present at the end: 'As I've said, I have no answers. But I've indicated some of the possibilities, some of the dangers that may lurk; some of the conundrums' (*Negotiating*, p. 108). Atwood's fictional mode in these texts belongs to traditions of eighteenth-century British satire. Not only does she perpetuate the legacy of Swift in the epigraphs to both her dystopias but their environments of disaster resemble nothing so much as the ending of Alexander Pope's *The Dunciad*, where his 'Universal Darkness', which 'buries all', is a staged scenario of prophecy and warning.

I have attempted to trace similar changes in Atwood's representations of femininity and the female body since the late 1960s, and in her use of Gothic narrative conventions, where there is a discernible shift from Joan Foster's wide-eyed Canadian responses to Europe as romantically Gothic, to *The Robber Bride* where European Gothic becomes Canadian Gothic, lodged right in Toronto. No longer can Canada be viewed as peculiarly safe and separate from the international community, for Atwood uses a Canadian location here as one more example of contemporary crisis, where 'something ordinary but horrifying is taking place' (*The Robber Bride*, p. 3). So it is with Atwood's Gothic versions of Canadian history in *Alias Grace* and *The Blind Assassin*, for 'nobody is exempt from anything', as Rennie Wilford realises in her prison cell on the Caribbean island or as Snowman realises in a devastated New New York where Paradise has been Lost once again.

'Revision', 'retrospection' and 'reconstruction' are related impulses of mind and artistic creativity, and we notice that Atwood's fictions are becoming increasingly retrospective themselves. Just as Elaine Risley in *Cat's Eye* is painting time in her pictures, so Atwood is writing time as she is writing about women and about Canada, mapping cultural shifts and changing fashions. Arguably, all Atwood's novels are retrospectives in the sense that they are narrative reconstructions of the past lives of their protagonists, but it is Atwood's 'continuously historicising consciousness'[3] which I wish to focus on briefly, a dimension that has only become explicit with her historical novels of the 1990s. A retrospective glance would show that Atwood's interest in history was always there, though it has been overshadowed by critical interest in Atwood's more fashionable topics like feminism, environmental issues, or postmodern narrative constructions. *Surfacing* is haunted by ghosts, not only of the narrator's parents but of Amerindian prehistory as well, just as *Life Before Man* is fascinated with the dinosaurs whose skeletons and footprints may be seen in the Royal Ontario Museum. Joan Foster's enthusiasm for Gothic bodice rippers is closely related to her devotion to nineteenth-century British costume history, while in *Bodily Harm* it is Caribbean colonial history which shapes the newly postcolonial present, and *The Handmaid's Tale* harks back to American colonial history. Atwood comes back to the local history of Toronto with *Cat's Eye* and *The Robber Bride*, though it is only with *Alias Grace* that she returns to nineteenth-century Canadian colonial history, followed by *The Blind Assassin*, with Iris's account of twentieth-century Canadian history. Yet the curious fact is that while her novels always acknowledge the legacies of history, she writes in a postmodern context that emphasises the constructedness of history and inherited cultural myths by recognising the different perspectives from which 'true stories' might be told. At first glance, *Oryx and Crake* may look like a supplement which disturbs this pattern, but what is a survivor's narrative if not an oral history haunted by memories of the past?

There is one further issue I would like to raise, and that is Atwood's figurings of women artists – writing women and painting women, with the woman as the 'I-witness', a pattern from which she has deviated only once, in *Oryx and Crake*. Interestingly Atwood's early women artists, like the protagonist in *Surfacing* or Joan Foster in *Lady Oracle*, are women who face crises of confidence in their own creative powers. The 'surfacer' is a failed painter who never trusts her own vision and as a narrator she struggles to find a language of her own. Yet she is also aware of the power locked inside herself, symbolised I believe in her clenched fist as she sits alone and silent on the other side of the wall, listening to her friends talking together: 'It was there in me, the evidence, only needing to be deciphered' (*Surfacing'*, p. 76). By the end, her visionary experiences have released the power to heal herself, though she has not yet found a voice to answer her lover's call. For Joan Foster, writer of popular Gothic romances, wordlessness is not the problem, though she is still struggling to find her own voice even as she takes enormous pains to disguise it through her slavish adherence to Gothic conventions and her automatic writing. At the end she is still seeking an appropriate language and subject matter: 'But maybe I'll try some science fiction.... I keep thinking I should learn some lesson from all of this, as my mother would have said' (*Lady Oracle*, p. 345). Rennie Wilford's position is not much better really, for she only manages to break out of her lifestyle journalism and to find her own voice when there is nobody to hear it, and she realises that she cannot think of a title for her story. In a similarly incarcerated situation, Offred in *The Handmaid's Tale* manages to reclaim her lost identity and to tell her story, but only in secret, and her history of life in Gilead only becomes available long after she is dead.

All these narratives represent the processes by which women write of their attempts to speak or to write or to paint, just as they also write in their difficulties and silencings. It is only with *Cat's Eye* and *The Robber Bride* that the middle-aged female artist and the female historian gain confidence in their vision and their own powers of interpretation. As Elaine looks at the world through her cat's eye marble, she 'sees more than anyone else looking' (*Cat's Eye*, p. 327), and she dares to paint a picture with the title 'Unified Field Theory'. For all that, she remains an elusive subject and at the end she flies off to the other side of Canada, leaving her life energy in her paintings: 'I'm what's left over' (p. 409). Only Tony is willing to assume full responsibility as a storyteller, assuming authority over the fragments of the story of Zenia, that arch-plotter who abused her superb narrative skills:

> She will only be history if Tony chooses to shape her into history. At the moment she is formless, a broken mosaic; the fragments of her are in Tony's hands, because she is dead, and all of the dead are in the hands of the living.   (*The Robber Bride*, p. 461)

Tony's inheritor is obviously Iris Chase Griffen, who writes her memoir at the end of her life, declaring that only she can offer the truth about history, though she writes 'a left-handed book' and it is, after all, a collaborative effort with her dead sister Laura. Then there is Snowman, Atwood's only male storyteller, though as I have noted, his story must have been written down by somebody else, an anonymous omniscient narrator.

I should like to end with a return to my opening questions, which are of course Atwood's: *Who are you writing for? Why do you do it? Where does it come from?* (*Negotiating*, p. xix). Some of the answers may be found, oddly enough, in *Oryx and Crake*, though for most of the novel it is assumed that this Last Man story is a tale addressed to nobody. Yet that futuristic scenario is itself a kind of simulacrum and the book is here in print, written by Nobody to Nobody.[4] What might this novel's function be in relation to its readers? I think that Atwood gave us an answer in her comments about narrative journeys to the Underworld in *Negotiating with the Dead*:

> The dead may guard the treasure, but it's useless treasure unless it can be brought back into the land of the living and allowed to enter time once more – which means to enter the realm of the audience, the realm of the readers, the realm of change. (*Negotiating*, p. 160)

Though there may be no readers as far as Snowman is concerned, there are for Atwood, and the end of *Oryx and Crake* turns out to be similar, in its stepping out of the textual frame, to that in *The Handmaid's Tale*, where 'Are there any questions?' (*The Handmaid's Tale*, p. 324) is paralleled by Snowman's dilemma, 'What do you want me to do?' (*Oryx and Crake*, p. 432). That question may be addressed to Nobody, though it may be answered not only by ghosts but by Atwood's readers as well.

Notes

Notes to Chapter 1: Introduction: A Writer on Writing

1. Margaret Atwood, *Negotiating with the Dead: A Writer on Writing* (London: Virago, 2003). This book is based on Atwood's Empson Lectures at the University of Cambridge in 2000.
2. Philip Howard, *The Times*, 13 March 1980, p. 14.
3. See Margaret Atwood, *Second Words: Selected Critical Prose* (Toronto: Anansi, 1982), p. 430.
4. *Margaret Atwood: Conversations*, ed. Earl G. Ingersoll (London: Virago, 1992), p. 108. All other references to *Conversations* will be included in the text.
5. Margaret Atwood, *Cat's Eye* (London: Virago, 1990), p. 332.
6. See Margaret Atwood, *Second Words: Selected Critical Prose*, p. 111.
7. 1967 marked the 100th anniversary of Canadian Confederation (1867), when Canada became a Dominion within the British Empire. In 1982 the Patriation of the Constitution established Canada as an independent nation within the British Commonwealth.
8. Philip Howard, Introduction to *Margaret Atwood: Conversations*, p. vii.
9. Jeremy Brooks, *The Sunday Times*, 27 May 1973.
10. Peter Prescott, *Newsweek*, 4 October 1976.
11. Marilyn French, *The New York Times Book Review*, 3 February 1980; Philip Howard, *The Times*, 13 March 1980; Lorna Sage, *The Times Literary Supplement*, 14 March 1980.
12. Atwood, *Second Words*, p. 14.
13. Margaret Atwood, *Cat's Eye* (London: Virago, 1990), p. 20.
14. Margaret Atwood, *In Search of Alias Grace* (Ottawa: Ottawa University Press, 1997), p. 4. Further references to *In Search of Alias Grace* will be given in the text.
15. Linda Hutcheon, *The Canadian Postmodern: A Study of Contemporary English-Canadian Fiction* (Toronto: Oxford University Press, 1988), p. 21.
16. Adrienne Rich, 'When We Dead Awaken: Writing as Re-Vision' (1971), in *On Lies, Secrets and Silence: Selected Critical Prose, 1966–1978* (London: Virago, 1980), pp. 33–50. Atwood reviewed Rich's work frequently during the 1970s.
17. Shannon Hengen, 'Zenia's Foreignness', in Lorraine M. York (ed.), *Various Atwoods: Essays on the Later Poems, Short Fiction, and Novels* (Toronto: Anansi, 1995), p. 275.
18. See C. A. Howells, *Contemporary Canadian Women's Fiction: Refiguring Identities* (New York: Palgrave Macmillan, 2003), pp. 9–23.
19. Northrop Frye, *The Bush Garden* (Toronto: Anansi, 1971). See also, Sandra Djwa, 'The Where of Here: Margaret Atwood and a Canadian Tradition',

in Arnold and Cathy Davidson (eds), *The Art of Margaret Atwood: Essays in Criticism* (Toronto: Anansi, 1981), pp. 15–34; and Sandra Djwa, 'Back to the Primal: the Apprenticeship of Margaret Atwood', in York (ed.), *Various Atwoods*, pp. 13–46.

20. Atwood, *Second Words*, p. 190.
21. M. Fulford (ed.), *The Canadian Women's Movement, 1960–1990: A Guide to Archival Resources* (Toronto: ECW Press, 1992); A. Prentice, P. Bourne, G. C. Brandt et al., *Canadian Women: A History*, 2nd edn (Toronto: Harcourt Brace Canada, 1996).
22. Betty Friedan, *The Feminine Mystique* (1963) (London: Gollancz, 1965).
23. For a brief account of 'second wave' feminism, see Ruth Robbins, *Literary Feminisms* (London: Macmillan, 2000).
24. Introduction to Margaret Atwood, *The Edible Woman* (London: Virago, 1979).
25. Hutcheon, *The Canadian Postmodern*, p. 110.
26. Gerry Turcotte (ed.), *Margaret Atwood: Entering the Labyrinth: The Blind Assassin* (Wollongong: University of Wollongong Press, 2003), p. 19.
27. Atwood, *Negotiating with the Dead*, p. 136.

Notes to Chapter 2: *The Edible Woman*

1. Betty Friedan, *The Feminine Mystique* (1963) (London: Gollancz, 1965). Page references will be to this edition and included in the text.
2. Margaret Atwood, *The Edible Woman* (London: Virago, 1980), p. 145. Page references will be to this edition and included in the text.
3. Graeme Gibson (ed.), *Eleven Canadian Novelists* (Toronto: Anansi, 1973), p. 25; repr. in *Margaret Atwood: Conversations*, ed. Earl E. Ingersoll (London: Virago, 1992), p. 15.
4. Noelle Caskey, 'Interpreting Anorexia Nervosa', in Susan Rubin Suleiman (ed.), *The Female Body in Western Culture: Contemporary Perspectives* (Cambridge, MA, and London: Harvard University Press, 1985), pp. 175–92.
5. Dennis Cooley, 'Nearer by Far: the Upset "I" in Margaret Atwood's Poetry', in Colin Nicholson (ed.), *Margaret Atwood: Writing and Subjectivity* (Basingstoke: Macmillan; New York: St Martin's Press, 1994), pp. 68–93.
6. Susan Bordo, 'The Body and the Reproduction of Femininity', in Katie Conboy, Naida Medina and Sarah Stanbury (eds), *Writing on the Body: Female Embodiment and Feminist Theory* (New York: Columbia University Press, 1997), pp. 90–110.
7. For fuller discussion of Marian's paranoia, see Sonia Mycak, *In Search of the Split Subject: Psychoanalysis, Phenomenology, and the Novels of Margaret Atwood* (Toronto: ECW Press, 1996), pp. 47–69.
8. See Dianne Hunter, 'Hysteria, Psychoanalysis, and Feminism: the Case of Anna O', in Conboy, Medina and Stanbury, *Writing on the Body*, pp. 257–76.
9. Adrienne Rich, 'When We Dead Awaken: Writing as Re-Vision', in *On Lies, Secrets and Silence: Selected Critical Prose, 1966–1978* (London: Virago, 1980), p. 42.

10. Gibson, *Eleven Canadian Novelists*, p. 21.
11. For a brief comprehensive discussion of the supernatural in relation to Duncan, see W. J. Keith, *Introducing Margaret Atwood's 'The Edible Woman': A Reader's Guide*, Canadian Fiction Series 3 (Toronto: ECW Press, 1989), p. 4.

Notes to Chapter 3: *Surfacing* and *Survival*

1. Margaret Atwood, *Survival: A Thematic Guide to Canadian Literature* (Toronto: Anansi, 1972), p. 13. All further page references will be to this edition and included in the text.
2. For a contemporary reassessment of *Survival* as one of the foundational texts for Canadian postcolonialism, see Cynthia Sugars, *Unhomely States: Theorizing English–Canadian Postcolonialism* (Peterborough: Broadview Press, 2004), pp. xiii–xx.
3. Margaret Atwood, 'Death by Landscape', in *Wilderness Tips* (London: Virago, 1992), pp. 107–29.
4. Atwood's unfinished novel *The Nature Hut* (*c*.1966) and her unpublished story 'Transfigured Landscape' are in the Margaret Atwood Papers MS Collection 200, Thomas Fisher Rare Book Library, University of Toronto, Box 17: Folder 6–7, and Box 79: Folder 26.
5. Margaret Atwood, *The Journals of Susanna Moodie* (Toronto: Oxford University Press, 1970), 'Afterword', p. 62.
6. Margaret Atwood, *Surfacing* (London: Virago, 1979), p. 11. All further page references will be to this edition and included in the text.
7. Critical discussion of *Surfacing* has focused on the following major topics: (a) quest narrative: Annis Pratt, 'Surfacing and the Rebirth Journey', in Arnold and Cathy N. Davidson (eds), *The Art of Margaret Atwood: Essays in Criticism* (Toronto: Anansi, 1981), pp. 139–57; Carol Christ, 'Margaret Atwood: the Surfacing of Women's Spiritual Quest and Vision', *Signs*, 2, 2 (Winter 1976): 316–30; (b) shamanism: Kathryn van Spanckeren, 'Shamanism in the Works of Margaret Atwood', in K. van Spanckeren and J. Garden Castro (eds), *Margaret Atwood: Vision and Forms* (Carbondale, IL: Southern Illinois University Press, 1988), pp. 183–204; (c) nationalism: Paul Goetsch, 'Margaret Atwood: a Canadian Nationalist', in R. Nischik (ed.), *Margaret Atwood: Works and Impact* (New York: Camden House, 2000), pp. 166–79; (d) feminist issues: Sherrill Grace, 'In Search of Demeter: the Lost, Silent Mother in *Surfacing*', in van Spanckeren and Garden Castro, *Vision and Forms*, pp. 35–47; Maggie Humm, *Border Traffic: Strategies of Contemporary Woman Writers* (Manchester and New York: Manchester University Press, 1991); Eleanora Rao, *Strategies for Identity: The Fiction of Margaret Atwood* (New York: Lang, 1993); (e) language and narrative structure: Peter Quartermaine, 'Margaret Atwood's *Surfacing*: Strange Familiarity', in C. Nicholson (ed.), *Margaret Atwood: Writing and Subjectivity* (Basingstoke: Macmillan, and New York: St Martin's Press, 1994), pp. 119–32; Shuli Barzilai, 'Who is He? The Missing Persons Behind the Pronoun in Atwood's *Surfacing*', *Canadian Literature*, 164 (Spring 2000): 57–79.

8. Kildare Dobbs, *Toronto Star*, 12 September 1972, p. 31.
9. Graeme Gibson (ed.), *Eleven Canadian Novelists* (Toronto: Anansi, 1973), pp. 30–1.
10. *North Bay Nugget*, 3 September 1976.
11. George Woodcock, *Introducing Margaret Atwood's Surfacing: A Reader's Guide* (Toronto: ECW Press, 1990), p. 69.
12. Atwood Papers, MS Collection 200, Box 22: Folder 12.
13. This useful term was coined by W. J. Keith, *A Sense of Style* (Toronto: ECW Press, 1989), p. 180.
14. Van Spanckeren, 'Shamanism in the Works of Margaret Atwood', in van Spanckeren and Garden Castro, *Margaret Atwood: Vision and Forms*, pp. 183–204.
15. Graeme Gibson (ed.), *Eleven Canadian Novelists*, p. 27.
16. Ronald B. Hatch, 'Margaret Atwood, the Land and Ecology', in Nischik, *Margaret Atwood: Works and Impact*, pp. 180–201.

Notes to Chapter 4: *Lady Oracle*

1. Margaret Atwood, *Murder in the Dark* (1984) (London: Virago, 1994), pp. 49–50.
2. For a comprehensive account of the genre, see Fred Botting, *Gothic* (London and New York: Routledge, 1996), pp. 1–20.
3. Eve Kosofsky Sedgwick, *The Coherence of Gothic Conventions* (New York and London: Methuen, 1986), pp. 4–5.
4. Sigmund Freud, 'The Uncanny' (1919), in *Art and Literature*, Penguin Freud Library, vol. 14 (London: Penguin, 1990), p. 363.
5. Margaret Atwood, *Lady Oracle* (1976) (London: Virago, 1993), p. 7. All page references will be to this edition and included in the text.
6. Sharon R. Wilson, 'Mythological Intertexts in Margaret Atwood's Works', in R. Nischik (ed.), *Margaret Atwood: Works and Impact* (New York: Camden House, 2000), pp. 215–28.
7. For accounts of criticism of *Lady Oracle*, see Margery Fee, *The Fat Lady Dances: Margaret Atwood's Lady Oracle* (Toronto: ECW Press, 1993), pp. 20–9; also Susanne Becker, *Gothic Forms of Feminine Fictions* (Manchester: Manchester University Press, 1999), pp. 151–98.
8. Margaret Atwood Papers, MSS Collection 200, Box 27. See also Marilyn Patton, '*Lady Oracle* and the Politics of the Body', *Ariel*, 22, 4 (1991): 29–50.
9. Atwood Papers, letter to Donya Peroff, 16 January 1974 (Box 27).
10. Janice Radway, *Reading the Romance: Women, Patriarchy and Popular Literature* (Chapel Hill: University of North Carolina, 1984); Scott McCracken, *Pulp: Reading Popular Fiction* (Manchester: Manchester University Press, 1998), pp. 75–101.
11. Margaret Atwood, 'Superwoman Drawn and Quartered: the Early Forms of She', in *Second Words: Selected Critical Prose* (Toronto: Anansi, 1982), pp. 35–54.

12. For further discussion of the 'Lady Oracle' poem as *mise-en-abîme* of the mother–daughter relationship, see Susanne Becker, *Gothic Forms of Feminine Fictions* (Manchester: Manchester University Press, 1999), pp. 166–70.
13. Botting, *Gothic*, pp. 81–5.

Notes to Chapter 5: *Life Before Man*

1. Margaret Atwood, *Life Before Man* (1979) (London: Virago, 1982), p. 30. All page references will be to this edition and included in the text.
2. Janice Kulyk Keefer, 'Hope against Hopelessness: Margaret Atwood's *Life Before Man*', in C. Nicholson (ed.), *Margaret Atwood: Writing and Subjectivity* (Basingstoke: Macmillan; New York: St Martin's Press, 1994), pp. 153–76.
3. Ibid., p. 15.
4. David Lodge, '*Middlemarch* and the Idea of the Classic Realist Text', in *After Bakhtin: Essays on Fiction and Criticism* (London and New York: Routledge, 1990), pp. 45–56.
5. Margaret Atwood Papers, MSS Collection 200, Box 32: Folder 6.
6. George Eliot, *Middlemarch* (1871) (Harmondsworth: Penguin, 1979), 'Prelude', p. 25.
7. Margaret Atwood, *Second Words: Selected Critical Prose* (Toronto: Anansi, 1982), p. 334.
8. Homi Bhabha, *The Location of Culture* (London and New York: Routledge, 1994), p. 181.
9. David Ketterer, *Canadian Science Fiction and Fantasy* (Bloomington and Indianapolis: Indiana University Press, 1992), pp. 19–22.
10. Atwood, *Second Words*, p. 333.
11. Graeme Gibson (ed.), *Eleven Canadian Novelists* (Toronto: Anansi, 1973), p. 27.

Notes to Chapter 6: *Bodily Harm*

1. Margaret Atwood, *Bodily Harm* (1981) (London: Virago, 1983). All references are to this edition and included in the text.
2. Quoted from Atwood's address at a conference held at Dyffryn House, Cardiff, in October 1982 when Atwood received the annual Welsh Writers Prize.
3. MSS Collection 200, Margaret Atwood Papers, Box 33: Folders 1–6, Box 34: Folder 1.
4. For the full quotation, see John Berger, *Ways of Seeing* (London: British Broadcasting Commission and Penguin, 1972), pp. 45–6.
5. Judith McCombs, 'Atwood's Haunted Sequences: *The Circle Game*, *The Journals of Susanna Moodie* and *Power Politics*', in Arnold and Cathy

Davidson (eds), *The Art of Margaret Atwood* (Toronto: Anansi, 1981), pp. 35–54.

6. Sonia Mycak, *In Search of the Split Subject: Psychoanalysis, Phenomenology, and the Novels of Margaret Atwood* (Toronto: ECW Press, 1996), pp. 161–2.

7. Lorna Irvine, 'Recycling Culture: Kitsch, Camp, and Trash in Margaret Atwood's Novels', in Reingard M. Nischik (ed.), *Margaret Atwood: Works and Impact* (New York: Camden House, 2000), pp. 202–14.

8. Luce Irigaray, *'This Sex which is Not One'* (New York: Cornell University Press, 1985), p. 26.

9. M. A. Caws, 'Ladies Shot and Painted: Female Embodiment in Surrealist Art', in S. R. Sulieman (ed.), *The Female Body in Western Culture* (Cambridge, MA, and London: Harvard University Press, 1985), p. 263.

10. Beverley Brown, 'A Feminist Interest in Pornography – Some Modest Proposals' (1981); quoted by Linda Williams, *Hard Core: Power, Pleasure, and the 'Frenzy of the Visible'* (London: Pandora, 1990), p. 269. Williams offers an extremely useful documentation and reinterpretation of the hard-core porn film genre, to which I am indebted for information, though my fictional material and interpretations differ in many respects from hers.

11. Susanne Kappeler, *The Pornography of Representation* (1986), quoted in ibid., p. 18.

12. Diana Brydon, 'Atwood's Postcolonial Imagination: Rereading *Bodily Harm*', in Lorraine York (ed.), *Various Atwoods: Essays on the Later Poems, Short Fictions and Novels* (Toronto: Anansi, 1995), pp. 89–116.

Notes to Chapter 7: *The Handmaid's Tale*

1. Margaret Atwood, *The Handmaid's Tale* (London: Vintage, 1996). All further page references will be to this edition and included in the text.

2. Linda Hutcheon, *The Canadian Postmodern* (Toronto: Oxford University Press, 1988), p. 110.

3. *Guardian* Review, 26 April 2003, p. 23.

4. For discussions of dystopian and feminist elements, see Krishan Kumar, *Utopianism* (Milton Keynes: Open University Press, 1991); Lynette Hunter, '"That Will Never Do": Public History and Private Memory in *Nineteen Eighty-Four* and *The Handmaid's Tale*', in Marta Dvorak (ed.), *The Handmaid's Tale: Margaret Atwood* (Paris: Ellipses, 1998), pp. 19–29; C. A. Howells, 'Transgressing Genre: a Generic Approach to Atwood's Novels', in R. M. Nischik (ed.), *Margaret Atwood: Works and Impact* (New York: Camden House, 2000), pp. 139–56.

5. Margaret Atwood Papers, MS Collection 200, University of Toronto, '*The Handmaid's Tale*: Before and After', November 1986, Box 96: Folder 11.

6. Atwood Papers, MS Collection 200.

7. 'Genesis of *The Handmaid's Tale* and Role of the Historical Notes', in J. M. Lacroix, J. Leclaire and J. Warwick (eds), *The Handmaid's Tale: Roman Protéen* (Rouen: Presses Universitaires de Rouen, 1999), pp. 7–14; Margaret Reynolds, 'Interview with Margaret Atwood', in M. Reynolds

and J. Noakes (eds), *Margaret Atwood: The Essential Guide* (London: Vintage, 2002), pp. 11–25. Interview also available on Random House website: www.randomhouse.com.

8. Zillah R. Eisenstein, 'The Sexual Politics of the New Right: Understanding the "Crisis of Liberalism" for the 1980s', in N. O. Keohane, M. Z. Rosaldo and B. C. Gelpi (eds), *Feminist Theory: A Critique of Ideology* (Brighton: Harvester, 1982), pp. 77–98; Priscilla Ollier Morin, '*The Handmaid's Tale* and American Protestant Fundamentalism', in M. Dvorak (ed.), *Lire Margaret Atwood: The Handmaid's Tale* (Rennes: Presses Universitaires de Rennes, 1999), pp. 33–46.

9. Margaret Atwood, 'Witches', in *Second Words: Selected Critical Prose* (Toronto: Anansi, 1982), pp. 329–33.

10. See Mark Evans, 'Versions of History: *The Handmaid's Tale* and its Dedicatees', in Colin Nicholson (ed.), *Margaret Atwood: Writing and Subjectivity* (Basingstoke: Macmillan; New York: St Martin's Press, 1994), pp. 177–88.

11. Lee Thompson cites Atwood's manuscript notation of Offred's birth date as 1978 though, significantly, Atwood has crossed it out. See Lee Briscoe Thompson, *Scarlet Letters: The Handmaid's Tale* (Toronto: ECW Press, 1997), p. 36.

12. Constance Rooke, 'Interpreting *The Handmaid's Tale*: Offred's Name and "The Arnolfini Marriage"', in *Fear of the Open Heart* (Toronto: Coach House, 1989), pp. 175–96.

13. Hélène Cixous, 'The Laugh of the Medusa' (1976), trans. Keith and Paula Cohen, repr. in *New French Feminisms: An Anthology*, ed. E. Marks and I. de Courtivron (Brighton: Harvester, 1981), pp. 245–54. All further page references to Cixous's essay will be taken from this edition and included in the text.

14. See Marta Dvorak, '"What's in a Name?" Readers as both Pawns and Partners, or Margaret Atwood's Strategy of Control', in J.-M. Lacroix and J. Leclaire (eds), *Margaret Atwood: The Handmaid's Tale/Le Conte de la servante: The Power Game* (Paris: Presses de la Sorbonne Nouvelle, 1998), pp. 79–97.

15. The name Denay, Nunavit, clearly signals the Canadian location of this second futuristic scenario, for Nunavut is the name of Canada's first aboriginal self-governing territory, which in the 1980s was scheduled to come into existence in 1999. This has now happened.

16. In the context, the choice of Pieixoto's name is significant. At a conference in Rouen, France, in 1998, Atwood revealed that she had found the Portuguese name in a Brazilian novel, referring to a man who keeps being reincarnated in the same form century after century. Pieixoto exemplifies the same sexist values as the Gilead regime, who modelled themselves on the Old Testament patriarchs.

Notes to Chapter 8: *Cat's Eye*

1. Margaret Atwood, 'Instructions for the Third Eye', in *Murder in the Dark* (London: Virago, 1994), p. 108.

2. Stephen Hawking, *A Brief History of Time* (London: Bantam, 1988), p. 28.
3. See Sherrill Grace, 'Gender as Genre: Atwood's Autobiographical "I"', in Colin Nicholson (ed.), *Margaret Atwood: Writing and Subjectivity*, (Basingstoke: Macmillan; New York: St Martin's Press, 1994), pp. 189–203.
4. In its use of paintings *Cat's Eye* focuses on a similar area of inquiry to that of Norman Bryson, *Word and Image: French Painting of the Ancien Régime* (Cambridge: Cambridge University Press, 1981). On narrative techniques, see also M. MacMurragh-Kavanagh, *Cat's Eye*, York Notes Advanced (London: York Press, 2000), pp. 78–80; and Nathalie Cooke, 'The Politics of Ventriloquism: Margaret Atwood's Fictive Confessions', in Lorraine York (ed.), *Various Atwoods: Essays on the Later Poems, Short Fiction, and Novels* (Toronto: Anansi, 1995) pp. 207–28.
5. Sharon R. Wilson has commented on Atwood's involvement with the visual arts in 'Sexual Politics in Margaret Atwood's Visual Art', in K. Van Spanckeren and J. Garden Castro (eds), *Margaret Atwood: Vision and Forms* (Carbondale: Southern Illinois University Press, 1988), pp. 205–14.
6. Margaret Atwood, *Cat's Eye* (1988) (London: Virago, 1990). All page references will be to this edition and included in the text.
7. MSS Collection 200, Box 102: Folder 2.
8. See also J. Brooks Bouson, *Brutal Choreographies: Oppositional Strategies and Narrative Design in the Novels of Margaret Atwood* (Amherst: University of Massachusetts Press, 2000), pp. 159–84.
9. Paul de Man, 'Autobiography as De-facement', *Modern Language Notes*, 94 (1979): 931–55.
10. Ibid., p. 926.
11. For a fuller analysis of Cordelia's role, see Arnold E. Davidson, *Seeing in the Dark: Cat's Eye*, Canadian Fiction Studies, 35 (Toronto: ECW Press, 1997), pp. 51–69.
12. De Man, 'Autobiography as De-facement', p. 920.
13. Ibid., p. 922.
14. See Mary K. Kirtz, '(Dis)unified Field Theories: the Clarendon Lectures Seen Through (a) *Cat's Eye*', in Sharon R. Wilson (ed.), *Margaret Atwood's Textual Assassinations* (Columbus, OH: Ohio State University Press, 2003), pp. 54–73.
15. For definitions of these terms, see Hawking, *A Brief History of Time*, a book to which Atwood draws attention in her Acknowledgements.
16. Atwood, 'Instructions for the Third Eye', pp. 109–10.
17. Ibid., p. 109.
18. Bryson, *Word and Image*, p. 13.
19. Dennis Lee's definition, quoted by Helen Tiffin, 'Post-Colonial Literature and Counter-Discourse', *Kunapipi*, 9, 3 (1987): 17–34.
20. For a glimpse into this territory, see Hawking, *A Brief History of Time*, pp. 155–69.
21. De Man, 'Autobiography as De-facement', p. 922.
22. Ibid., p. 922.
23. MSS Collection 200, Box 99: Folder 8.
24. Elaine's final words echo Stephen's (p. 104); see also Hawking, *A Brief History of Time*, p. 28.

Notes to Chapter 9: *The Robber Bride*

1. Margaret Atwood, *The Robber Bride* (London: Virago, 1994). All further references will be to this edition and included in the text.
2. Anne Williams, *The Art of Darkness: A Poetics of Gothic* (Chicago: University of Chicago Press, 1995), p. 171.
3. Hayden White, 'The Historical Text as Literary Artifact', in *Tropics of Discourse: Essays in Cultural Criticism* (Baltimore, MD, and London: Johns Hopkins University Press, 1978), pp. 81–100.
4. Margaret Atwood, 'Speeches for Dr Frankenstein', in *Eating Fire: Selected Poetry, 1965–1995* (London: Virago, 1998), p. 46.
5. Shannon Hengen, 'Zenia's Foreignness', in Lorraine York (ed.), *Various Atwoods: Essays on the Later Poems, Short Fiction, and Novels* (Toronto: Anansi, 1995), pp. 271–86.
6. Sonia Mycak, *In Search of the Split Subject: Psychoanalysis, Phenomenology and the Novels of Margaret Atwood* (Toronto: ECW Press, 1996), pp. 212–42.
7. Margaret Atwood, 'Spotty-Handed Villainesses: Problems of Female Bad Behaviour in the Creating of Literature' (1994) www.web.net/owtoad/vlness.htm.
8. Alison Light, 'Returning to Manderley – Romance Fiction, Sexuality and Class', *Feminist Review*, 16 (1984): 7–25. See also, Avril Horner and Sue Zlosnik, 'Daphne du Maurier and Gothic Signatures: Rebecca as Vamp(ire)', in *Body Matters: Feminism, Textuality, Corporeality* (Manchester: Manchester University Press, 1998), pp. 209–22.
9. For a fascinating discussion of Zenia as Snake Goddess, see Sharon R. Wilson, 'Mythological Intertexts in Margaret Atwood's Work', in R. M. Nischik (ed.), *Margaret Atwood: Works and Impact* (New York: Camden House, 2000), pp. 215–28.
10. For discussion of *The Robber Bride* as a postcolonial novel, see Shannon Hengen, 'Zenia's Foreignness', pp. 271–86; Eleanora Rao, *Heart of a Stranger: Contemporary Women Writers and the Metaphor of Exile* (Naples: Liguori Editore, 2002), pp. 107–19; C. A. Howells, 'The Robber Bride; or, Who is a True Canadian?' in Sharon R. Wilson (ed.), *Margaret Atwood's Textual Assassinations: Recent Poetry and Fiction* (Columbus: Ohio State University Press, 2003), pp. 88–101.
11. Rao, *Heart of a Stranger*, p. 110.

Notes to Chapter 10: *Alias Grace*

1. Margaret Atwood, *In Search of Alias Grace* (Ottawa: University of Ottawa Press, 1997), p. 19. References will be included in the text, under *In Search*.
2. Margaret Atwood, *Alias Grace* (London: Virago, 1997). All page references will be to this edition and included in the text.
3. Grace Marks's story clearly fascinates Atwood, who has written two earlier versions of it: *The Servant Girl* (1974), a play for CBC television based on Susanna Moodie's account in her *Life in the Clearings* (1853), and *Grace*, an unpublished play for the theatre in the late 1970s.

4. See Sigmund Freud, 'Repression' (1915), in *On Metapsychology*, Penguin Freud Library, vol. 11 (London: Penguin, 1991), p. 148.
5. Earl G. Ingersoll, 'Engendering Metafiction: Textuality and Closure in Margaret Atwood's *Alias Grace*, *American Review of Canadian Studies* (Autumn 2001): 385–401.
6. For a detailed discussion of frustrated discourse and erotic undertones in the novel, see Christie March, 'Crimson Silks and New Potatoes: the Heteroglossic Power of the Object Atwood's *Alias Grace*', *Studies in Canadian Literature*, 22, 2 (1997): 66–82.
7. Jenny Bourne Taylor and Sally Shuttleworth (eds), *Embodied Selves: An Anthology of Psychological Texts, 1830–1890* (Oxford: Clarendon, 1998), p. xiii.
8. Jenny Bourne Taylor, 'Obscure Recesses: Locating the Victorian Unconscious', in J. B. Bullen (ed.), *Writing and Victorianism* (London and New York: Longman, 1997), pp. 137–79. In my discussion of nineteenth-century theories of mind, I am much indebted to this essay.
9. See Taylor and Shuttleworth, *Embodied Selves*, pp. 266–80, for medical discourses by Henry Maudsley and John Charles Bucknill on the relation between insanity and criminality.
10. Shuli Barzilai, 'Who is He? The Missing Persons behind the Pronoun in Atwood's *Surfacing*', *Canadian Literature*, 164 (Spring 2000): 57–79.
11. See Roxanne Rimstead, 'Working-Class Intruders: Female Domestics in *Kamouraska* and *Alias Grace*', *Canadian Literature*, 175 (Winter 2002): 44–65.
12. Margaret Rogerson, 'Reading the Patchworks in *Alias Grace*', *Journal of Commonwealth Literature*, 33, 1 (1998): 5–22.
13. Coomi Vevaina, 'Quilting Selves: Interpreting Atwood's *Alias Grace*', in C. Vevaina and C. A. Howells (eds), *Margaret Atwood: The Shape-Shifter* (New Delhi: Creative Books, 1998), pp. 64–74.
14. Jennifer Murray, 'Historical Figures and Paradoxical Patterns: the Quilting Metaphor in Margaret Atwood's *Alias Grace*', *Studies in Canadian Literature* (2001): 65–83.
15. Ingersoll, 'Engendering Metafiction', p. 390.
16. Sharon R. Wilson, 'Quilting as Narrative Art: Metafictional Construction in *Alias Grace*', in Sharon R. Wilson (ed.), *Margaret Atwood's Textual Assassinations* (Columbus: Ohio State University Press, 2003), p. 134.
17. C. A. Howells, *Contemporary Canadian Women's Fiction: Refiguring Identities* (New York and Basingstoke: Palgrave Macmillan, 2003), pp. 37–40.

Notes to Chapter 11: *The Blind Assassin*

1. Margaret Atwood, *The Blind Assassin* (London: Virago, 2001). Page references are to this edition and will be included in the text.
2. Margaret Atwood, *Negotiating with the Dead: A Writer on Writing* (London: Virago, 2003), p. 142. All further references to this edition will be included in the text. These essays are based on Atwood's Empson Lectures, given at Cambridge in the spring of 2000.
3. Margaret Atwood, 'Entering the Labyrinth: Writing *The Blind Assassin*', in G. Turcotte (ed.), *Margaret Atwood: Entering the Labyrinth: The Blind Assassin* (Wollongong: University of Wollongong Press, 2003), p. 23.

4. For discussion of this novel's use of history to challenge traditional notions of national identity, see C. A. Howells, *Contemporary Canadian Women's Fiction: Refiguring Identities* (Basingstoke: Palgrave Macmillan, 2003), pp. 40–52.

5. Dorothy Jones, 'Narrative Enclosures', in Turcotte (ed.), *Margaret Atwood: Entering the Labyrinth: The Blind Assassin*, pp. 47–69.

6. Kenneth C. Dewar, 'Where to Begin and How: Narrative Openings in Donald Creighton's Historiography' (1991), in G. Roberts (ed.), *The History and Narrative Reader* (London and New York: Routledge, 2001), pp. 337–53.

7. Sigmund Freud, 'The Uncanny' (1919), in *Art and Literature*, Penguin Freud Library, vol. 14 (London: Penguin, 1990), pp. 335–76.

8. The photograph appears near the beginning as the Prologue to Laura's novel (p. 7) and again at the end as its Epilogue (p. 631); it is also there in Laura's notebooks under 'History' (p. 610) and in Iris's description of how Laura obtained the negative (p. 238).

9. Jones, 'Narrative Enclosures', p. 63.

10. Karen F. Stein, 'A Left-Handed Story: *The Blind Assassin*', in Sharon R. Wilson (ed.), *Margaret Atwood's Textual Assassinations: Recent Poetry and Fiction* (Columbus: Ohio State University Press, 2003), pp. 135–53.

11. There are several other science fiction plots here, namely the pulp magazine instalment of *The Lizard Men of Xenor* and 'The Peach Women of Aa'A'. For fuller discussion of these, see C. A. Howells, 'Sites of Desolation', and D. Jones, 'Narrative Enclosures', both in Turcotte (ed.), *Entering the Labyrinth*, pp. 31–46 and pp. 47–67.

12. Hayden White, 'Historical Emplotment and the Problem of Truth', in *The History and Narrative Reader*, ed. Geoffrey Roberts (New York and London: Routledge, 2001), p. 376.

Notes to Chapter 12: *Oryx and Crake*

1. Margaret Atwood, *Wilderness Tips* (London: Virago, 1992).

2. Margaret Atwood, *Oryx and Crake* (London: Virago, 2004), p. 256. Page references are to this edition and will be included in the text.

3. Margaret Atwood, *Negotiating with the Dead* (London: Virago, 2003), p. 148. All further references to this edition will be included in the text.

4. *Margaret Atwood: Conversations*, ed. Earl G. Ingersoll (London: Virago, 1992), p. 193.

5. The genesis of this novel, according to Atwood, stems from her sighting of a red-necked crake in North Queensland in March 2001. See Margaret Atwood, 'Writing *Oryx and Crake*', in *Moving Targets: Writing with Intent, 1982–2004* (Toronto: Anansi, 2004), pp. 328–30.

6. Margaret Atwood, 'Writing *Oryx and Crake*', p. 330. See also www.random house.com/features/atwood/essay.html

7. Robert Potts, 'Profile Margaret Atwood', *Guardian Review*, 26 April 2003, pp. 20–4.

8. Margaret Atwood, 'Writing *Oryx and Crake*', p. 329.

9. Atwood interview, 29 May 2003. www.mcclelland.com/features/oryxand crake/interview_atwood.html

10. Noah Richler, 'Atwood's Ground Zero', *Saturday Post*, 26 April 2003, p. BK4.
11. Jean Baudrillard, 'Simulacra and Simulations', in Mark Poster (ed.), *Jean Baudrillard: Selected Writings* (Oxford: Polity Press, 1988), p. 168.
12. Ibid., p. 178.
13. Margaret Atwood, 'Genesis of *The Handmaid's Tale* and Role of the Historical Notes', in J.-M. Lacroix, J. Leclaire and Jack Warwick (eds), *The Handmaid's Tale: Roman Protéen* (Rouen: Presses Universitaires de Rouen, 1999), p. 8.
14. Lisa Appignanesi, review of *Oryx and Crake*, *The Independent*, 26 April 2003, www.enjoyment.independent.co.uk/books/reviews/story.
15. Brian Bethune, 'Atwood Apocalyptic', *Macleans*, 28 April 2003, http://web6. epnet.com.
16. See J. Brooks Bouson, ' "It's Game Over Forever": Atwood's Satiric Vision of a Bioengineered Posthuman Future in *Oryx and Crake'*, *Journal of Commonwealth Literature*, 39, 3 (2004): 139–56.
17. Nicholas Royle, *The Uncanny* (Manchester: Manchester University Press, 2003), pp. vii–viii.

Notes to the Conclusion

1. W. B. Gallie, 'Narrative and Historical Understanding', in Geoffrey Roberts (ed.), *The History and Narrative Reader* (London and New York: Routledge, 2001), p. 42.
2. Margaret Atwood, 'True Stories', in *Eating Fire: Selected Poetry, 1965–1995* (London: Virago, 1998), p. 244.
3. Colin Nicholson, 'Living on the Edges', in Colin Nicholson (ed.), *Margaret Atwood: Writing and Subjectivity* (Basingstoke: Macmillan, and New York: St Martin's Press, 1994), p. 15.
4. This is Atwood's formulation of Emily Dickinson's description of the writer–reader relationship, *Negotiating with the Dead: A Writer on Writing* (2002) (London: Virago, 2003), p. 120.

Bibliography

PRIMARY SOURCES

All references in this text to Margaret Atwood's novels, short stories and poetry* are to Virago Press Ltd editions. Note: the current edition of *The Handmaid's Tale* is now published by Vintage.

The Edible Woman (1969) (London: Virago, 1980).
Surfacing (1972) (London: Virago, 1979).
Lady Oracle (1976) (London: Virago, 1993).
Life Before Man (1979) (London: Virago, 1992).
Bodily Harm (1981) (London: Virago, 1983).
Murder in the Dark: Short Fictions and Prose Poems (1983) (London: Virago, 1994).
The Handmaid's Tale (1985) (London: Vintage, 1996).
Poems: 1976–1986 (1987) (London: Virago, 1992).
Bluebeard's Egg and Other Stories (1987) (London: Vintage, 1997).
Cat's Eye (1988) (London: Virago, 1994).
Wilderness Tips (1991) (London: Virago, 1992).
Good Bones (1992) (London: Virago, 1993).
The Robber Bride (1993) (London: Virago, 1994).
Alias Grace (1996) (London: Virago, 1997).
Eating Fire: Selected Poetry, 1968–1995 (London: Virago, 1998).
The Blind Assassin (2000) (London: Virago, 2001).
Negotiating with the Dead: A Writer on Writing (2002) (London: Virago, 2003).
Oryx and Crake (2003) (London: Virago, 2004).
Margaret Atwood: Conversations, ed. Earl E. Ingersoll (London: Virago, 1992).

* Texts from which I quote that are not available in Virago:

The Journals of Susanna Moodie (Toronto: Oxford University Press, 1970).
Survival: A Thematic Guide to Canadian Literature (Toronto: Anansi, 1972).
Second Words: Selected Critical Prose (1982) (Toronto: Anansi, 1996).

Strange Things: The Malevolent North in Canadian Literature (Oxford: Clarendon, 1995).

In Search of Alias Grace (Ottawa: University of Ottawa Press, 1997).

Bottle (Hay on Wye: Hay Festival Press, 2004).

Moving Targets: Writing with Intent, 1982–2004 (Toronto: Anansi, 2004).

SECONDARY SOURCES

Barzilai, Shuli, 'Who is He? The Missing Person Behind the Pronoun in Atwood's *Surfacing*', *Canadian Literature*, 164 (Spring 2000): 57–79.

Baudrillard, Jean, 'Simulacra and Simulations', in *Jean Baudrillard: Selected Writings*, ed. Mark Poster (Oxford: Oxford University Press, 1988).

Becker, Susanne, *Gothic Forms of Feminine Fictions* (Manchester: Manchester University Press, 1999).

Belsey, Catherine and Jane Moore (eds), *The Feminist Reader: Essays in Gender and the Politics of Literary Criticism*, 2nd edn (London: Macmillan, 1997).

Berger, John, *Ways of Seeing* (London: British Broadcasting Corporation and Penguin Books, 1972).

Bhabha, Homi K., *The Location of Culture* (London and New York: Routledge, 1994).

Botting, Fred, *Gothic* (London and New York: Routledge, 1996).

Bouson, J. Brooks, *Brutal Choreographies: Oppositional Strategies and Narrative Design in the Novels of Margaret Atwood* (Amherst: University of Massachusetts Press, 1993).

——, '"It's Game Over Forever": Atwood's Satiric Vision of a Bioengineered Posthuman Future in *Oryx and Crake*', *Journal of Commonwealth Literature*, 39, 3(2004): 139–56.

Braidotti, Rosi, *Nomadic Subjects: Embodiment and Sexual Difference in Contemporary Feminist Theory* (New York: Columbia University Press, 1994).

Brydon, Diana, 'Atwood's Postcolonial Imagination: Rereading *Bodily Harm*', in Lorraine M. York (ed.), *Various Atwoods* (Toronto: Anansi, 1995), pp. 89–116.

Bryson, Norman, *Word and Image: French Painting of the Ancien Régime* (Cambridge: Cambridge University Press, 1981).

Castle, Terry, *The Female Thermometer: Eighteenth-Century Culture and the Invention of the Uncanny* (New York and Oxford: Oxford University Press, 1998).

Caws, Mary Ann, 'Ladies Shot and Painted: Female Embodiment in Surrealist Art', in Susan Rubin Suleiman (ed.), *The Female Body in Western Culture: Contemporary Perspectives* (Cambridge, MA, and London: Harvard University Press, 1985), pp. 262–87.

Cixous, Hélène, 'The Laugh of the Medusa' (1976), repr. in *New French Feminisms: An Anthology*, ed. Elaine Marks and Isabelle de Courtivron (Brighton: Harvester, 1981), pp. 245–64.

Conboy, Katie, Nadia Medina and Sarah Stanbury (eds), *Writing on the Body: Female Embodiment and Feminist Theory* (New York: Columbia University Press, 1997).

Cooke, Nathalie, *Margaret Atwood: A Biography* (Toronto: ECW Press, 1998).

Davey, Frank, *Margaret Atwood: A Feminist Poetics* (Vancouver: Talonbooks, 1984).

——, *Post-National Arguments: The Politics of the Anglophone-Canadian Novel* (Toronto: University of Toronto Press, 1993).

Davidson, A. E. and Cathy N. Davidson (eds), *The Art of Margaret Atwood: Essays in Criticism* (Toronto: Anansi, 1981).

——, *Seeing in the Dark: Margaret Atwood's 'Cat's Eye'* (Toronto: ECW Press, 1997).

Dvorak, Marta (ed.), *'The Handmaid's Tale': Margaret Atwood* (Paris: Ellipses, 1998).

——, *Lire Margaret Atwood: 'The Handmaid's Tale'* (Rennes: Presses Universitaires de Rennes, 1999).

Fee, Margery, *The Fat Lady Dances: Margaret Atwood's 'Lady Oracle'* (Toronto: ECW Press, 1993).

Freud, Sigmund, 'The Uncanny' (1919), in *Art and Literature*, Penguin Freud Library, vol. 14 (London: Penguin, 1990), pp. 335–76.

Friedan, Betty, *The Feminine Mystique* (1963) (London: Gollancz, 1965).

Frye, Northrop, *The Bush Garden* (Toronto: Anansi, 1971).

Fulford, Margaret (ed.), *The Canadian Women's Movement, 1960–1990: A Guide to Archival Resources/Le Mouvement Canadien des Femmes, 1960–1990: Guide des resources archivistiques* (Toronto: ECW Press, 1992).

Fullbrook, Kate, *Free Women: Ethics and Aesthetics in Twentieth-century Women's Fictions* (Hemel Hempstead: Harvester-Wheatsheaf, 1990).

Gibson, Graeme, *Eleven Canadian Novelists* (Toronto: Anansi, 1973).

Grace, Sherrill and Lorraine Weir (eds), *Margaret Atwood: Language, Text and System* (Vancouver: University of British Columbia, 1983).

Hawking, Stephen, *A Brief History of Time* (London: Bantam, 1988).

Hengen, Shannon, 'Zenia's Foreignness', in Lorraine M. York (ed.), *Various Atwoods: Essays on the Later Poems, Short Fiction, and Novels* (Toronto: Anansi, 1995), pp. 271–86.

Horner, Avril and Angela Keane (eds), *Body Matters: Feminism, Textuality, Corporeality* (Manchester: Manchester University Press, 2000).

Howells, Coral Ann, *Love, Mystery and Misery: Feeling in Gothic Fiction*, 2nd edn (London: Athlone Press, 1995).

——, *Private and Fictional Words: Canadian Women Novelists of the 1970s and 80s* (London: Methuen, 1987).

——, *Contemporary Canadian Women's Fiction: Refiguring Identities* (New York and Basingstoke: Palgrave Macmillan, 2003).

——, *The Handmaid's Tale*, York Notes Advanced (London: York Press, 2003).

Humm, Maggie, *Border Traffic: Strategies of Contemporary Women Writers* (Manchester and New York: Manchester University Press, 1991).

—— (ed.), *Feminisms: A Reader* (New York and London: Harvester-Wheatsheaf, 1992).

Hutcheon, Linda, *The Canadian Postmodern: A Study of Contemporary English-Canadian Fiction* (Toronto: Oxford University Press, 1988).

Ingersoll, Earl G., 'Engendering Metafiction: Textuality and Closure in Margaret Atwood's *Alias Grace*', *American Review of Canadian Studies* (Autumn 2001): 385–401.

Irigaray, Luce, *This Sex which is Not One*, trans. Catherine Porter (New York: Cornell University Press, 1985).

Jameson, F., '"If I find one good city I will spare the man": Realism and Utopia in Kim Stanley Robinson's Mars Trilogy', in Patrick Parrinder (ed.), *Learning from Other Worlds: Estrangement, Cognition and the Politics of Science Fiction* (Liverpool: Liverpool University Press, 2000), pp. 208–32.

Jones, Dorothy, 'Narrative Enclosures', in Gerry Turcotte (ed.), *Margaret Atwood: Entering the Labyrinth: Writing The Blind Assassin* (Wollongong: University of Wollongong Press, 2003), pp. 47–69.

Keith, W. J., *Introducing Margaret Atwood's 'The Edible Woman': A Reader's Guide* (Toronto: ECW Press, 1989).

Keohane, N. O., M. Z. Rosaldo and B. G. Gelpi (eds), *Feminist Theory: A Critique of Ideology* (Brighton: Harvester, 1982).

Ketterer, David, *Canadian Science Fiction and Fantasy* (Bloomington and Indianapolis: Indiana University Press, 1992).

Kumar, Krishan, *Utopianism* (Milton Keynes: Open University Press, 1991).

Lacroix, J.-M. and J. Leclaire (eds), *Margaret Atwood: The Handmaid's Tale/Le Conte de le servante: The Power Game* (Paris: Presses de la Sorbonne Nouvelle, 1998).

Lacroix, J.-M, J. Leclaire and J. Warwick (eds), *The Handmaid's Tale: Roman Protéen* (Rouen: Presses Universitaires de Rouen, 1999).

Light, Alison, 'Returning to Manderley: Romance Fiction, Sexuality, and Class', *Feminist Review*, 16 (1984): 7–25.

Lodge, David, *After Bakhtin: Essays on Fiction and Criticism* (London and New York: Routledge, 1990).

Man, Paul de, 'Autobiography as De-facement', *Modern Language Notes*, 94 (1979): 931–55.

Marks, Elaine and Isabelle de Courtivron (eds), *New French Feminisms: An Anthology* (Brighton: Harvester, 1981).

McCombs, Judith (ed.), *Critical Essays on Margaret Atwood* (Boston, MA: G. K. Hall, 1988).

Moi, Toril, 'Feminine, Female, Feminist', in *The Feminist Reader*, ed. Catherine Belsey and Jane Moore, 2nd edn (Basingstoke: Macmillan, 1997), pp. 104–16.

Murray, Jennifer, 'Historical Figures and Paradoxical Patterns: the Quilting Metaphor in Margaret Atwood's *Alias Grace*', *Studies in Canadian Literature*, 26, 1 (2001): 65–83.

Mycak, Sonia, *In Search of the Split Subject: Psychoanalysis, Phenomenology, and the Novels of Margaret Atwood* (Toronto: ECW Press, 1996).

Nicholson, Colin (ed.), *Critical Approaches to the Fiction of Margaret Laurence* (Basingstoke: Macmillan, 1990).

—— (ed.), *Margaret Atwood: Writing and Subjectivity* (Basingstoke: Macmillan; New York: St Martin's Press, 1994).

Nischik, Reingard M. (ed.), *Margaret Atwood: Works and Impact* (New York: Camden House, 2000).

Patton, Marilyn, '*Lady Oracle* and the Politics of the Body', *Ariel*, 22, 1 (1991): 29–50.

Prentice, Alison, Paula Bourne et al. (eds), *Canadian Women: A History*, 2nd edn (Toronto: Harcourt Brace, 1996).

Radway, Janice, *Reading the Romance: Women, Patriarchy and Popular Literature* (Chapel Hill: University of North Carolina Press, 1984).

Rao, Eleanor, *Heart of a Stranger: Contemporary Women Writers and the Metaphor of Exile* (Naples: Liguori Editore, 2002).

Reynolds, Margaret and J. Noakes (eds), *Margaret Atwood: The Essential Guide* (London: Vintage, 2002).

Rich, Adrienne, *On Lies, Secrets and Silence: Selected Critical Prose, 1966–1978* (London: Virago, 1980).

Roberts, Geoffrey (ed.), *The History and Narrative Reader* (London and New York: Routledge, 2001).

Rogerson, Margaret, 'Reading the Patchworks in *Alias Grace*', *Journal of Commonwealth Literature*, 33, 1 (1998): 5–22.

Rooke, Constance, *Fear of the Open Heart: Essays on Contemporary Writing* (Toronto: Coach House, 1989).

Royle, Nicholas, *The Uncanny* (Manchester: Manchester University Press, 2003).

Sedgwick, Eve Kosofsky, *The Coherence of Gothic Conventions* (New York and London: Methuen, 1986).

Stein, Karen, 'A Left-Handed Story: *The Blind Assassin*', in Sharon R. Wilson (ed.), *Margaret Atwood's Textual Assassinations: Recent Poetry and Fiction* (Columbus: Ohio State University Press, 2003), pp. 135–53.

Suleiman, Susan Rubin (ed.), *The Female Body in Western Culture: Contemporary Perspectives* (Cambridge, MA, and London: Harvard University Press, 1985).

Sullivan, Rosemary, *The Red Shoes: Margaret Atwood Starting Out* (Toronto: Harper Flamingo, 1998).

Taylor, Jenny Bourne, 'Obscure Recesses: Locating the Victorian Unconscious', in J. B. Bullen (ed.), *Writing and Victorianism* (London and New York: Longman, 1997), pp. 139–79.

Taylor, Jenny Bourne and Sally Shuttleworth (eds), *Embodied Selves: An Anthology of Psychological Texts, 1830–1890* (Oxford: Clarendon, 1998).

Thompson, Lee Briscoe, *Scarlet Letters: Margaret Atwood's 'The Handmaid's Tale'* (Toronto: ECW Press, 1997).

Tiffin, Helen, 'Post-colonial Literature and Counter-discourse', *Kunapipi*, 9, 3 (1987): 17–34.

Turcotte, Gerry (ed.), *Margaret Atwood: Entering the Labyrinth: Writing 'The Blind Assassin'* (Wollongong: University of Wollongong Press, 2003).

Van Spanckeren, Kathryn and Jan Garden Castro (eds), *Margaret Atwood: Vision and Forms* (Carbondale: Southern Illinois University Press, 1988) .

Vevaina, Coomi and C. A. Howells (eds), *Margaret Atwood: The Shape-Shifter* (New Delhi: Creative Books, 1998).

White, Hayden, 'The Historical Text as Literary Artifact', in R. H. Canary and K. Kozicki (eds), *The Writing of History: Literary Form and Historical Understanding* (Madison: University of Wisconsin Press, 1978), pp. 41–62.

——, 'Historical Emplotment and the Problem of Truth' (1996), reprinted in *The History and Narrative Reader*, ed. Geoffrey Roberts (London and New York: Routledge, 2001), pp. 375–89.

Williams, Anne, *Art of Darkness: A Poetics of Gothic* (Chicago: University of Chicago Press, 1995).

Williams, Linda, *Hard Core: Power, Pleasure, and the Frenzy of the Visible* (London: Pandora, 1990).

Wilson, Sharon Rose (ed.), *Margaret Atwood's Textual Assassinations: Recent Poetry and Fiction* (Columbus: Ohio State University Press, 2003).

Woodcock, George, *Introducing Margaret Atwood's 'Surfacing': A Reader's Guide* (Toronto: ECW, 1990).

York, Lorraine M. (ed.), *Various Atwoods: Essays on the Later Poems, Short Fiction, and Novels* (Toronto: Anansi, 1995).

Index